T0330858

Marx for the 21st Century

This collection surveys current research on Marx and Marxism from a diverse range of perspectives.

Marx is rescued from 'orientalism', evaluated as a socialist thinker, revisited as a theorist of capitalist development, heralded as a necessary ethical corrective to modern economics, linked to ecologism, and claimed as an inspiration to 'civil society' theorists. There are also major scholarly revisions to the 'standard' historical accounts of Marx's work on the *Communist Manifesto*, his relationship to the contemporary theories of Louis Blanc and P.-J. Proudhon, and new information about how he and Engels worked together.

Hiroshi Uchida researches and teaches at Senshu University, Tokyo, Japan.

Routledge frontiers of political economy

Marx for the 21st Century

Edited by Hiroshi Uchida

With a special introduction by Terrell Carver

Routledge
Taylor & Francis Group

LONDON AND NEW YORK

First published 2006
by Routledge
2 Park Square, Milton Park, Abingdon, Oxon OX14 4RN

Simultaneously published in the USA and Canada
by Routledge
711 Third Avenue, New York, NY 10017

Routledge is an imprint of the Taylor & Francis Group

© 2006 Editorial matter and selection, Hiroshi Uchida; individual
chapters, the contributors

Typeset in Times by Wearset Ltd, Boldon, Tyne and Wear

British Library Cataloguing in Publication Data
A catalogue record for this book is available from the British Library

Library of Congress Cataloging in Publication Data
A catalog record for this book has been requested

ISBN 0-415-30530-6

Contents

Contributors

Daisuke Arie, Yokohama National University, and author of: *Labour and Justice: A History of Socio-Economic Theory from Aristotle to Loemer.* Sofusha Press 1991 (Japanese); 'Collapse of socialism and Japanese scholarship of social science', *Kanagawa University Bulletin*, no. 21, pp. 38–45, 1995 (Japanese); and 'Japanese reception of utilitarianism II', in *Practical Possibility of Social Justice and Utilitarianism*, pp. 3–17, Japanese Society for Promotion of Sciences 2001.

Makoto Itoh, Kokugakuin University, The Japan Academy, and author of: *The Basic Theory of Capitalism.* Macmillan, and Barnes & Noble, 1988; *Political Economy for Socialism.* Macmillan, and St. Martin's Press, 1995; and *The Japanese Economy Reconsidered.* Palgrave, 2000.

Hideaki Kudo, Chiba University, and author of: 'A note on the concept of cycle in ecological economics,' *Economic Journal of Chiba University* 19:2, 2004 (Japanese); and 'The recycling-based society and the society embedded in natural cycles (1)', *Economic Journal of Chiba University*, 19:3, 2004 (Japanese).

Akihiro Matoba, Kanagawa University, and author of: *A Social History of Trier: Karl Marx and his Environment.* Miraisha Publishers, 1986 (Japanese); *Marx in Paris.* Ochanomizu Publishers, 1995 (Japanese); and *Rereading Marx.* Gogatsu Publishers, 2004 (Japanese).

Shohken Mawatari, Miyagi University, and author of: 'The Uno school: A Marxian approach in Japan', *History of Political Economy*, 17:3 (1985); *The Economics of J. S. Mill.* Ochanomizu Publishers, 1997 (Japanese); and *History of Economics.* Yuhikaku Publishers, 1997 (Japanese).

Hiroshi Mizuta, The Japan Academy, and author of: *Adam Smith's Library: A Catalogue* (ed.) with an introduction and note. Clarendon Press, 2000; and 'Adam Smith in Japan'. In *The Rise of Political Economy in the Scottish Enlightenment*, T. Sakamoto and H. Tanaka (eds). Routledge, 2003.

Makoto Nishibe, University of Hokkaido, and author of: *A Genealogy of Market – Images – Visions in the Economic Calculation Debate*. Toyokeizai Publishers, 1996 (Japanese); *Ethics in Exchange and Reciprocity, Trust, Cooperation and Competition: A Comparative Study* (ed. with Shinoyama and Yagi). Springer-Verlag 2000; and *Frontiers of Evolutionary Economics* (ed.). Nihonhyoron Publishers 2004 (Japanese).

Makoto Noguchi, (d. 2003), formerly of Senshu University, and author of: *Modern Capitalism and Theories of Effective Demand*. Shakaihyoronsha, 1990 (Japanese); and 'The evolution of Japanese capitalism under global competition', in *Capitalism in Evolution – Global Contentions – East and West*, G. Hodgson, M. Itoh and N. Yokokawa (eds). Edward Elgar, 2001.

Masanori Sasaki, Wakkanai Hokusei Gakuen College, and author of: *Denuded Businessman: Creation of New Public Space*. Gendaikikakushitsu Publishers 1997 (Japanese); and *Alternative Society: Recover Time-Sovereignty*. Gendaikikakushitsu Publishers 2003 (Japanese).

Tadashi Shibuya, Kagoshima University, and author of: *The German Ideology*, ed. and trans., Shinnihon Publishers, 1998 (Japanese); 'Editorial problems of the German ideology', *MEGA-Studien*, 1996/1 (German); and 'The economic studies of the young Marx and his notebooks of 1844–47', *Keizai*, 2002, nos 81, 83, 84, 85, 86 and 87; and 2003, nos 89, 90, 93 and 95 (Japanese).

Akitoshi Suzuki, Senshu University Hokkaido College, and author of: *The Future of Weberian Methods*. Nihonkeizai-hyoronsha Publishers, 2001 (Japanese); and 'Keynes and some economic thoughts', *Journal of Hokkaido College, Senshu University*, no. 20, 1987 (English).

Koichi Takakusagi, Keio University, and author of: *Impact of the Revolution of 1848* (co-editor). Ochanomizu Publishers, 1998 (Japanese); *A Perspective from Minorities* (co-editor). Koubundou Publishers, 2000 (Japanese); and *Eye on the Family* (co-editor). Koubundou Publishers, 2001 (Japanese).

Hiroshi Uchida, Senshu University, and author of: *A Study of Marx's Grundrisse*. Shinhyoronsha Publishers, 1982 (Japanese); *Marx's Grundrisse and Hegel's Logic*. Routledge, 1988; and *Kiyoshi Miki: Imagination of Individuality*. Ochanomizu Publishers, 2004 (Japanese).

Kunihiko Uemura, Kansai University, and author of: *Schulz and Marx on Modernity*. Shinhyoron Publishers, 1990 (Japanese); *Assimilation and Emancipation: 'The Jewish Question' Controversy in 19th Century Germany*. Heibonsha Publishers, 1993 (Japanese); and *Reading Marx*. Seidosha Publishers, 2001 (Japanese).

Acknowledgements

This is the fourth volume in the series 'Collected Essays in English' produced by the Japan Society for the History of Economic Thought. The society nominated me at the 2002 Annual Meeting at Hitotsubashi University as chief editor for a collection of essays on Marx. Subsequent to that occasion, I appointed Professor Makoto Itoh at Kokugakuin University and Professor Akihiro Matoba at Kanagawa University as associate editors. We, the three editors, discussed the theme, content and construction of the essays and agreed to treat Marx with reference to 20th century experiences in the theory and practice of Marxism, and to apply a 21st century perspective to him and his work. Therefore we chose the title *Marx for the 21st Century*. Aiming at a compact and well-balanced collection, we organised the work into four parts: 'Marx for the 21st century'; 'Contemporary problems in Marx studies'; 'The reception of Marx into modern Japan'; and 'New horizons of Marxology'. Each part is composed of several chapters as detailed in the Contents.

We asked fourteen members of the society to contribute to this work on Marx and, to our pleasure, all of them accepted. Every author has been very cooperative, and thus this has been a very smooth process. Makoto Noguchi, author of Chapter 11, sadly died on 2 April 2003. Professor Nobuharu Yokokawa of Musashi University checked the copy-edited typescript for him. All contributors share in a deep grief for the late Noguchi.

From 7 January to 26 March 2004 I was able to collaborate with Professor Terrell Carver at the Department of Politics, University of Bristol, UK. When I stayed previously in Bristol some eighteen years ago (1986–87), I was able to pursue my research with him in conjunction with my first book in English, *Marx's Grundrisse and Hegel's Logic*, published by Routledge in 1988. Terrell has always kindly improved and polished my clumsy English with amazingly accurate understanding. Then, as Head of Department, and sparing precious time from a very tight schedule, he was been able to engage in specialist copy-editing for all the Japanese authors. He has also shown his goodwill by writing a special introduction for the volume. All of the Japanese contributors, including myself, are very grateful to him.

xiv *Acknowledgements*

My sincere gratitude is also expressed to Warden Donald Shell at Wills Hall, University of Bristol, where I stayed for these three months in 2004. My life at Wills Hall has been very interesting, productive and enjoyable. His invitations to Formal Dinner on Friday evening have brought me many opportunities to become acquainted with students not only from the United Kingdom but also from many other countries. It has been wonderful for me to be with students who are acquiring professional skills, academic knowledge and genial sociability under the Warden's warm and deliberate guidance. I will remember my happy stay at Wills Hall for a very long time.

I am very grateful to Elaine Newcombe and Robert Holbeche of the Support Staff at the Department of Politics, and to Sue Smith, the Warden's Secretary at Wills Hall. They all kindly assisted me with highest professionalism.

Last but not least, I would like to express my gratitude to the Routledge editors Rob Langham and Terry Clague. They accepted our project with generous understanding, and have been patient while waiting for the manuscript to be completed. As chief editor, I hope that the essays will be widely welcomed by English-speaking audiences.

Hiroshi Uchida
Bristol, March 2004

Special introduction

Terrell Carver

This is a landmark work. It surveys current research on Marx and Marxism from an unusual variety of perspectives, asking an unusual range of questions. In these days of globalised capitalist hegemony, the contributors find Marx more interesting, and more relevant, than ever. Moreover this is the first collection assembled by scholars in Japan for international publication in English. Marx was received in Japan in the late 19th century, almost as soon as anywhere else in the world (with the exception of Germany, France and Belgium). Scholarly and political activity has been intense and continued almost unabated, despite notable eras of intense repression. Very little of this commentary, exploration and textual work, other than in the specific field of Marxist economics, has reached the West and the Anglophone world. This volume is an exceptional showcase, and indeed a window on preceding Japanese and international scholarship, in the four main areas detailed below.

Marx for the 21st century

The first two chapters look forward to a world enriched analytically, and politically, by rereading and reabsorbing central ideas from Marx's vision.

In Chapter 1 'Marx and modernity' Kunihiko Uemura examines world history and the interplay of nationalisms as seen by Marx, and asks if he is the successor to the Eurocentric project of 'modernity', or a critic of it. Uemura argues that Marx is not an orientalist, as Edward Said claimed (in his famous and controversial book *Orientalism*). In fact Marx was a critic of 'fantasies' of linear historical development and/or necessary stagnation for cultural or 'racial' reasons – both features of orientalist thinking. Marx's schema detailing different 'modes of production' was quite different in terms of its structure and content within his 'guiding thread' for historical studies. Moreover, for Marx the nation was a construct of the bourgeois/capitalist era (not a teleological outcome of historical or 'racial' 'developments'), and his political viewpoint was characteristically and relentlessly internationalist, scathingly critical of nationalisms. Marx was therefore a thorough-going critic of modernity in both national and economic terms. Uemura, like Marx, looks forward to a deconstruction of the nation state.

In Chapter 2 Makoto Itoh examines 'Marx's economic theory and the prospects for socialism', and enquires whether a conception of socialism, based on Marx, can be developed for the 21st century. Marx addressed himself to a social object – capitalist society – and interpellated a social subject – the proletariat, but did not leave a blueprint for socialism, or any 'recipes for the cookshops of the future', as he put it in his 'Afterword' to the second German edition of *Capital*, vol. 1. The Soviet planned economy did not carry through the productivity of capitalist society to an era of socialist transition (such as Marx sketched out), nor did it abolish those features of exploitation and privilege (which he had expected it to). Itoh examines Uno's critique of Stalin's economic policies and related debates concerning the continuance of the 'law of value' under socialism. He concludes that in Stalin's system there was neither equilibrium pricing nor labour-time exchange of useful goods and services. Instead there was a system of quasi-prices and quasi-money, closest perhaps to Piero Sraffa's neo-Ricardian price theory than to anything in Marx's *Capital*. Looking at contemporary Russia and China, Itoh asks if it is possible to use Marx's value theory today to envisage a democratic form of market socialism. His answer is a qualified yes, giving due attention both to anti-corruption controls and to the need for socialist market economies to tax sufficiently for adequate services.

Contemporary problems in Marx studies

The next five chapters tackle a range of problems in which Marx studies has an important role. These include the 'theory of history' extrapolated from, or implied by, his major political and theoretical works; the future of capitalist society, a question which Marx famously raised and answered in the negative; the relation of Marx's views to political theories of justice, highly controversial since Marx dissociated himself from 'fair' distributive frameworks and moralising political slogans; environmental issues – a conceptualisation that postdates Marx but to which his work can nevertheless be made to speak; and, rather against the grain, an argument within Marx's terms for labour-money that draws his work closer to Proudhonian socialism than he himself would probably have liked.

In Chapter 3, 'Marx's theory of history reappraised', Hiroshi Uchida argues that Marx's theory of capitalist development is applicable to present-day developing societies where monetary funds, land, labour power and technology are being commercialised. He conceptualises this as either rentier-state capitalism or developmental dictatorship, and considers England, Japan, Iran, Taiwan and China, showing the coherence of the major variants within an overall scheme derived from Marx. In that way he is able to trace phases of worker unfreedom similar to those sketched by Marx when he considered capitalist development in England.

In Chapter 4 Masanori Sasaki considers 'Marx and the future of post-capitalist society'. He surveys a post-capitalist alternative to American neo-liberal productivism – the free time model. He examines this in relation to consumer society with its insidious 'work and spend' dynamic, and its tendency to ecological crisis. His vision is developed not just in relation to leisure time but also in relation to domestic labour and childcare. This takes unpaid work into account, in contrast to traditional masculine presumptions. The reduction of labour-time is thus crucial for the future, and Marx's work on cooperation and association points the way.

In Chapter 5, 'Marx and distributive justice', Daisuke Arie traces the Aristotelian view of justice in Western thought and argues that Marx's critical target was negative or commutative justice. This offers a clue to contemporary questions of social distribution. Marx's successive principles of distribution, marking a transition from socialism to communism, were distribution 'according to contribution' and distribution 'according to need'. Arie explicates these two principles in an Aristotelian context, arguing that this is the way to put ethics back into modern economics, which has become impoverished without this dimension.

In Chapter 6 Hideaki Kudo tackles 'Marx and the environmental problem'. He examines environmental disasters and difficulties caused by capitalism, but in the light of Marx's economic thought. He interprets this as an economics free of human-centric triumphalism over nature and therefore more inclined to an inclusive view, seeing humanity as part of nature. He finds an ontological naturalism relevant to ecological concerns in Marx's doctoral dissertation and in his early 'Paris' manuscripts of 1844. Tracing this outlook in *Capital*, vol. 1, he argues for a unification of a new Marxist economics with ecologism.

In Chapter 7, 'The theory of labour money: Implications of Marx's critique for the Local Exchange Trading System (LETS)', Makoto Nishibe theorises an associative and cooperative market using alternative money, despite Marx's criticisms of labour money and of Proudhonian socialisms. He thus draws out the positive aspects of Proudhon's vision of freedom and individual independence, despite the latent authoritarianism that Marx found there. Nishibe endorses Marx's critique of Owen's and Ricardo's theories of labour money in relation to regulating values and market prices, but notes that Marx argued for a general change to a system of cooperative labour en route to socialism. An alternative form of money would allow free trade and would be founded on mutual trust. This would not only create a market but would also encourage cooperation rather than competition. The Canadian 'LETS' (Local Exchange Trading System) or alternative money would not in fact create interest or self-expand as capital.

The reception of Marx into modern Japan

This volume includes four chapters on the intellectual reception of Marx into modern Japan, following the Meiji 'restoration' of 1868. While Western scholars and Marxists are likely to have some knowledge of the reception of Marx in France, Germany, Russia, China and even Vietnam and Cuba, the history of repression and lively political debate in Japan is still largely unknown. Note that this episode in intellectual history includes comparisons between Marx and other social theorists in rather more balanced and compromising terms than Western Marxist debate has generally sanctioned.

In Chapter 8 Hiroshi Mizuta considers 'The Japanese concept of civil society and Marx's *bürgerliche Gesellschaft*', noting that many Japanese Marxists understood *bürgerliche Gesellschaft* in the tradition of Smith and Ferguson, that is, an array of independent institutions in a civilized and civilizing society. Out of sympathy with Stalinists and the Comintern line, and persecuted by reactionary authorities during the imperial period before World War II, they nonetheless found inspiration in Marx for their vision of radical democracy and extraparliamentary politics. For these Japanese Marxists, revolution would not abolish what is 'civil' in society, but rather realise it.

In Chapter 9 Shohken Mawatari considers 'Marx and J.S. Mill on socialism'. He traces important distinctions and changes in Mill's thinking with respect to socialism and communism, and argues that this accounts for differing opinions amongst commentators since Mill's time. He then contrasts Marx and Mill with respect to their views on ethics and science, recounting Mill's views on Fourierism and communism, and noting that his social theory proceeds from important values of choice and liberty. In conclusion, Mawatari argues that Mill was a socialist, but in a very different way from Marx, not least because he left the factuality and desirability of communism as open questions.

In Chapter 10 Akitoshi Suzuki presents 'A bioeconomic Marx–Weber paradigm'. The Japanese reception of Marx presents a particularly clear example of the confrontation and complementarity between Marx and Weber, and of the variants of their respective theories that develop as a result. In the first instance the issue was whether post-Meiji Japan was ripe for socialist development, or whether the semi-feudal elements there would have to be expunged in the first instance. This discussion draws on Weber's concept of 'civil society' and its relationship to developing capitalism and attendant 'liberal' structures. In the second instance the issue was the role of the post-war Japanese economy within 'world system' economic structures of capitalist development that might tend towards socialist outcomes, or within a more revolutionary perspective on international economic and political relations driven by proletarianised 'third world' countries in the grip of globalised class struggle. In conclusion Suzuki offers his own perspectives on world government and its relation to Weberian individualism.

In Chapter 11 Makoto Noguchi considers 'Japanese "cultural eclecticism" and a reinterpretation of Marx and Keynes on the instabilities of capitalism'. Methodological eclecticism, specifically a reworking of Marxian political economy along Keynesian lines, is an important offshoot of debates in Japan concerning the general nature of economic and political 'backwardness' and modernisation. Diverse instabilities in capitalism can best be analysed as phases in an evolutionary process, rather than as apparent contradictions to a monistic scheme. In that way, Marxist debates in Japan have been influential in economic methodology and are transferable elsewhere.

New horizons of Marxology

The final three chapters showcase historical and textual scholarship on Marx in Japan. Meticulous textual and archival research is something that is particularly cultivated in Japan, and these three chapters open up new vistas with respect to the production of the *Communist Manifesto*, the relationship between Marx's thought and Louis Blanc's, and finally a contribution to a particularly innovative and distinguished area of achievement in Japan: the deciphering, interpretation and reproduction of the text of *The German Ideology*.

In Chapter 12, 'The Brussels Democratic Association and the *Communist Manifesto*', Akihiro Matoba argues that Marx and Engels were not the only writers of the *Communist Manifesto*, which was in fact published anonymously. The document was produced for a committee and so emerged from a number of related sources. These were in turn derived from a collaboration between émigré German workers in an association (to which Marx and Engels belonged) and Belgian democratic socialists, whose fervent internationalism and distinctive ideas about cross-class coalition contributed significantly to this famous text.

In Chapter 13, 'Louis Blanc, associationism in France, and Marx', Koichi Takakusagi suggests that for Marx's thought to take on a new life in the 21st century it must be re-positioned in our view of the 19th. While Marx is famously said to have absorbed and revivified 'French revolutionary socialism', this claim is as yet under-researched. In particular the *Communist Manifesto* uses the term 'association', which derives from the work of Louis Blanc, specifically from his critique of Alexis de Tocqueville's classic *Democracy in America*. These theorisations specify future economic and political formations but within certain constraints, namely those of democratic participation and national centralisation. This is a nexus of theory and practice that occupies us politically today.

In Chapter 14 Tadashi Shibuya considers 'Editorial problems in establishing a new edition of *The German Ideology*'. This manuscript work presents formidable problems of interpretation: handwriting, authorship, typographical representation and interpretation. Shibuya reviews the five major editions that precede his own, and explains how his new research, and his focus on clear presentation, can reveal new information about the Marx–Engels collaboration. In particular his method enables us to see Engels and Marx working alternately on particular sentences, each stopping the other to revise the work in hand. Shibuya's own edition exhibits a clear presentation of any deletions in each sentence, yet the use of bold type enables the reader to see at a glance the text as Marx and Engels revised it.

Overview

The conjunction of Japanese scholarship with Marx and Marxism has been an extraordinarily productive one, yet until now almost unknown in the Anglophone West. This volume marks the beginning of a new era in international discussion and debate about Marx's work, his thought, and its relevance to the present day and new century as events unfold. The questions tackled by the contributors to this book will all be familiar ones to Western readers, but the historical, political and intellectual resources brought to these issues will be somewhat unfamiliar, yet intelligible and refreshing. This is all to the good in a globalised world, something that Marx himself predicted and openly welcomed, as his career, ambitions and outlook were not just internationalist in spirit but decidedly practical and explicit in generating collaboration, translations and controversy. The editor, sponsor and contributors to this outstanding collection have all done their job. Now it is up to Anglophone readers to do theirs, and push forward in making contact, generating dialogue and pursuing issues with colleagues in Japan.

Part I

Marx for the 21st century

1 Marx and modernity

Kunihiko Uemura

Introduction

Everyone knows that Marx was a critic of capitalism, but what did he think about 'modernity'? Was he the successor to 'an incomplete project of modernity', or a critic of it?

The shaping of modernity coincided with the genesis of the Eurocentric capitalist world system. The idea of modernity is obviously Eurocentric, though it also promulgates universality. It relates very directly to the capitalist world system; however, it should not be identified with the capitalist superstructure. The idea of modernity has three aspects.

The first is the 'civil society' model, consisting of free and equal individuals. This was established by social contract theories based on methodological individualism. It declared the emancipation of the individual from the restraints of older communities, and motivated individuals to participate voluntarily in social formations. However, it was an ideology that made social and economical inequality a matter of individual self-responsibility as well as social responsibility.

The second is the idea of 'world history' based on twin dualisms of 'civilised/savage' and 'progressive/stagnant'. It put peoples and cultures into a chronological order and evaluated them by those dualisms. Therefore it justified ideologically the colonisation of 'stagnant and savage' areas by 'progressive and civilised' countries.

The third is nationalism, imagining the 'nation' as the highest form of being in the global inter-state system. In this way national identity generated a powerful, emotional fellowship based on the imagined sharing of language and blood, and it mobilised people to engage in warfare for 'us as a nation'.

These three aspects are related closely to one another. 'World history' tried to prove European predominance over other societies by considering European 'civil society' as the latest stage of historical progress. At first it took the form of 'the history of civil society', for example, by Adam Ferguson. Then, in the age of nationalism, it metamorphosed into 'the stages of national economic growth', for example, in works by W.W. Rostow.

The aim of this chapter is to explore how Marx responded to these ideas. It is well-known that his life-work is a criticism of the capitalist theory of civil society found in Adam Smith as well as laying bare 'the anatomy of bourgeois society' itself (Marx 1996: 159). My goal is to make clear how Marx examines Eurocentric 'world history' and 'nationalism'.

Is Marx an orientalist?

Was Marx a representative of Eurocentric 'world history', or a critic of it? Since Edward W. Said counted Marx among the 'orientalists', some have argued that Marx's view of world history was obviously Eurocentric. Said pointed out that 'Orientalism as a Western style for dominating, restructuring, and having authority over the Orient ... can accommodate Aeschylus, say, and Victor Hugo, Dante and Karl Marx' (Said 1979: 3). As proof that Marx was an orientalist, Said pointed to his notorious article on 'the British rule in India' in the *New York Daily Tribune* (25 June 1853):

> We must not forget that these idyllic village-communities, inoffensive though they may appear, had always been the solid foundation of Oriental despotism, that they restrained the human mind within the smallest possible compass, making it the unresisting tool of superstition, enslaving it beneath traditional rules, depriving it of all grandeur and historical energies ... We must not forget that these little communities were contaminated by distinctions of caste and by slavery, that they subjugated man to external circumstances instead of elevating man the sovereign of circumstances, that they transformed a self-developing social state into never changing natural destiny, and thus brought about a brutalizing worship of nature, exhibiting its degradation in the fact that man, the sovereign of nature, fell down on his knees in adoration of Hanuman, the monkey, and Sabbala, the cow ... England, it is true, in causing a social revolution in Hindustan, was actuated only by the vilest interests, and was stupid in her manner of enforcing them. But that is not the question. The question is, can mankind fulfill its destiny without a fundamental revolution in the social state of Asia? If not, whatever may have been the crimes of England she was the unconscious tool of history in bringing about that revolution.
>
> (Marx and Engels 1979: 132)

There seems to be no room for defence. Said referred to this as 'a piece of pure Romantic Orientalism', and used Marx 'as the case by which a non-Orientalist's human engagements were first dissolved, then usurped by Orientalist generalizations' (Said 1979: 154, 156). As a European of the 19th century, Marx could not have escaped a Eurocentric stereotype: 'progressive or enlightened' Europe versus 'stagnant or superstitious' Asia.

Facing such criticism, we could hardly expect to get something new from a reconsideration of Marx's view of world history. However, was Marx really an 'orientalist' in the first place?

In a letter dated 14 June 1853 Marx tells Engels that he has read a new book *The Slave Trade, Domestic and Foreign: Why it exists, and How it may be extinguished* (London 1853) by Henry Charles Carey, an American economist. According to Marx's summary, Carey insists that:

> all ills are blamed on the centralising effect of big industry ... But this centralising effect is in turn blamed on England, who has made herself the *workshop* of the world and has forced all other countries to revert to brutish agriculture divorced from manufacturing.

Regarding Carey's characterisation of 'England's sins' as 'Sismondian-philanthropic-socialist anti-industrialism', Marx continues:

> Your article on Switzerland was, of course, a direct swipe at the Tribune's 'leaders' (anti-centralisation, etc) and *their* man Carey. I continued this clandestine campaign in my first article on India, in which England's destruction of native industries is described as *revolutionary*. This they will find very *shocking*. Incidentally the whole administration of India by the British was detestable and still remains so today.
>
> (Marx and Engels 1983: 345–6)

Engels's article on Switzerland appeared in the same *Tribune* (17 May 1853) about a month earlier than Marx's first article on India. Engels argues there that the pastoral society of Switzerland, based on 'a petty and sporadic sort of manufactures mixed up with agricultural pursuits', is politically reactionary, because it is 'among the least civilized populations of Europe' and 'stationary' (Marx and Engels 1979: 87–8). Marx says in his letter that Engels's article was a deadly blow to Carey and the *Tribune*'s leaders, who try 'to counter centralisation with localisation and the union – a union scattered throughout the land – of factory and farm' (Marx and Engels 1983: 346), and his own article was also an intentional criticism of them, rather like shock therapy.

Marx's seemingly 'orientalist' side is therefore intentional and concerned with his revolutionary strategy, which insists that 'philanthropic-socialist and anti-industrialist' criticism of British imperialism is wrong. Marx criticises Carey again in *Grundrisse: Foundations of the Critique of Political Economy* of 1857–58. In the fragment 'Bastiat and Carey' he criticizes Carey's 'naiveté' in mentioning 'the destructive influence of England, with its striving for industrial monopoly' and asserting 'the harmonious cooperation of town and countryside, industry and agriculture'. Marx continues:

This naiveté apart, with Carey the harmony of the bourgeois relations of production ends with the most complete disharmony of these relations on the grandest terrain where they appear, the world market, and in their grandest development, as the relations of producing nations ... If patriarchal gives way to industrial production within a country, this is harmonious, and the process of dissolution that accompanies this development is conceived in its positive aspect alone. But it becomes disharmonious when large-scale English industry dissolves the patriarchal or petty bourgeois or other lower stages of production in a foreign country ... What Carey has not grasped is that these world-market disharmonies are merely the ultimate adequate expressions of the disharmonies which have become fixed as abstract relations within the economic categories or which have a local existence on the smallest scale.

(Marx 1973: 886–7)

Marx's thinking is now clear for us. Carey is contradictory because he blames the British for their colonisation in India, though at the same time he is in favour of industrialisation and civilisation in England. In other words, the British colonisation of India represents a part of the worldwide violent dissolution of 'pastoral' rural societies (the primary accumulation of the capital), which had already occurred in England. Therefore, on the one hand, Marx appreciates that 'Carey sees the contradictions in economic relations as soon as they appear on the world market as English relations', but on the other hand, he blamed him for other faults:

As a genuine Yankee, Carey absorbs from all directions the massive material furnished him by the old world, not so as to recognize the inherent soul of this material, and thus to concede to it the right to its peculiar life ... Hence both [Carey and Frédéric Bastiat, a French economist] are equally unhistorical and anti-historical.

(Marx 1973: 888)

The words 'unhistorical and anti-historical' here mean that Carey does not consider present 'world-market relations' in connection with the 'real historic transitions' that have already occurred in Europe. On the contrary, the word 'historical' for Marx means understanding actually existing relations genealogically. 'In real history', that is, with the genesis of capitalism in England, 'wage labour arises ... out of the decline and fall of the guild economy, of the system of Estates, of labour and income in kind, of industry carried on as rural subsidiary occupation, of small-scale feudal agriculture etc' (Marx 1973: 891). At present, this same 'history' is repeated globally as the 'dissolution of the patriarchal or petty bourgeois or other lower stages of production in a foreign country' by English industry. Why is this so? Because, according to Marx, 'the tendency to create the world market is directly given in the concept of capital itself' (Marx 1973: 408):

> Hence, the great civilizing influence of capital ... In accord with this tendency, capital drives beyond national barriers and prejudices as much as beyond nature worship, as well as all traditional, confined, complacent, encrusted satisfactions of present needs, and reproductions of old ways of life. It is destructive towards all of this, and constantly revolutionizes it, tearing down all the barriers which hem in the development of the forces of production, the expansion of needs, the all-sided development of production, and the exploitation and exchange of natural and national forces.
>
> (Marx 1973: 409–10)

It is capital that destroys all the old modes of life and traditions and brings a revolution. Now we can easily understand that Marx's first article on India was an application of this 'universal tendency of capital' theory. Marx is not an 'orientalist' as judged by his recognition of the capitalist world market. His paradigm is not 'Occident versus Orient,' nor 'progressive Europe versus stagnant Asia'. It is not 'us versus them' in the first place, but 'capital' versus 'modes of production preceding capital'. And from this standpoint, India is equivalent to present-day Switzerland and to England itself in former days.

World history as a structure

The 'domestic combination of agriculture and industry', which Marx sees as a general economic form in India and China, is not for him a typical Asiatic characteristic, but is rather observed generally in pre-modern societies. Marx himself says:

> History shows that agriculture never *appears in pure form* in the modes of production preceding capital, or which correspond to its own underdeveloped stages. A rural secondary industry, such as spinning, weaving etc. must make up for the limit on the employment of labour time posited here.
>
> (Marx 1973: 669)

The question for Marx is not a so-called 'Asiatic peculiarity' compared with Europe. India and China are dominated by the British, not because they are typical 'Asiatic' societies quite different from Europe, but because of their pre-capitalist modes of production, 'whether in Hindustan or in England' (Marx 1973: 885). On that point, Marx's view of Asia is decisively different from the contemporary European view of Asia, for example, Hegel's.

In *The Philosophy of History*, published in 1837 and then exerting a great influence on German intellectuals, Hegel says that in the Orient, especially in China and India, 'every change is excluded, and the fixedness of a character which recurs perpetually, takes the place of what we should call the truly historical' (Hegel 1900: 116). As for the political system, the imagined 'Oriental despotism', under which all people seem to be the emperor's slaves, is compared with an ideal of Germanic freedom. 'Stagnation' and 'despotism' as a fate are the substance of 'the Asiatic' for Hegel. Thus he justifies the European colonisation of Asia in the name of historical necessity:

> The English, or rather the East India Company, are the lords of the land; for it is the necessary fate of Asiatic Empires to be subjected to Europeans; and China will, some day or other, be obliged to submit to this fate.
>
> (Hegel 1900: 142–3)

This amounts to a prophecy of the Opium War of 1839–42.

The object of Hegel's description is 'One Individuality as the Spirit of a People' (Hegel 1900: 53), so he presumes the eternal nature of 'the Indian'. Hegel's thinking represents what Said calls 'essentialization' or 'Orientalizing the Oriental for an indefinite time and with no alternative' (Said 1993: 311). On the contrary, the issue for Marx is not the eternal nature or peculiarity of 'the Indian', but the village community system in India. Indeed, in his second article on India (8 August 1853) Marx insists:

> The Hindoos are allowed by British authorities themselves to possess particular aptitude for accommodating themselves to entirely new labour, and acquiring the requisite knowledge of machinery.

And then he also points out the possibility that 'the Hindoos themselves shall have grown strong enough to throw off the English yoke altogether' (Marx and Engels 1979: 220–1).

If Hegel's view of 'the Oriental' is a typical case of orientalism, Marx's view of Asian societies is obviously different from it. Therefore, we can say that Marx's view of world history itself is also different from Hegel's. But how?

'The so-called historical presentation of development', says Marx in the introduction to the *Grundrisse*, 'is founded, as a rule, on the fact that the latest form regards the previous ones as steps leading up to itself, and, since it is only rarely and only under quite specific conditions able to criticize itself, it always conceives them one-sidedly' (Marx 1973: 106). He insists that the theory of linear historical development is an ideology through which 'the latest form regards the previous ones as steps leading up to it'.

We can understand Marx's intention most easily if we remember, for example, Adam Smith's model of historical development. 'There are four distinct states', says Smith in his *Lecture on Jurisprudence* at Glasgow University of 1762–63, 'which mankind pass thro'; 1st, the Age of Hunters; 2ndly, the Age of Shepherds; 3dly, the Age of Agriculture; and 4thly, the Age of Commerce'. According to him, the age of hunters shifts to the age of shepherds 'in process of time', and then:

> we find accordingly that in almost all countries the age of shepherds preceded that of agriculture ... But when a society becomes numerous ... they would naturally turn themselves to the cultivation of land ... As society was farther improved ... they would exchange with one another what they produced more than was necessary for their support.
>
> (Smith 1978: 14–15)

Marx calls such a fantasy of escalating development, which occurs 'naturally' and 'in process of time', 'an infinite bourgeois progress' (Marx 1973: 890).

Hegel's 'world history' is also divided into four stages: 'the Oriental, Greek and Roman and German World', and is still depicted as 'a process of necessary progress' as much as Smith. Hegel writes:

> According to this abstract definition [that Freedom is the sole truth of Spirit], it may be said of Universal History, that it is the exhibition of Spirit in the process of working out the knowledge of that which it is potentially ... The application of the principle [liberty] to political relations; the thorough moulding and interpenetration of the constitution of society by it, is a process identical with history itself ... The History of the world is none other than the progress of the consciousness of Freedom; a progress whose development according to the necessity of its nature, it is our business to investigate.
>
> (Hegel 1900: 17–19)

Althusser and Balibar described linear 'infinite bourgeois progress' as 'an ideological concept of historical time', or fantasy, which permeates our consciousness as common sense (Althusser and Balibar 1970: 96). According to them, presuming 'historical time' in a specific way is the premise of the hierarchical dualism 'forward/backward' or 'progressive/stagnant', which is the core of orientalism or Eurocentrism.

'World history', Marx says similarly in the introduction to the *Grundrisse*, 'has not always existed; history as world history a result' (Marx 1973: 109). It is just the history of the capitalist world system, because capital creates it by creating a world market. With the so-called 'civilizing influence of capital', it is articulated from 'mere local developments of humanity' which 'have their own time and history' as 'the site peculiar to such and such an element of such and such a structural level in the complexity of the whole' (Althusser and Balibar 1970: 99, 106). In this way, it is articulated into 'the structure of an *organic hierarchized whole*' (Althusser and Balibar 1970: 98). Marx could escape the ideology of an evolutionary 'historical time', insofar as he saw world history as a structure itself.

Surely it cannot be denied that Marx's classification 'Asiatic, antique (Roman) and Germanic' forms is similar to Hegel's historical stages 'the Oriental, Greek, Roman and German World', but the resemblance is purely formal. Marx's 'forms' are not 'stages' of escalating development. They are simply the 'primary equations that point towards a past lying behind this [capitalist] system' (Marx 1973: 461), or variations in 'the identity of labour with property' (Marx 1973: 470–1).

In Marx's preface to *A Contribution to the Critique of Political Economy* of 1859 we find the following sentence as well: 'In broad outline Asiatic, ancient, feudal and modern bourgeois modes of production can be designated as progressive epochs in the economic development of society' (Marx 1996: 160). Surely these modes of production seem to be in historical order, but they are still not escalating stages in the sense of Smith and Hegel. In other words, it is not presumed here that these four modes of production follow one after another 'naturally' (Smith) or 'necessarily' (Hegel) in the continuity of time. Rather Marx presumes differences in the conditions that define each form. Therefore we had better consider Marx's 'outline' as 'an ideal construct of a developmental sequence', or 'the logical classification of analytical concepts', in Max Weber's words (Weber 1949: 102–3). For example, 'the Asiatic Mode of Production', as Gayatri C. Spivak says:

> has revealed itself to be neither historico-geographically 'Asiatic' nor logically a 'mode of production' ... The Asiatic Mode and primitive Communism, then, are names that inhabit the pre-historical or para-geographical space/time that remark the outside of the feudalism-capitalism circuit.
>
> (Spivak 1999: 82–3)

Is Marx a nationalist?

Let us now go on to the second question. How does Marx conceptualise the relations between class and nation? In his *Manifesto of the Communist Party* of 1848 he famously insisted that 'workers have no nation of their own' and appealed to 'proletarians of all countries' to unite. However, Horace B. Davis asserts that 'Marx and Engels did not intend to imply that proletarian internationalism excluded a decent affection for one's own country, even if not for the bourgeois version of it ... They may have been unconscious nationalists' (Davis 1967: 13, 20).

Was Marx really a nationalist, or a critic of nationalism? He actually did not discuss ethnic communities sharing a language, religion, customs etc. What he discussed was rather the role of the bourgeoisie in completing a capitalist world system, and the implications of nation-formation within that world system.

First, let us examine the context of the sentence 'workers have no nation of their own'. We find it in the second chapter of *Manifesto*:

> Communists have been further criticized for wanting to abolish the nation ['fatherland' in German original text] and nationalities ... Workers have no nation ['fatherland' in German original text] of their own. We cannot take from them what they do not have. Since the proletariat must first of all take political control, raise itself up to be the class of the nation, must constitute the nation itself, it is still nationalistic, even if not at all in the bourgeois sense of the term ... National divisions and conflicts between peoples increasingly disappear with the development of the bourgeoisie, with free trade and the world market, with the uniform character of industrial production and the corresponding circumstances of modern life ... The rule of the proletariat will make them disappear even faster.
>
> (Marx 1996: 17–18)

According to Marx, the proletariat is 'still nationalistic', though it has 'no nation, no fatherland'. How can these two propositions be compatible? We must first enquire into the meaning of 'nation as a fatherland'. We have a clue in the following sentences in *Manifesto*, though we cannot find a definite explanation:

> The circumstances necessary for the old society to exist are already abolished in the circumstances of the proletariat. The proletarian is without property; his relationship to his wife and children no longer has anything in common with bourgeois family relations; modern industrial labour, modern servitude to capital, which is the same in England as in France or America as in Germany, has stripped him of all national characters.
>
> (Marx 1996: 11)

Some German socialists in the 1840s have already said that workers have no fatherland, because they have no 'father's land', literally, no inheritance. In his *Eighteenth Brumaire of Louis Bonaparte* of 1852 Marx also analyses the historical process through which the French smallholding peasantry acquired 'nationality' by getting their 'inheritance' because of the Revolution, and then later becoming supporters of 'imperialism':

The army was the *point d'honneur* for the smallholding peasantry; it transformed them into heroes, defended their new possessions from outside threats, glorifying their recently acquired nationality, plundering and revolutionizing the world. The dazzling uniform was its own national dress, was its poetry, the smallholding, extended and rounded off in the imagination, was its fatherland, and patriotism was the ideal form of their sense of property.

(Marx 1996: 122)

In that sense, then, the proletariat has 'no fatherland'.

Second, what does Marx mean when he says that 'the proletariat must raise itself up to be the class of the nation and constitute the nation itself'? In order to answer that question we must examine Marx's view of the world system. He sees this dualism in the contemporary capitalist world system. On the one hand, through the exploitation of the world market the bourgeoisie has made the production and consumption of all countries cosmopolitan. On the other hand, however, agglomerating the population, centralising the means of production and concentrating property in a few hands, it has intensified political centralisation. In other words, the bourgeoisie invented 'a nation' as a political unit, whereas it scrapped the 'national basis of industry' and built the global economy at the same time. Why so? Because the bourgeoisie has been involved in a constant battle against the aristocracy, against a part of the bourgeoisie itself and against the bourgeoisie in foreign countries. 'In all those struggles it finds it necessary to appeal to the proletariat, to enlist its aid, and thus to draw it into political action' (Marx 1996: 10). Therefore the struggle of the proletariat against the bourgeoisie would be 'at the outset a national one in form, although not in content. Naturally the proletariat of each country must first finish off its own bourgeoisie' (Marx 1996: 11).

It is important to interpret this sentence precisely. We can easily understand that the class struggle is 'national in form'. For example, Marx says:

The real result of their battles is not some immediate success but a unity amongst workers that gains ever more ground. This is furthered by improved communications, which are generated by large-scale industry, and which put workers from different localities in touch with one another. But this unity is all that is needed to centralise the many local struggles of a generally similar character into a national struggle, a class struggle. Every class struggle, however, is a political struggle.

(Marx 1996: 9)

As for 'national' here, Marx undoubtedly means it to be not local but 'nationwide', or spatially in the frame of a nation state. If so, then, what does it mean that the proletarian class struggle is 'not national in content'? This is concerned with Marx's view of world, as has been mentioned. If capitalism is 'within the bounds of the world market economically and within the bounds of the state-system politically' (Marx 1996: 217), then the class struggle of the proletariat against the bourgeoisie must be a global one beyond nationality and border.

Therefore, if necessary, class struggle will not be 'national in form'. Marx explains this in *The Class Struggles in France* of 1850:

> The task of the worker is not accomplished anywhere within the national walls; the class war within French society turns into a world war, in which the nations confront one another. Accomplishment begins only when, through the world war, the proletariat is pushed to the fore in the nation that dominates the world market, to the fore-front in England. The revolution, which finds here not its end, but its organisational beginnings, is no short-lived revolution.
>
> (Marx and Engels 1978: 117)

Now we can make the meaning of the phrase: 'national in form, although not in content' definite as far as 'the proletarian class struggle' is concerned. However, a question about 'the proletariat's own national character' remains. Why and how 'must the proletariat constitute the nation itself'?

It is obvious that Marx wants the proletariat 'to take political control' and 'to raise itself up to be the class of the nation and constitute the nation itself' (Marx 1996: 17–18). The proletariat can constitute the nation itself, as long as it succeeds in representing 'a national interest' at one with its own class interest in order to take political control nationwide just as the bourgeoisie once did. In the battle against the aristocracy and foreign bourgeoisie it was necessary for the bourgeoisie 'to appeal to the proletariat'. To whom must the proletariat appeal in turn? It must 'arouse the mass of the nation, the peasants and petty bourgeois, standing between the proletariat and the bourgeoisie, against this order, against the rule of capital, and to force them to attach themselves to the proletarians as their protagonists' (Marx and Engels 1978: 57). 'Nation' is therefore a political and ideological concept that represents a class interest as a universal one. Insofar as he thinks this, Marx is without doubt not a nationalist.

Conclusion

Marx's argument concerning the world market was a criticism of the Euro-centric view of world history that considered European civilised society to be 'the latest stage of history'. Since he saw capitalism as a world system, he understood the nation to be a political form through which the bour-geoisie adapted to the worldwide inter-state system. 'Nation' was merely an ideological idea in the capitalist world system for him. In that sense,

Marx's 'Critique of political economy' is not only the criticism of the capitalist world system, but also the criticism of Eurocentric modernity.

However, in the present day, 120 years after Marx's death, most workers seem to have a fatherland to belong to, though they still have no 'father's land' to inherit. Contrary to Marx's expectation, the working class seems to be 'nationalistic in the bourgeois sense of the term', and does not yet constitute 'the nation itself'. Now we must ask why it is so.

Explaining the articulation of the class formation and national integration of workers, Balibar and Wallerstein point out that 'the hegemony of the dominant classes was based on their capacity to organise the labour process and, beyond that, the reproduction of labour-power itself in a broad sense which includes both the workers' subsistence and their cultural formation' (Balibar and Wallerstein 1991: 4). In other words, the hegemony of the dominant class culturally constructs the workers not only as 'the labour-power commodity' but also as 'a nation', by means of a state that takes care of the labour market, unemployment, social security, health, schooling and training. The nationality of the proletariat is therefore an ideological product of 'the social (or "hegemonic") functions of the bourgeoisie tied to national or quasi-national institutions' (Balibar and Wallerstein 1991: 176). Nationality itself is nothing but 'fictive ethnicity' invented by ideological state apparatuses (including the school and the family) and imagined as 'the language community and the race community'.

According to Balibar and Wallerstein, no nation possesses an ethnic basis by nature. But as social formations are nationalised, the populations included within them are 'ethnicized – that is, represented in the past or in the future *as if* they formed a natural community, possessing of itself an identity of origins, culture and interests which transcends individuals and social conditions' (Balibar and Wallerstein 1991: 96).

The problem of constituting the 'nation' must be posed as a problem of internal hegemony. This is the outcome of the dispute concerning 'the nationality' of the proletariat. However, insofar as class is prescribed on the basis of position in the capitalist world system, workers could not be dissolved into a 'national' identity alone. The first necessary condition for workers to liberate themselves as a class would be to realise the social relations of their own that deviate from their 'nationality' as required by the hegemony of the dominant class. That is the deconstruction of 'nationality', a process that promotes international solidarity in the actual relations of life.

It is not a coincidence that some people represent xenophobic nationalism in the present day when we can all obviously see the worldwide relations of the capitalist economy in the activity of multinational enterprises and the immigration of foreign workers. Because of those developments, the dominant classes have become sharply conscious of the crisis of internal hegemony within the imagined community. That crisis represents a chance to deconstruct 'nationality' among the workers and all the rest of us.

References

Althusser, L. and Balibar, É. (1970) *Reading Capital*, trans. B. Brewster. New York: Pantheon.

Balibar, É. and Wallerstein, I. (1991) *Race, Nation, Class: Ambiguous Identities*. London and New York: Verso.

Davis, H.B. (1967) *Nationalism and Socialism: Marxist and Labor Theories of Nationalism*. New York: Monthly Review Press.

Hegel, G.W.F. (1900) *The Philosophy of History*, trans. J. Sibree. New York: Wiley.

Marx, K. (1973) *Grundrisse: Foundations of the Critique of Political Economy*, trans. M. Nicolaus. Harmondsworth: Penguin.

Marx, K. (1996) *Later Political Writings*, ed. and trans. T. Carver. Cambridge: Cambridge University Press.

Marx, K. and Engels, F. (1978) *Collected Works*, vol. 10. London: Lawrence & Wishart.

Marx, K. and Engels, F. (1979) *Collected Works*, vol. 12. London: Lawrence & Wishart.

Marx, K. and Engels, F. (1983) *Collected Works*, vol. 39. London: Lawrence & Wishart.

Said, E.W. (1979) *Orientalism*. New York: Vintage.

Said, E.W. (1993) *Culture and Imperialism*. New York: Vintage.

Smith, A. (1978) *Lectures on Jurisprudence*. Oxford: Clarendon Press.

Spivak, G.C. (1999) *A Critique of Postcolonial Reason: Toward a History of the Vanishing Present*. Cambridge: Harvard University Press.

Weber, M. (1949) *The Methodology of the Social Sciences*, trans. E.A. Shils and H.A. Finch. New York: The Free Press.

2 Marx's economic theory and the prospects for socialism

Makoto Itoh

Traditional Marxism and K. Uno's view

How are we now to conceive of socialism for the 21st century? In most of the 20th century, socialism seemed a clear alternative to capitalism, and Marx's economic theory in *Capital* was regarded as a solid scientific ground for socialism.

Through critical analysis of the capitalist economy, including its historical and contradictory character, Marx's theoretical system in *Capital* has generally been interpreted as suggesting a completely planned economy without any elements of the market. However, Marx did not draw up a blueprint for an ideal society, nor did he expect the middle and upper classes to make it a reality, as opposed to the utopian socialists who preceded him. Instead, he concentrated in a scientific way on the theoretical basis of socialism by clarifying both its target (revolutionising the capitalist market economy), and the potential social subject for realising it (the working class).

However, the relevance of Marx's economic theory in *Capital* for socialism today is not confined to these two points only. While *Capital* presents a systematic, theoretical analysis of the capitalist economy within a longer perspective on human history, it further demonstrates which elements of that economy are to be carried over to a socialist economy of the future. For example, he points to the following as trans-historical socio-economic factors not limited to the commodity economy, nor to the capitalist economic order: use-value as the material content of wealth; the essence of the labour-process as human action mediating the metabolism between human beings and nature; the social necessity to allocate labour-time in accordance with various social needs; and even a directing authority to secure harmonious co-operation in workplaces.

According to the traditional Marxist view, after a revolutionary change of ownership of the major means of production – from private property to state ownership – a socialist economic order could be constructed relatively easily in the form of a centrally planned economy. By abolishing the market and the capitalist economic order, a socialist economy would be subject to social planning, which would manage the trans-historical rules and elements in human economic life. The role of political economy (or economics) would terminate in such a socialist planned economy, since economic science was hitherto almost exclusively limited to the study of the capitalist market economy (Engels 1878: 191). The Soviet economy was usually taken to be a representative model for such a socialist planned economy.

Orthodox Marxists, who followed Soviet Marxism, were not critical of the Soviet model of socialism. Even K. Uno, an original Japanese Marxian economist who attempted to solve many methodological and theoretical confusions in Marxian political economy, took a similar position. They all disagreed with the idea of applying the notions of economic science, such as the law of value, to the construction of a socialist economy. In this regard, Uno's famous essay 'Economic law and socialism' (1953), which decisively criticised Stalin (1952) three years before Khrushchev's de-Stalinisation, was basically in accord with the traditional Marxist understanding of this matter. Against Stalin's assertion that economic laws, just like the laws of nature, should be utilised in the construction of a socialist economy, Uno argued that a socialist economy should aim at the abolition of economic laws, such as the law of value, dominant in capitalist society, and should instead consciously organise and manage in a planned way the basic trans-historical social rules for economic life. In Uno's view, this way of constructing a socialist economy should not be understood as a way to utilise economic laws at all.

The economic laws in a capitalist society actually work anarchically through the market, which is based on the commodity form of labour-power. In Uno's understanding, a fundamental task of socialism is the self-liberation of workers. This means abandoning the commodification of labour-power as well as anarchical economic laws, so as to make the workers true masters of their own society. However, Uno (1953) in a sense made a concession to Stalin and agreed to his admission that a part of the commodity economy must survive within the Soviet one, against an argument that commodity production should be immediately and totally excluded. Stalin and his followers believed in the continued existence of commodity and money in the Soviet system, so long as ownership of the means of production had not yet been totally concentrated into state hands, but was still divided between the state and the *kolkhozi* (collective farms). In the next section, we shall come back to this point and enquire into the nature of the price system and the status of the ruble in the Soviet economy.

On the other hand, Uno (1968: 170) suggested that a socialist economy must generate a social mechanism for replacing capitalist economic devices in order to flexibly mobilise idle capital through the functioning of interest and credit. With this suggestion Uno implied that a simple abandonment of the capitalist market economy would not suffice for constructing a socialist economy. He presented a conscious need to conceive and promote positive socialist alternatives to capitalist economic mechanisms in order to organise a socialist economy. From this point of view, Marx's economic theory must be applied and extended to socialist economies, so as to form an essential part of what Engels had suggested would be needed for 'political economy in a wider sense' (Engels 1878: 191).

The nature of the Soviet economy

With the deepening crisis and final collapse of the Soviet system, there has been considerable interest in rethinking the nature of the Soviet economy and society, including attempts by Japanese economists. In this context, the controversy over economic calculation under socialism has been revisited.

In the controversy, von Mises (1920) and Hayek (1935) represented the neo-classical school, and denied both the possibility of determining and the practicality of calculating rational prices for the means of production under public ownership in a socialist economy, and therefore any rational economic calculation of costs among different methods of production. Thus they argued that collectivist economic planning, as in the Soviet system, cannot exist rationally, and is thus destined to collapse. In addition, Hayek (1949) later emphasised also that a central planning authority would be unable to mobilise the spontaneous and innovative motivation of individuals with locally limited knowledge and information, unlike economic agents in a market economy (Lavoie 1985). According this neo-classical view, the collapse of Soviet-type economies would be only natural.

Taylor (1929) and Lange (1936–37) were opposed to von Mises and Hayek, and argued instead that rational prices for the means of production under public ownership could be determined in a socialist economy through trial and error revisions of the central authority's price list. This could be done by observing the feedback from individual firms in demanding and supplying the means of production. A socialist economy with public ownership of the means of production could thus be defended as feasible in order to form a 'market socialism' with flexible prices in accord with the balance between demand and supply among relatively independent firms. As Taylor and Lange depended upon the neo-classical general equilibrium theory of prices in their defence of socialism, the controversy seemed to lie outside the Marxist theoretical paradigm, and it generally bypassed most Marxists in the world at large, as well as in Japan, until recently.

Von Mises and Hayek followed Böhm-Bawerk's (1896) critique of the labour theory of value by denouncing Marx's idea of using labour-time in socialist economic calculations. They pointed, among other things, to the difficulty of reducing complex labour-time to simple labour-time. Hayek's point on the practical infeasibility for a socialist central authority to gather necessary information and calculate equilibrium prices would be applicable to a similar difficulty in calculating the labour-time embodied in each product by formulating and solving hundreds of thousands of simultaneous equations representing physical input–output co-relations. Although the controversy about how to defend Marx's labour theory of value from Böhm-Bawerk's critique was a focal point of theoretical concern among Marxists, including Japanese Marxists, these attempts to defend and deepen Marx's labour theory of value were somehow unconnected with the socialist economic calculation controversy, or with defences of socialism against the von Mises and Hayek type of criticism.

Besides the impression that Taylor and Lange successfully defended the feasibility of a socialist economy incorporating public ownership of the means of production, without relying on Marx's theory of value, the seemingly successful growth of the Soviet economy was generally believed empirically to have proven the feasibility of a centrally planned economy, as against von Mises and Hayek. Nevertheless, the nature of the Soviet economy left complex problems to be reconsidered both in its growth and in its final collapse.

One problem concerns the nature of prices in the Soviet economy. Although the Soviet economy grew rather successfully for several decades with public ownership of the means of production, against the prediction by von Mises and Hayek, it was not run in accordance with the Taylor and Lange model of flexible revisions of price lists so as to realise equilibrium between demand and supply. Prices in the Soviet economy actually followed the pattern of the pre-World War I period, and were subsequently officially altered from time to time on the cost-plus principle. Such officially fixed ruble prices, together with physical input–output data, were used for planning the distribution of products and services, and for selection by consumers. So far as the price-form of commodities and money appears in principle only within the anarchical free market economy, these officially fixed prices in the Soviet system could not be for real commodities, but could only be socialist quasi-prices, and the ruble was therefore quasi-money. In this regard, Stalin's and the Soviet orthodox position – that commodities and money remained in the Soviet system – was in my view not theoretically correct, despite Uno's endorsement. It is noteworthy, however, that such quasi-prices were also useful as units of account for measuring macro-economic growth (representing the conventional aggregate of the physical growth of products), independent of labour-time, as well as for economic planning and income distribution. In retrospect, real economic growth was theoretically and conventionally measured by either market prices or by public prices, but not simply by labour-time alone.

At the same time, we have to admit that the nature of prices in the Soviet system was different from Marx's prescription for a socialist economy, which was to use direct labour-time as units of account for co-operative planning of production and distribution through the application of the labour theory of value. Indeed, official prices in the Soviet system were theoretically and practically unrelated to the labour-time embodied in products. A theoretical difficulty concerning how to reduce complex labour to simple labour remained unsolved, and the practical difficulty of calculating the labour-time embodied in products from the physical input–output data must also have been a real obstacle to Marx's prescription.

Thus, the nature of prices in the Soviet system was neither that of the neo-classical price theory nor that of a deductive application of Marx's labour theory of value. In my view, Sraffa's (1960) neo-Ricardian price theory, based on physical data of input and output for viable social reproduction without reference to labour-time, was closest to it. If I dare say without evidence, Sraffa's price theory may even have been given encouragement through the experience of economic reproduction in Soviet society. The socialist economic calculation controversy was unfortunately not merely disconnected from Marxian value theory, but was also not yet able to make use of Sraffian price theory. It is worth emphasising that an economic calculation for choosing the most economical method of production can theoretically be performed not only by the neo-classical pricing model, but also by using either labour-time as a unit of account (following Marx), or a Sraffian type of pricing model, though the resultant pattern of rationality would not be identical.

A problematic point in Sraffian theory in relation to the Soviet economy was the degree of freedom contained in determining a real wage rate in relation to a general rate of profit. As the free or cheap supply of social communal consumption was extended in the spirit of socialism, a wage rate could be relatively low, covering a smaller and smaller portion of the labour-time necessary for its own reproduction over generations. A result was that a mark-up in the form of an economic surplus over costs in such a socialist economy could be inflated or could be apparently much greater, and subject to more bureaucratic manipulation, compared to the average profit in a capitalist economy with similar levels of technological development and living standards.

Another result was a tendentious bias for overstaffing with lower levels of technology in order to avoid the introduction of new machinery for economising on costs with lower wage rates. At least part of the inefficiency and stagnation during the period toward the end of the Soviet economy must be fundamentally related to that kind of problem.

Marx's prescription to use labour-time as a unit of account in a socialist economy, if realisable, could be superior in that context, but now it remains unutilised, though still worth considering for the future, despite the failure of the Soviet economic model. If we reverse the Soviet model of wages, and set up a model of what I call a full s-wage (socialist quasi-wage), where net national product is completely distributed to s-wages; and if we take an egalitarian socialist position in seeing abstract labour-time expended in various forms of concrete labour as being based on the common human ability to labour and measured homogeneously simply by time regardless of degrees of complexity, then the prices of products in equilibrium either in a planned economy or in market socialism must necessarily be proportional to the labour-time necessary to reproduce them (Itoh 1995: 52, 130). Then Marx's idea of realising transparent social relations of production and distribution in a socialist economy can be achieved through prices in either planned or market socialism. Various funds necessary to sustain accumulation, common consumption, adminis-trative activities, social care and education, including various necessary kinds of complex labour-power, must then be directly contributed by workers or taxed on their s-wage income. This system would avoid the biased underestimation of labour costs in the Soviet economy, and would promote instead a democratic and socially co-operative sense in society, so as to place workers in the position of real masters of their own society.

Compared with Marx's notion of socialism as 'an association of free men' with common ownership of the means of production (Marx 1867: 171), there was also another anomaly in the Soviet system. This took the form of hypertrophy of the state and party bureaucrats, who were called *nomenklatura* or red aristocrats, as against a de-politicised and suppressed mass of people. How are we to understand the nature of Soviet society and to save Marx's ideas for socialism after the failure of the Soviet Union? There have been two different positions on this issue, with minor variants.

The first type denounced the characterisation 'socialism' in Soviet society. The position of the Japanese Communist Party has largely changed, and has shifted to this type of view. Correspondingly, a group of Japanese Marxists, such as Otani *et al.* (1996), began to assert that the Soviet system was a type of state capitalism. The same characterisation was presented by Bettelheim (1974), as well as by the Chinese critique of the Soviet Union in the period of the Chinese Cultural Revolution. Against a popular and especially neo-classical opinion identifying the col-lapse of the Soviet system with the general failure of socialism, this type of assertion represents one of several attempts to save socialism for the future. However, it is not very persuasive to identify the Soviet state and party bureaucrats, who did not have private ownership of means of pro-duction or shares in firms, with capitalists. Their pattern of behaviour in managing individual firms or the whole economy was quite different from that of capitalists or their agents, who would be always motivated to increase efficiency or productivity. Workers were generally immune from the threat of unemployment, unlike the situation in a real capitalist economy. Moreover, if there was state capitalism, why has the transition to a capitalist market economy been so difficult and even self-destructive?

Sweezy (1980) presented an argument against Bettelheim, outlining another notion of a post-revolutionary society with a new type of class structure that could define the Soviet model of society. It required certain revisions to Marx's theory or his historical materialism. In Marx's formula for historical materialism, a capitalist society is conceived as the last form of class society, in which the social bases of the ruling classes have been in certain forms of ownership or possession of land and of other means of production. Against this, Sweezy argued that a new type of class society can be born and grow, even after a socialist revolution has abolished capitalism, and that the basis of a new ruling class can be in a privileged education and promotion system for *nomenklatura* families. Amin (1985) followed Sweezy and defined the Soviet type of ruling class as a state class. Although Sweezy's view was translated into Japanese and then gathered a certain amount of attention among Japanese Marxists, somehow it did not attain much continuous support, probably due to their hesitation in revising Marx's formula for historical materialism.

The second type of conceptualisation of the nature of the Soviet society is that the Soviets had formed a type of socialism, even though there were anomalies or distortions in various aspects, such as immaturity at an early stage of socialism (Fujita 1980), the Stalin phenomenon (Ellenstein 1976), or the revolution having been betrayed by technocratic bureaucrats who were initially placed in the position of managing agents for an immature working people (Trotsky 1937). Those points are not mutually exclusive. Military statism, necessitated by anti-communist intervention, fascist invasion and the strictures of the Cold War, could also be added to these issues. Anyway, this second type of view, in comparison with the first type, is more or less favourable to the socio-economic achievements in the Soviet system undertaken within the spirit of socialism.

Indeed, Soviet society had achieved economic growth higher than most advanced capitalist countries, despite heavier military burdens. It had removed the threat of unemployment and guaranteed relatively egalitarian living conditions, including pensions, medical care and childcare, and an extended education system that produced the largest number of engineers in the world, and greatly expanded jobs for women, enhancing their positions at workplaces in accord with the socialist idea. So long as there was relatively easy access to rich natural resources and to mobilisable work forces in the process of industrialisation to construct heavy industries on a large scale, the Soviet economy could grow suitably within the form of central planning based on the co-operation of workers, who were motivated by improving living conditions in the spirit of socialism. The stagnation since the middle of 1970s and the failure of the Soviet system must be profoundly related to the historical fact that such favourable conditions for economic growth were used up, and also that technological, industrial and systemic changes were so difficult to realise within the Soviet social framework under the rule of a hypertrophied bureaucracy.

If the historical experience of the Soviet economy can thus be positively assessed in certain ways, the programme of the current Russian Communist Party, which throughout the 1990s has occasionally begun to gather broader support among the people again, cannot simply be denounced as old-fashioned. Rather it should be warmly applauded as one of the feasible options for socialism in the 21st century, arguing for the reconstruction of the planned economy with public ownership of the means of production in a democratic political order. Insofar as the main reason for the failure of the Soviet economy lies in undemocratic political oppression under hypertrophied bureaucrats, and in a resultant loss of co-operation among the workers, a centrally planned economy with public ownership of the means of production under a democratic political system, mobilising workers as true masters of a society in the spirit of Marx's idea for realising an association of free persons, is actually a socio-economic model which has not yet been tried even experimentally. Therefore it remains an option for the new century.

The possibilities of the Chinese road to socialism

A popular view is that China is already going over to capitalism as its market economy expands. This view is generally supported by neoclassical economists, among others, since they believe that a market economy is the natural order of things and is identical with a capitalist economy. Such a view is against not just the Chinese official position as reflected in their Constitutional Law, but is also against the expectations of those in the world who are seeking a future for socialism, even after the collapse of the Soviet system.

Is it possible to utilise Marx's economic theory in order to demonstrate the feasibility of a socialist market economy? In this regard, the following things need to be re-examined with a view to the future of socialism and a more flexible understanding of various models of socialism amongst which people could choose: the basic distinction in history between a market economy and capitalism; the social function of the labour market in market socialism; and the possibilities for socialist forms of taxation on profit, ground rent and personal income.

If a market economy is an inevitable result of a natural human propensity to exchange, as A. Smith (1776: 15) stated, and if this is naturally completed in a capitalist economy, a socialist market economy with public ownership of the major means of production and a certain degree of planning must therefore be an unnatural and artificially distorted economic order. In contrast, Marx (1867: 182) pointed out that commodity exchange began historically 'where communities have their boundaries, at their points of contact with other communities, or with members of the latter', thus co-existing with various social orders very broadly from previous, even ancient periods. Marx (1867: 125–280) further presented commodities, money and capital initially as simple forms of a market economy prior to his analysis of capitalist process of production. Uno (1950; 1964) regarded this theoretical treatment very highly and clarified those parts of his work to make a genuine theory of circulation, without referring to social relations of labour as the substance of value. Such theoretical compositions surely demonstrate an important recognition that the forms of the market economy have a historical nature much older and broader than the capitalist market economy. At the same time, they offer an important theoretical ground for the possibility of incorporating and utilising the forms, adjustment functions, and stimulus of a market economy within a socialist economy, based on public ownership of the means of production at various levels and in various forms, being subject to a certain degree of planning. This view is clearly opposed to naturalising theories in the tradition of both classical and neo-classical economics, which identify a capitalist market economy with a market economy in general, as well as with a natural order of liberty.

The social functions of forms of the market economy have greatly changed throughout the history of capitalism. Capitalist economies have not just completed the full market economy, but have also attempted to regulate it, in order to reduce its violent fluctuations, unequal and unfair income distribution, and economic crimes. The currency management system is an example that will serve for such purposes, if not always successfully. The Chinese road for a socialist market economy will have to learn the lessons of such historical experiences of capitalist economies, so as to realise more self-consciously the institutional settings needed for more desirable social functions of the market economy, as opposed to a simple neo-liberal belief in the harmonious efficiency of the free market order. In the area of currency management, for example, the Chinese government has been relatively successful in maintaining stability in the fields of money and finance, by comparison with surrounding Asian countries, including Japan and the USA, due to its control of both the international and the domestic supply of money and finance.

On the other hand, encouragement to make money individually through simple, free market trading tends to go hand-in-hand with economic crimes. As commodity trade originated from inter-social transactions, merchant capital tended to raise profit by defrauding and cheating others in defiance of communal regulations within each society. Thus Marx (1894: 448–9) pointed out that:

> commercial capital, when it holds a dominant position, is thus in all cases a system of plunder, just as its development in the trading peoples of both ancient and modern times is directly bound up with violent plunder, piracy, the taking of slaves and subjugation of colonies; as in Carthage and Rome, and later in the Venetians, Portuguese, Dutch, etc.

A critical recognition of these dark depths of the market economy, which is apt to induce unfair trade and economic crimes, is very necessary as a point of reference for the Chinese road to a socialist market economy. It is now especially relevant as the Chinese Communist Party is striving to tighten discipline in order to overcome increasing corruption and economic crimes, though mainly by restudying socialist thought and ethics at various levels. Socialist thought may not be sufficient by itself in this context, and should always be grounded on critical and scientific recognition of the historical nature of the market economy and capitalism, so as to construct socialist institutional devices (such as policing and the legal system) for ordinary people that are much fairer than those found in capitalist market economies.

Capitalist economies have grown up on the basis of commodifying the labour-power of a mass of workers, who are generally excluded from private ownership of the means of production. Socialism has traditionally aimed at abandoning the commodity form of labour-power so as to make workers the true masters of their society, on the basis of public ownership of the means production. However, in the process of making economic reforms in order to bring about a socialist market economy, specific forms of the labour-market began to reappear in the Chinese economy.

As rural township and village enterprises in China grew from 1.52 million in 1978 to 20.04 million enterprises in 1998, they absorbed an excess labouring population from agricultural farming families and increased their workers from 28 million to 125 million. Their share in rural industrial employment became 28.6 per cent in 1995 (Meng 2000: 37). In city areas, various non-state-owned enterprises grew and absorbed a large number of workers through the labour market. State-owned enterprises have attempted to restructure and reduce the excess working population. As a result, the share of state-owned enterprises in the employment of working people in city areas has declined from 78.3 per cent in 1978 to 40.8 per cent in 1999 (Minami and Makino 2001: 103). At the same time, unemployment has become a serious social problem in urban areas (Marukawa 2000). In 1997, the number of registered unemployed workers in urban areas reached 5.76 million (3.1 per cent). Besides this, the number of workers out of jobs from state-owned enterprises in the form of layoffs (on which they are paid basic subsistence wages for three years in order to seek other jobs) amounted to 9.37 million in 1999. In total, the practical unemployment figure in urban areas is estimated to have reached at least fifteen million (8.1 per cent). That figure is paradoxical against the high economic growth of the Chinese socialist market economy.

It is often argued, with a certain amount of truth, that a fluid labour market with efficient information and communication is desirable and necessary for a more effective market economy (Meng 2000). In such an argument, possible differences between the capitalist labour market and the socialist labour market in theory are apt to be neglected. In a capitalist economy, instability and difficulty in personal lives due to a fluctuating labour market, including unemployment, are basically an individual responsibility. In a socialist market economy, with public ownership of the means of production, instability and difficulty in personal lives in relation to a function of the labour market should not be attributed theoretically to an individual worker's own risk and responsibility, because workers are fundamentally the masters of society by collectively owning the major means of production.

In the socialist economic calculation controversy, Lange's (1936–37) famous model of market socialism presented an idea for making up the income of working people – preserving free choice of occupation in a labour market – from two different parts: one part would be remuneration for their labour, and the other part would be derived from collectively owned natural resources and the means of production. The latter part should not affect the choice of occupation of an individual or the social allocation of labour, and therefore it could be distributed either equally to each person or according to family structure and the age of family members.

That model is very useful in making clear the notion of a labour market in a socialist market economy, in distinction from that notion in a capitalist economy. Although the function of a labour market – to enable the flexible reallocation of workers across industries and workplaces – is necessary for a socialist market economy, it should be combined with a solid social security system in order to ensure stability in the economic life of workers as the masters of a society. In practice, however, the idea and the reality of the social security system in China are far from what they should be in a socialist market economy.

A serious problem in constructing a social security system outside the historical functions of Chinese state-owned enterprises and Chinese people's communes is the shortage of government income. The Chinese government has continually run up a large deficit on tax revenue since the latter half of the 1980s, despite successive years of high economic growth. The share of government revenue in the Chinese GDP has declined from 31.2 per cent in 1978 to 11.6 per cent in 1997 (Ma 2000: 18). It is lower than in most capitalist countries. Partly it reflects a strategic decentralisation, shifting various public functions to local authorities. However, it must have come largely from negligence, both theoretically and institutionally, in raising taxes in a socialist way, and instead following a neo-liberal trend among advanced capitalist countries of reducing taxes for corporations and wealthier persons, so as to induce multinational investment and to reactivate individualistic market principles. It is clearly against the egalitarian spirit and programme for socialism, as the market economy under such a policy stance inevitably expands income differentials corresponding not to effort or labour but rather to fortunate or unfortunate initial endowment or market circumstances.

So long as land is basically owned by the whole people in China, to be utilised by individual family farms and various enterprises under the Contract Responsibility System, socialist forms of differential rent should explicitly be estimated and collected as a socialist form of tax from the excess-revenue or excess-profit accruing to better quality land or to the location of land in use. The amount of differential rent in a socialist form must surely be increased as the land in use becomes more profitable in relation to a growing market in a nearby city, or in relation to the whole process of national economic growth, especially when there is an inflationary bias. It should not remain unchanged or prepaid for a long lease period, say fifteen years or more, in a rapidly changing economy. Similarly, so long as the means of production are mainly held in public ownership, a substantial part of the profit of various enterprises should be socialised, by being paid to the central or local government as another form of socialist tax, though some part of this profit must certainly be retained as an incentive to the enterprises under the Contract Responsibility System. Theoretically, the share of such a socialist form of tax must be greater than the proportion of corporate tax to profit in capitalist enterprises with privately owned means of production. A third form of socialist tax is a progressive income tax and inheritance tax. In conformity with the socialist principles of egalitarianism, they should also be substantially heavier than in capitalist countries.

Without constructing both theoretical grounds and fair social institutions for collecting socialist taxes, the Chinese socialist market economy will not be able to achieve its goal of making working people the true masters of society. The social welfare or safety net system that supplements the workings of the labour market, a desirable education system that realises free or cheap opportunities for younger generations to develop, and medical services guaranteed for all people in case of necessity, are surely to be realised only on the basis of increased public revenue in a socialist market economy. These reflections suggest that the Chinese progression to a socialist market economy cannot proceed toward its original goal simply by means of macro-level economic growth.

Marx's economic theory in my view is thus worthy of reconsideration as a direct and indirect frame of reference for feasible socialism in the 21st century, including the current Chinese path. The complex problems inherent in this should be resolved in the spirit 'by the people, and for the people'.

References

(Titles in square brackets [ ] are my translation from Japanese.)

Amin, S. (1985) 'The prospects for socialism', in M. Nicolic (ed.) *Socialism on the Threshold of the Twenty-first Century*. London: Verso.

Bettelheim, C. (1974) *Les Luttes de Classes en USSR*, 4 vols. Paris: Maspero Seuil.

Böhm-Bawerk, E. von (1896) *Zum Abschluss des Marxschen Systems.* English trans. in P. Sweezy (ed.) (1966) *Karl Marx and the Close of His System by E. Von Böhm-Bawerk and Böhm-Bawerk's Criticism of Marx by R. Hilferding.* New York: M. Kelley.

Ellenstein, J. (1976) *The Stalin Phenomenon,* trans. P. Lantham. London: Lawrence and Wishart.

Engels, F. (1878) *Herrn Eugen Dührings Umwälzung der Wissenschaft.* English trans. Peking: Foreign Language Press, 1976.

Fujita, I. (1980) [*The Theory of Socialist Societies*]. Tokyo: University of Tokyo Press.

Hayek, F.A. (ed.) (1935) *Collectivist Economic Planning.* London: Routledge and Kegan Paul.

Hayek, F.A. (1949) *Individualism and the Economic Order.* London: Routledge and Kegan Paul.

Itoh, M. (1995) *Political Economy for Socialism.* London and New York: Macmillan and St. Martin's.

Lange, O. (1936–37) 'On the economic theory of socialism', Part 1 and Part 2, *Review of Economic Studies* 4: 53–71, 123–42.

Lavoie, D. (1985) *Rivalry and Central Planning.* Cambridge: Cambridge University Press.

Ma, J. (2000) *The Chinese Economy in the 1990s.* Harmondsworth and New York: Macmillan and St. Martin's.

Marx, K. (1867, 1885, 1894) *Capital,* vol. 1, 2, 3, trans. B. Fowkes and D. Fernbach (1976, 1978, 1981). Harmondsworth: Penguin.

Marukawa, T. (2000) ['Present and future of the unemployment problem'], in W. Nakagane (ed.) [*Structural Changes in Contemporary China*], vol. 2. Tokyo: University of Tokyo Press.

Meng, X. (2000) *Labour Market Reform in China.* Cambridge: Cambridge University Press.

Minami, R. and Makino, F. (eds) (2001) [*Introduction to Chinese Economy*]. Tokyo: Nihonhyoron-sha.

Otani, T., Onishi, H. and Yamaguchi, M. (eds) (1996) [*What was Soviet 'Socialism'?*]. Tokyo: Otsuki-shoten.

Smith, A. (1776) *The Wealth of Nations,* ed. E. Cannan (1922), vol. 1. London: Methuen.

Sraffa, P. (1960) *Production of Commodities by Means of Commodities.* Cambridge: Cambridge University Press.

Stalin, J.V. (1952) *Economic Problems of Socialism in the U.S.S.R.* English trans. (1972). Peking: Foreign Language Press.

Sweezy, P.M. (1980) *Post-Revolutionary Society.* New York: Monthly Review Press.

Taylor, F.M. (1929) 'The guidance of production in a socialist state', *American Economic Journal* 19: 1–8.

Trotsky, L. (1937) *The Revolution Betrayed,* trans. M. Eastman. London: Faber and Faber.

Uno, K. (1950, 1952) [*Principles of Political Economy*], 2 vols. Tokyo: Iwanami-shoten.

Uno, K. (1953) ['Economic law and socialism'] in K. Uno [*Marx's Capital and Socialism*] (1958). Tokyo: Iwanami-shoten.

Uno, K. (1964) *Principles of Political Economy*, trans. T. Sekine (1980). Brighton: Harvester Press.
Uno, K. (1968) ['A theory of interest'] in Hosei University, *Shakai-Rodou Kenkyu* 14: 150–79.
von Mises, L. (1920) 'Economic calculation in the socialist commonwealth', in F.A. Hayek (1935): 89–130.

Part II

Contemporary problems in Marx studies

3 Marx's theory of history reappraised

Hiroshi Uchida

Introduction

Marx's theory of history, as set out in the chapters on 'primitive accumulation' in *Capital*, is still valid when expanded into a historico-theoretical conception of the capitalist mode of production worldwide. His account of primitive accumulation, especially in Chapter 24, 'So-called primitive accumulation', in volume one and in Chapter 47, 'Genesis of capitalist ground-rent', in volume three (Marx 1965, 1966), should not be read simply as a history of English capitalism as a unique phenomenon. In *Capital* Marx (1965: 8) identified England as the 'classic case' for his study of capitalism in general. He argued that advanced English capitalism presaged the future for other developing nations; he maintained that vision from the time of his early works in the 1840s. His account of primitive accumulation thus has the potential to generate a theory of history that would enable us to understand the structure and trends of primitive accumulation in contemporary developing nations. His theory reveals that these nations are following basically the same path as past Western primitive accumulation. In the process of primitive accumulation, capitalism generally forms 'rentier-state capitalism', sometimes referred to as 'developmental dictatorship'. Early English capitalism offers a classic example of 'rentier-state capitalism'. In the present chapter I define and illustrate this.

Capitalism and manufacture

Marx writes that industrial capital, having outgrown older modes of production, is derived from an articulation of monetary funds. These have been accumulated in the hands of merchants, so largely concentrating labour power and technology and thus causing guilds to reorganise. Industrial capital generates manufacture par excellence, especially the production of luxuries, such as glass, metal, ships etc., for large-scale foreign trade. However, it was the peasants' ancillary work in spinning wool or weaving woollen clothes, articles of necessity, which enabled manufacture to rise on its first broad basis. This rural manufacture originated as a transitory form in the putting-out system between merchant managers and peasants who did the weaving. Later, merchants deprived peasants of land and organised them as wage-workers in manufacture (Marx 1973: 510–11; Marx and Engels 1974: 98ff.). 'The old self-employed possessors of land themselves thus give rise to a nursery for capitalist tenants, whose development is conditioned by the general development of capitalist production beyond the bounds of the countryside' (Marx 1966: 799).

In generalising Marx's view of the formation of the capitalist mode of production, I suggest that there are four elements:

1   monetary funds;
2   labour power;
3   technology;
4   land.

These are organised into commercialised forms for profit. Technology and monetary funds are determining factors that I will illustrate with several examples below. Technology is the material mediator for labour power in action and the means through which labour gains higher productivity. Monetary funds are the formal mediator for commercialised elements of labour power and the means of production, because they embody technology in order to raise profitability. Contemporary transnational capital is powerful enough to integrate developing nations into the system, because it monopolises technology and monetary funds. Commercialisation of land, labour power and technology, the manifestation of money, and the establishment of the capitalist mode of production, are simultaneous. Capitalist commercialisation begins with the commercialisation of land.

Land is the most basic element in the formation of capitalism in which almost all existence tends to be commercialised. When serfs purchased a long-use right to land from a feudal landlord, they became independent and the land was commercialised. Thus agriculture became commerce, and its products, that is, the means of life and the materials for industry, began to be commercialised, moving from a surplus part of the whole product to a necessary part.

When the necessary part of the product started to be commercialised, labour power inevitably became a commodity, because it was reproduced through the consumption of the necessary and now commercialised means of life. After agriculture became commercialised, industry also changed in this way. Industrial technology had been prepared for this through a proto-industrial age that then advanced through the period of the industrial revolution. During this revolution, technology was developed not by 'workmen in manufacture, but by learned men, handicraftsmen and even peasants' (Marx 1965: 348). The industrial revolution drastically changed agriculture as commerce:

Modern industry alone and finally supplies in machinery the lasting basis of capitalist agriculture, expropriates radically the enormous majority of the agricultural population, and completes the separation between agriculture and rural domestic industry.

(Marx 1965: 748–9)

Later, the development of technology brought higher profits, and technology itself became a commodity. Money was invested in research and development, and technology was socially utilised with a royalty on inventions. Military demand accelerated industrial development and established a 'military-industrial complex' (McNeill 1982: 223ff.).

Monetary funds were accumulated in the hands of merchants during the Middle Ages. The European continent received an abundant supply of gold and silver from the new world, revolutionising prices in the 17th century. The gold rush of the 19th century met the needs of monetary funds in commercialising almost all wealth. Thus all four of the basic elements of the capitalist mode of production, i.e. land, labour power, technology and monetary funds, were commercialised, producing rent, wages, royalties and interest, respectively. The ways in which the four elements are obtained depends on the historical stage of development of world capitalism. English capitalism developed technology by itself, and obtained other elements from within and without, whereas contemporary developing nations provide land and labour power, both of them available in abundance at cheap prices, for transnational capital, which in turn introduces the determining factors, monetary funds and technology, that are in its possession.

Workers' conditions were divided into four stages in English economic history. They were:

1   unfree as serfs in the Middle Ages;
2   free as independent peasants for a short period about the beginning of the 16th century;
3   unfree as wage workers under the 'bloody' legislation introduced between the first half of the 16th century and the middle of the 19th century;
4   free as wage workers from the middle of the 19th century when they obtained citizenship.

Amongst many other kinds of unfree workers, serfs became free peasants independent from feudal landlords by purchasing land use right for a long period. After enjoying 'a golden age' of short duration around the beginning of the 16th century, peasants were then organised as unfree wage workers in manufacture par excellence, the point at which Marx set the beginning of capitalist mode of production. Under the later 'bloody' legislation, they became subordinate. Despite bourgeois revolutions in the

17th century, most English wage workers were unfree and so without modern civil rights about for 300 years, until the middle of the 19th century, when wage workers emancipated themselves through civil conflict. This was the second civil revolution in England, in solidarity with the Chartists. The 'bloody' legislation had been introduced in order to maintain absolute monarchy. However, it had the unexpected effect of forcing proletarians, violently separated from land and community, to become unfree wage workers, and of making wages cheaper to accumulate monetary funds. In the age of manufacture par excellence, when the capitalist mode of production had become strong enough to render legal regulation of wages impractical and unnecessary, the ruling classes were unwilling to renounce the old weapons in critical situations. The history of labour legislation had already begun in 1349 with the Statue of Labourers of Edward III, and it ended in the 1813 with the repeal of wage regulation and in the 1825 laws against trade unions. Referring to the primitive accumulation chapters of *Capital*, Mochizuki divides the founding process of the capitalist mode of production into three stages, starting with its foundation, an acceleration of the process and then adding the basic elements of the capitalist mode of production, labour power and monetary funds etc. (Mochizuki 1982). Contemporary world capitalism is still adding labour power from the peripheral countryside to developmental dictatorships in peripheral cities or to capitalist world cities in the centre in order to continue the expansion of capitalist mode of production. Developmental dictatorships force wage workers into unfreedom and enforce cheap wages through oppressions similar to the 'bloody' legislation.

The role of the early bourgeois state was indispensable for accelerating the establishment of the capitalist mode of production, in order to win commercial wars against foreign rivals. The state constructed modern tax systems, transportation-communication systems, the education system and sanitation, and introduced factory regulations, a protection policy for domestic industry and a colonial policy, as mentioned in the primitive accumulation chapters of *Capital*. The state was under the rule of the landed class who utilised land rent or merchants' profits gained by investing land rent in commerce. Therefore, the early English state was a state for primitive accumulation, in other words, a landowner-monarchy (squirearchy), after Jiro Iinuma's categorisation of English capitalism from the early 16th century until the 1870s (Iinuma 1978: 125), or 'landowner-system based capitalism', after Kenji Kawano's characterisation of the agrarian capitalism of England or France (Kawano 1966: 39).

Developmental dictatorship as rentier-state capitalism

Reference to Max Weber's *Economy and Society* gives us a suggestion for redefining the term rent (*die Rente*) or rentier (*der Rentner*), because he abstracted all kinds of revenue into rent in general; that is, land rent, mine rent, freight, interest, dividend, profit etc., that are gained through owner-ship of land, mines, hire-purchase (factories and equipment), ships, credi-tors (of livestock, grains or money), securities and men (in case of slave-owners) (Weber 1978: 303). Weber included in 'rentier' landed inter-ests, moneyed interests, commercial capitalists, industrial capitalists and even slave masters (slavery was abolished 1833 within the British Empire). However, the landed class distinguished themselves from other rentiers, because they took the initiative in supplying from the agricultural sector the four main elements of the capitalist mode of production, or introduc-ing monetary funds and technology from transnational capital, utilising land rent. The redefinition of 'rent' and 'rentier' opens up a new perspect-ive and scope for locating on the same long transitory stage of primitive accumulation not only contemporary developing nations, but also Western agrarian capitalism of the past.

So-called 'developmental dictatorship' that aims for capitalist industri-alisation under a dictatorial party-state armed with the military (Marx 1965: 750ff.) can generally be observed in the history of primitive accumu-lation, both in present-day developing nations and in Western nations of the past. The concept of 'developmental dictatorship' can be illustrated with examples not only from contemporary developing nations, but also from the history of Western nations. Even socialist nations like China in its 'socialist market economy' or Vietnam in its 'Doimoi developmental strategy' may be categorised under developmental dictatorship (as detailed below). This is a system where the landed class or bureaucrats in a landed state establish the capitalist mode of production. The state that supports or accelerates the formation of capitalism is termed a 'rentier-state' in order to analyse the elements and roles of the state.

The rentier-state is categorised into the following two types:

A   States ruled by a landed class or rentier (A1) who owns most national land as private property, expropriates rent (land rent) from peasant tenants, grasps political power in the state by paying part of the rent as land tax to the state as rentier (A2) for constructing infrastructure, and turns the rest of the rent into funds for obtaining and organising the four elements of capitalism.

B   Landed states or rentier that immediately own and rule the entire national land as state property and gain rent (land tax) by releasing a right of land use to the nation or transnational capital especially for monetary funds and technology.

Rentier in state (A) are categorised into a landed class or rentier (A1) and the state or rentier (A2). The state expends rent (land tax), supplied by the landed class for capitalist industrialisation, having extracted it as a land tax from peasants. Rentier in state (B) are the state itself extracting rent as land tax immediately from peasants. When private ownership of land changes into state-ownership, the landed class (A1) ceases to exist and the state (A2) is replaced by state (B). The landed state (B) then separates itself into the landed class or rentier (A1) and the state or rentier (A2), when state ownership of land (B) changes into private ownership. When the state (A) or the state (B) colonises other nations, the state (A) or (B) becomes the imperial state (A') or (B'); as the Victorian British state (A) occupied India, or the pre-war Japanese state (A) dominated Korea, or the Soviet Union (B) ruled East European nations under the Warsaw Pact and COMECON.

In spite of the difference in land ownership, whether private property or state property, the landed class or landed state share the same mission to found the capitalist mode of production. Under 'the great civilising influence of capital' (Marx 1973: 409), they are forced to become the head of the rentier-state, utilising agricultural surplus as basic funds for constructing the economic, political and social infrastructure, and investing in capitalist industrial sectors. Agriculture ruled by the landed class or the landed state supplies food, industrial materials (including mineral resources, such as oil and gas) and labour power to the capitalist industrial sector, and it simultaneously supplies manpower as bureaucrats and members of military forces of the state for primitive accumulation. Both states maintain ideological national integration in order to maintain political stability for the founding of the capitalist mode of production.

Rentier-state capitalism illustrated

This section illustrates the concept of rentier-state capitalism by giving several examples of nations in the process of primitive accumulation.

England

From the civil revolutions of the 17th century until the 1870s English capitalism has been a rentier-state. Landowners, merchants and moneylenders exercised hegemony in the early English state in order to establish a capitalist industrial sector. The Petition of Right of 1628 originated the principle that a land tax should be imposed on landowners as law through Parliament, and so the king's household and the Treasury should be clearly separated from this. 'The socio-economical significance of the bourgeois revolution exists in the *legal* establishment of private property' (Iinuma 1978: 120; my italics). Marx paid attention to the Treasury (*Fiskus*) as early as *The German Ideology* (Marx and Engels 1974: 104) and the *Grundrisse* (Marx 1973: 509). He recognised the English state de facto as a rentier-state, both domestic and foreign; indeed, he detailed the facts in Chapter 35 of volume three of *Capital* and in his essays of the 1850s on current events. In his theoretical perspective, English capitalism needed to rid itself of the aspect of rentier-state and would become industrial capitalism; at the same time, he realised that English capitalism was in fact maintaining this aspect even in 1870s.

English capitalism began economic development and improvement under the English constitutional monarchy from the time of the Glorious Revolution of 1689. English large-scale landowners were not feudal, but rather belonged to a bourgeoisie that was progressive in agricultural commodity production and in the business of commerce and finance. They developed agriculture in order to provide an advanced industrial sector with labour power, food and materials; thus they enjoyed a golden age (1850s to 1870s) and so shared interests with the industrial bourgeoisie until the 1870s. Therefore, English capitalism in the 19th century, during Marx's period, was built on a class alliance between industrial capitalists and the landed aristocracy. Industrial capitalists constructed a structure of coal, steel, machine and cotton industry that reproduced itself. However, even after the middle of the 19th century, capitalists were not entirely independent of commercial, landed and monied interests in the economic sphere, because industrial capital required monetary funds. Monetary funds were supplied to industry by landowners and commercial capitalists through the City of London. Capitalists were thus further dependent on loan-interest for export of their products and import of materials and foods for their industry. Revenue from rentiers holding national bonds flowed as money funds to merchants and industrial capitalists. With networks of commerce, railway, marine trade, telecommunication, insurance and material productive powers, England extracted huge rent in the form of dividends, share allocations and interest from within and without England, India, Australia and the Americas. English capitalism built world order as a *Pax Britannica* and grasped worldwide hegemony, as the London Exhibition of 1851 symbolically demonstrated. Marx noted this spectacle (Marx and Engels 1978: 500). 'England is the demiurge of the bourgeois cosmos' (Marx and Engels 1978: 509).

Japan

From the Meiji Restoration (1868) until defeat in World War II (1945) Japan was a rentier-state capitalism, founding itself on a revision of the land tax system (1873–81). This was a springboard for funding capitalist industrialisation. Japan was an articulation of three sub-systems: the Emperor state; the landowner system; and the capitalist mode of production in formation. Japan had to accelerate and compress the process of capitalist industrialisation under pressure from the Euro-American powers. It was almost in the same situation as nations on the periphery of Europe (Berend and Ránki 1982) and non-Euro-American nations. This included severe regulation of the civil liberties of Japanese working people by a strong oppressive state power, like England during the period of manufacture par excellence. State bureaucrats took over leadership in

establishing capitalist industrialisation. They were social elites or intellectuals; some of whom were educated in advanced nations, as can be
observed in many other developing nations. Bureaucrats protected the
landed class in order to expropriate high-rate rent in kind from peasant
tenants, and they established a finance system in order to transform this
land tax into monetary funds for industrial sectors, or public funds for
infrastructural development. This forced the agricultural sector to supply
not only monetary funds, but also labour power, food, industrial materials,
and so almost all resources necessary to build up capitalist industrial
sectors. Japanese capitalism during the period 1868–1945 may be termed
'landowner-monarchy capitalism', or 'rentier-state capitalism'.

The Meiji state expropriated huge amounts of common land in villages
dating from the Edo era of the 17th century into Meiji-era state property.
State-owned land comprised 67.5 per cent of all land in 1883, but
decreased to 51.6 per cent in 1924 (Inoma 1930: 118). During these 41
years (1883–1924), 16.9 per cent of state-owned land was sold off to Japanese nationals, private companies and the Meiji Emperor (Ten'no). This
decreasing trend in state-owned land indicated an expansion of the sphere
of industrial capitalism. The government deeded the Meiji Emperor vast
lands of 365,400 hectare *gratis*, that is, 3.7 per cent of the gross area of
Japan (Toda 1947: 77). The General Headquarters of the Japan Occupation Army reported just after World War II that the household of the
Emperor accounted for about 1,590,615,500 yen at current prices. 'It gives
an evident characteristic of the Emperor in the period of "landowner-
monarchy" that he was both the biggest landowner and capitalist of pre-
war Japan' (Iinuma 1978: 129; my italics).

Iran

Iranian history gives a typical case of concept of rentier-state capitalism.
During the interwar period of the Reza Shah regime (1925–41), landowners
took the initiative in independent industrialisation policies through an
import substitution strategy, modernising the bureaucracy, military forces
and transportation system. Financed by customs duties, an agriculture tax
was extracted from peasants through the landowner system, revenue from
state monopoly enterprises in tea and sugar etc., revenue from the disposal
of state-owned land, special revenues from oil concessions and an oil tax.
These state revenues were based on state power or state ownership of land
(based not only on agriculture but on the oil industry). A few landowners,
the state and the royal family possessed some 90 per cent of the entire land.
The Iranian state then belonged basically to state (A); the two kinds of
rentier (A1 and A2) carried the formation of capitalism. Goto categorises
the Iranian regime as a 'landowner-monarchy' or 'squirearchy', though he
does not refer to Jiro Iinuma who originated these terms (Goto 2002: 274).

The king Muhammad Reza Pahlavi declared a 'White Revolution'

(1962–79) involving land reform, nationalisation of forests and cattle farms, disposal of state-owned enterprise to private firms, distribution of profits to industrial workers, giving suffrage to women, founding of an education corps etc. Land reform was the most important, because it destroyed traditional pre-modern survivals, for instance, the landowner-peasant system (mālek-ra'īyat), in order to give political foundations to the king and the state, and to enforce policies necessary to develop a capitalist national economy. Although land reform was a halfway house, because it left half the land in the hands of absentee landowners and excluded landless peasants (khosh-neshīn), the reform took away landowners' rule from small peasant-owners, who now faced the bureaucracy and market directly (Hara 2000: 181–2). Goto thinks that this land reform had historical significance because it eradicated the 'landowner-monarchy' that had become a hindrance to the establishment of a capitalist national economy (Goto 2002: 275).

As the system gained political stability, the king gradually became a dictator, backed by bureaucrats, military authorities and aid from the USA. Goto thinks that the state began radical reforms under a 'monarchial developmental dictatorship', producing non-democratic industrialisation, almost the same as in other many developing nations (Goto 2002: 298–9). The Iranian state deprived peasants of vital water irrigation rights and forced them into public cooperation in agriculture through 'state enclosure' of land, and it supplied the labour power of ex-peasants to industry, increasing the labour productivity of agriculture supplying food. The Iranian state then became a landed state. Thus the Iranian land system from the interwar period to the age of the White Revolution had changed from private ownership to state ownership. Goto distinguishes 'landowner-monarchy' from 'developmental dictatorship', probably thinking that the landed class and the landed state are essentially different and not interchangeable with each other, and that the 'landowner-monarchy' is ruled by the landed class and the 'developmental dictatorship' by the Iranian landed state. However, the two systems are interchangeable with each other, sharing the same mission for capitalist industrialisation.

Taiwan

Taiwan provides an interesting case of rentier-state capitalism in which the landed state takes the initiative for capitalist industrialisation, essentially the same type as China in the 'socialist market economy'. Just after the end of World War II, the USA promoted land reform in Japan, Taiwan and Korea, in order to avoid the impact of land reform in mainland China and to sweep away the remains of Japanese imperialism, judging that the landowner-peasant tenant system in Japan and the two colonised areas had been one of the causes of, and bases for, Japanese imperialism. Land reform in Taiwan is significant in that disposal of the landowners' land furthered the transformation of landed capital into industrial capital. Also, by eliminating the landowners, the Taiwanese state expropriated peasants' surplus outside the market through an unequal barter system between peasants' rice and the state's chemical fertilisers, and this accelerated a transition of capital from agriculture to industry through a low price policy on rice. Hand in hand with technological instruction assisted by American aid (4,000 million dollars in total between 1950 and 1974), land reform further stimulated the productive morale of the peasants, increased agricultural productivity and supplied industrial sectors with plenty of cheap labour, the most important factor in Taiwanese industrialisation.

Wakabayashi suggests that, with the USA's Iron Curtain policy against communism, Taiwan constructed an 'anticommunism military dictatorship' that gradually transformed itself into an 'economic developmental dictatorship'. This dictatorship was founded on cheap labour and land developed for industrial use and on the USA's provision of a large market for Taiwanese products in exchange for the USA's technology and financial aid. Wakabayashi writes:

> A developmental dictatorship in Taiwan formed the political conditions of the Asian NIES type of development; from the viewpoint of centre-periphery theory, this dictatorship made use of *capital funds* and *technology* from the centre and of cheap *labour* from the periphery.
>
> (Wakabayasi 1992: 165–6; my italics)

Taiwan developed land and offered it to transnational direct investors as an essential element in setting up pioneering bases for capitalist industrialisation, export processing zones (Sklair 1995: 107–15), for instance, in Gao Xiong.

Union of the party (Guo Min Dang) with the Taiwan state created a hegemonic regime over local political factions and established a ruling coalition with them, providing them with various 'rent seeking' systems, including the Agricultural Association (Nong Hui). The Association spread its wings over villages and managed the state commission business both for rice pickup points and for distributors of fertiliser in the rice–fertiliser barter system. The Taiwanese state originated the barter system (1948–73) as a policy of commandeering supplies of rice, sugar cane and chemical fertilisers in order to gain rent, that is, a rent-in-kind system, or a 'rent seeking system'. The Association also undertook financial business, including agricultural finance founded on American aid. Similar to Japan and Korea after the war, US aid was given to support land reform in order to distribute small-scale land to peasants and to supply monetary funds for landowners that would have been supplied if the landowner system had been maintained. In this period the state monopolised about one-third of the peasants' rice through the tax system, compulsory purchase, the barter system and by controlling sales routes to both domestic and foreign markets (Sumiya *et al.* 1992: 69–76). The Taiwanese state obtained 28.6 per cent of the gross rice product during the fifteen years 1951–65. Liu Jin Qing writes:

> This amount is larger in scale than that which landlords under the rule of Imperial Japan obtained as rent from tenants of their land. In this sense, at least during this period, *the state has taken place of the landlords.*
>
> (Sumiya *et al.* 1992: 73; my italics)

Notably these systems limited the peasants' property rights in land not only in terms of use right, but also in terms of gaining a right to their own land and labour and to a right of disposal of their own, in order to expropriate the peasants' surplus product as a fund for accelerating primitive accumulation in Taiwan. The case that these rights are extremely limited was also analysed in Chinese state ownership of the entirety of national land and other Soviet types of land ownership. Liu suggests that Taiwanese industrialisation through the expropriation of peasants is based on a transfer of value from the agricultural surplus produced by them to the industrial sector (Sumiya *et al.* 1992: 79). The peasants were guaranteed civil rights *de jure*, but de facto they were not enforced. The Taiwanese state (*c.*1948–78) was the owner of Taiwanese land, or a rentier-state for industrial capitalism.

China

The People's Republic of China gives another example of the fact that landed states promote capitalist industrialisation. When China argues that it is now constructing a 'socialist market economy', the 'socialism' de facto consists of macro control of the market economy, state ownership of land and enterprise, and communist ideology. Macro control is almost the same role as that obtaining in Western socialist democratic states. State ownership is the core of Chinese socialism, but state-owned enterprises will sooner or later have to be privatised under the influence of the WTO. Communist ideology will soon become socialist democracy including not only wage workers and peasants, but also entrepreneurs in private enterprises as 'one of the representatives of Chinese broadest people's interests'. After that, Chinese socialism will identify itself with state ownership of land.

The Chinese state alone has property rights in the entirety of national land, and so it alienates natural or juristic personal land use rights with a time limit. Lately these rights have been guaranteed through a conveyance right in borrowed land use and a mortgage right in borrowed land use. Notably, time limitations on land use right are never nominal. When the period for land use right is over, land that has been lent must be returned to the Chinese state. The recent restoration of Hong Kong and Macao to China is propaganda that the Chinese state unconditionally holds land ownership. Simultaneously, researchers of land law in China are now disputing whether or not the creation of a use right in state-owned land for individual or private companies is an administrative or civil contract. The latter opinion has gained a dominant position (Oda 2002: 82). Use rights in state-owned land are converting to stock, in order to force surplus population in the countryside to emigrate for urban areas, where labour power is demanded for industrialisation. However, peasants often block the land policy with a traditional land-attached mentality. Misako Oda writes:

> Selling of land use rights brings China large-scale *capital and techno-
> logy* which it needs for the transition from a planned economy to a
> market economy ... The total income from the *release of land use
> rights* is estimated at not less than 1,000,000 million yuan ... Because
> China has been promoting industrialisation based on *agriculture*, it has
> primitively accumulated almost zero capital since the foundation of
> the People's Republic [until the 1978 introduction of Socialist Market
> Economy]; therefore the introduction of foreign capital that the
> release of land use rights brings for domestic needs is the pivotal point
> for Chinese economic development. That is why the credibility and
> stability of land use rights must be firmly guaranteed to the land users.
>
> (Oda 2002: 7; my italics)

Indeed, foreign monetary funds and technology have been vital for China in the developing stage but, in fact, especially since the 1978 introduction of the 'socialist market economy', the Chinese state has been expropriating huge economic surpluses from the agricultural sector. Associate professor at Nanjing University, Zhang Yu Lin writes:

> The Chinese state is now in transition, giving priority over any other
> matter both to maintenance of the communist regime and to modern-
> isation of the economy and society, because of 'stability' in politics
> and society. This strategy is very close to the regime of 'developmental
> dictatorship' that may be observed in the contemporary 'socialist
> states' of Indonesia or Malaysia.
>
> (Zhang 2001: 10)

As emancipator of the Chinese people, the Chinese communist state has always defended its various expropriations of economic surplus from the peasants for primitive accumulation. Zhang describes three ways of doing this: agriculture tax, reserve funds of villages, and labour duty for maintenance of the village and accumulation of resources for it. From 1978 to 1998, Chinese peasants paid an agriculture tax of 600,000 million yuan.

And for twenty years (1979–98), about 2,000,000 million yuan has been extracted from them through unequal exchange between the agricultural sector and the industrial sector, similar to the 'rice-fertiliser barter system' of Taiwan. Through financial routes, they have provided 749,300 million yuan. In total, over about twenty years, the Chinese state has extracted 3,349,300 million yuan.

Lower-level executives in the villages force peasants to pay heavy charges. Indeed, the nominal agriculture tax to the state is not particularly heavy, but many other charges, for instance, for the reserve fund of the village, labour duty for maintenance and accumulation, and a reckless 'cost' levy, have been forced onto peasants, and executives have embezzled this from them. For example, in 1995 a peasant in a village of Shangdon Sheng was ordered to pay marriage registration fees of 1,220.50 yuan in total, that is, equivalent to a peasant's yearly income, although the formal marriage registration fee was only eighteen yuan (Zhang 2001: 81). The system is traditional. Before the communist revolution, the Chinese state had long left the administration of villages to clan elders and executives, and had refrained from direct management of villages and so entrusted taxation on villages to leaders who expropriated tenant rent from peasants and paid part of it as tax to the central state (M. Shimizu 1939: 104–14). The Chinese communist party has tried to change the traditional system, but lower-level executives of the communist party control village administrations as a 'rent seeking' system. Therefore, Chinese ownership of land is two-fold; state ownership and de facto ownership by lower-level executives. China is a rentier-state capitalism that may exercise legitimacy so long as it utilises an agricultural surplus for 'co-prosperity among the Chinese people'.

To sum up, 19th century England was state (A) and imperial state (A') that ruled India etc. Meiji Japan started as state (B) that expropriated most common land, and then changed into state (A), sharing state-owned land with the ruling class, and then colonising East Asian nations as an imperial state (A'). The Iranian state was state (A) allied with the landed class, but then released state-owned land to the peasants as state (A), and later changed to state (B). Taiwan under the rule of the Guo Min Dang was state (B), limiting peasants' private ownership of land by politico-economic rent seeking systems. China since the 1949 revolution was also state (B), extracting huge agricultural surpluses as land tax from peasants who were forced to live within rural communities.

References

Berend, I.T. and Ránki, G. (1982) *European Periphery and Industrialisation 1780–1914*. Cambridge: Cambridge University Press.

Goto, A. (2002) *The Agricultural Community and the State of Middle-East Nations; Village in the Iranian Modern History*. Tokyo: Ochanomizushobo.

Hara, R. (2000) 'The development of agricultural policies and rural changes in Iran', in R. Hara and Y. Iwasaki (ed.) *Dynamism of Iranian National Economy*. Tokyo: The Institute of Developing Economies, 179–217.

Iinuma, J. (1978) 'Landowner-monarchy (squirearchy)', *Keizaihyoron* (*Economic Review*). Tokyo: Nihonhyoronsha, 118–29.

Inoma, K. (1930) *Charts of Japanese Economy*. Tokyo: Nihonhyoronsha.

Kawano, K. (1966) *French Revolution and Meiji Restoration*. Tokyo: NHK Publishers.

McNeill, W.H. (1982) 'The pursuit of power: technology, armed force and society since AD 1000'. Chicago: University of Chicago Press.

Marx, K. (1965) *Capital*, vol. 1. Moscow: Progress Publishers.

Marx, K. (1966) *Capital*, vol. 3. Moscow: Progress Publishers.

Marx, K. (1973) *Grundrisse*. London: Penguin Books.

Marx, K. and Engels, F. (1974) *The German Ideology*, W. Hiromatsu (ed.). Tokyo: Kawadeshoboshinsha.

Marx, K. and Engels, F. (1978) *Collected Works*, vol. 10. Moscow: Progress Publishers.

Mochizuki, S. (1982) 'Perspective and view of primitive accumulation', *Shiso* (*Thought*) 695. Tokyo: Iwanamishoten, 79–95.

Oda, M. (2002) *The Use Right and Property Right of Land in China*. Kyoto: Horitsubunkasha.

Shimizu, M. (1939) *A Study of Chinese Society*. Tokyo: Iwanamishoten.

Shimizu, Y. (2002) *Revolts of Chinese Peasants*. Tokyo: Kodansha.

Sklair, L. (1995) *Sociology of the Global System*. London: Prentice Hall.

Sumiya, M., Liu, J. and Tou, Z. (1992) *Economy of Taiwan*. Tokyo: University of Tokyo Press.

Toda, S. (1947) *An Analysis of Economic Basis of Ten'no System*. Tokyo: San'ichishobo.

Wakabayashi, M. (1992) *Taiwan: Democratisation in a Divided Country*. Tokyo: University of Tokyo Press.

Weber, M. (1978) *Economy and Society*, 2 vols. Berkeley: University of California Press.

Zhang, Y.L. (2001) *Chinese State and Peasants in the Period of Transition (1978–1998)*. Tokyo: Norintokeikyokai.

4 Marx and the future of post-capitalist society

Masanori Sasaki

Introduction

The structure of modern capitalism is changing dramatically, leaving behind the model of capitalist development known as Fordism. This development model was the typical form of capitalism in the early to mid 20th century, but it faced a serious structural crisis in the 1970s, and after that capitalism began to seek a new direction during the 1980s, at least in the central parts of the world economy. At present, a dominant tide has developed on a global scale, known as American 'liberal productivism'.

However, 'liberal productivism' has not resolved the contradiction and the crisis faced by Fordism in the 20th century. On the contrary, it is amplifying them on a global scale. They are expressed as social polarisation in the wage relation and an ecological crisis due to over-consumption. Therefore, for us to design a post-capitalistic model today, we must engage with other post-Fordist models which differ from 'liberal productivism'. The key concept in this chapter is 'free time', and the aim is to form a new model describing a social space which recognises 'time-sovereignty'.

Kiyoaki Hirata was one of the first scholars in Japan to appreciate fully Marx's theory of free time. He writes that in Marx's version of post-capitalism workers will 'establish time-sovereignty as a fundamental of citizenship and human rights individually and co-operatively' (Hirata 1993: 349). In other words, a developmental model that is founded on an increase in free time presents us with the future of post-capitalism in the 21st century. But it was Marx who intended to form the society that could make free time mankind's wealth in order to reform 'the capitalist mode of production'.

From the above point of view, in the first section of this chapter, I summarise the contents of Marx's free time argument, and I present a path for post-capitalism that he considered, one which is founded on an increase in free time. The relation between Fordism and the consumer society will be examined in the second section. The capitalism of the 20th century created a consumer-oriented society through a change in the wage relation, and this evolved as Fordism. The characteristics of this development model are that it gets its dynamics by structuring 'consumer society' where 'the insidious cycle of work-and-spend' becomes a popular phenomenon. Juliet B. Schor says that 'the consumerist treadmill and long hour jobs have combined to form an insidious cycle of work-and-spend' (Schor 1993: 9). I define the society where this cycle has become a mass phenomenon as 'consumer society'. However, this leads to 'the conversion of disposable time into superfluous labour time' that Marx pointed out, and a serious crisis arises in the wage relation. Following this, an ecological crisis becomes serious as well. This is the theme of the third section. Then, in conclusion, the modern struggle to recover free time will be examined, and the possibility of a sustainable path for the 21st century will be considered.

Marx's free time theory

It is in the *Grundrisse*, which became the first draft of *Capital*, that Marx brought up the free time argument in earnest. He analysed the production of absolute and relative surplus value from the viewpoint of the circular movement of capital, and said that it tends to mechanise the whole process of production and circulation. He saw this tendency as the 'development of fixed capital', and indicated that this development transforms the system of social production remarkably. This was expressed as 'the transformation of the production process from the simple labour process into a scientific process'.

In the first instance, the weight of direct labour in the production of material wealth decreases gradually in this transformation. In other words, 'the power of the agencies set in motion during labour time', such as an automatic system of machinery, takes the lead in the production process. In the second instance, 'the powerful effectiveness' of these agencies does not always depend on the direct labour time that is spent to produce them, but rather depends more on levels of the general social intellect outside of the direct labour process: for example, scientific and technical knowledge and their application to production. This means that in the production process as transformed into a scientific process, the production of wealth is carried out through the social division of labour, and this social labour is founded on the development of general intelligence in society in fields of study such as science and art. This social combination of labour and the general state of intellect enable the forces of production to develop and increase. That is, the development of fixed capital indicates that general social knowledge has become a direct force of production. It also indicates the development of 'all the powers of social combination and of social intercourse'. Marx defined it as 'the development of the social individual'. Human beings become relatively free from the restraint of material labour in this process (Marx 1977: 704–6).

Human beings have to assign a fixed portion of their time to material labour in order to fulfil individual desires and to maintain and reproduce life. This labour time is also needed in order for society to reproduce itself and is a requirement common to the history of all human beings. With the development of human beings as social individuals, 'the realm of physical necessity' expands, because desires also expand. However, at the same time, the forces of productive labour that satisfy these wants increase. The reduced portion of 'the necessary labour time of society', which may be generated by the increase of these forces of production, is 'disposable time'. It is time secured to human beings who are relatively free from the natural necessity to labour in a direct material process of production, and it is potential time that can be used for other purposes. It offers human beings room to live and an abundance of life.

However, in the mode of production founded on capital, the creation of disposable time took the form of the development of fixed capital. The development of fixed capital creates a huge quantity of disposable time and is also the result of the intellectual practice of human beings in this time. That is, disposable time is converted into surplus labour time and is realised as the development of fixed capital. Fixed capital ('objectified labour') functions as a means to absorb 'living labour' and thus to produce more surplus value. The development of fixed capital is realised as the development of power over living labour. Therefore, in the direct process of production in which an automatic system takes the lead, labourers are disempowered and debilitated (Marx 1977: 702). Furthermore, fixed capital functions as a means for reducing 'the necessary labour time for producing surplus labour', eliminates living labour from the process of production, and makes it superfluous. In short, reduction of the 'necessary labour time of society' appears as reduction of 'the necessary labour time for producing surplus labour', and the creation of 'disposable time' functions as an increase in 'superfluous labour time'. Marx points out three forms of 'superfluous labour time':

1   surplus labour time exceeding necessary labour time for reproducing labour-power: this time serves as free time for the owner of capital as a 'non-labourer', and a fund for accumulating of capital;
2   superfluous labour time as a fund which maintains the huge unproductive labour forces which are parasitic on a capitalist mode of production;
3   relative surplus population as the portion of labour eliminated from the process of production with the development of productive labour forces.

(Marx 1977: 401–2, 608–9)

The transformation of disposable time into superfluous labour time is a question of life or death for labourers who are made the personified existence of 'the necessary labour time to posit surplus labour'. Disposable time, which offers human beings room to live and an abundance of life, appears as time which guarantees the 'not-labour' for the capital owner and maintains huge numbers of 'surplus idlers, consuming without producing'. Disposable time as 'time for the full development of the individual' (Marx 1977: 711) appears as superfluous labour time, debilitating and eliminating labourers compulsorily. This is the repressive character of capital's productive force. So, the object for Marx was to reform the productive force of capital that takes on a repressive character into a form that contributes to the 'development of the social individual'. This would happen by recapturing the 'disposable time' that is now transformed into 'superfluous labour time' as, in future, a labourer's own realistic free time.

In the first instance, disposable time is the resource for solving the social problems produced by the existence of relative surplus population and a huge unproductive population. And this time is also the resource for reforming the capitalist regime of accumulation that inevitably produces such social problems. Capital produces the problems itself by transforming time into 'surplus labour time', creating 'disposable time'. This is the self-contradiction of capital that it cannot solve. In other words, the greatest restriction in trying to solve such problems is capital itself (Marx 1977: 704–6). In the second instance, the appropriation of their own surplus labour as free time enables people who exist only to labour ('personification of labour time') to change their styles of work and life, and to raise themselves up to a humane existence. In the capitalist mode of production, labour time is the 'sole measure and source of wealth' (Marx 1977: 706). So, labour is a dominant social bond and serves as the only fountainhead of social identity. Recovery of free time conquers such a 'labour-oriented society' and enables not only labour but also various activities in non-labour time to become the source of bonding and identity for the social individual. This would be the 'full development of the social individual' as 'the free blossom of humanity' (Gorz 1988; Méda 1995).

So Marx's perspective on post-capitalism is to present an alternative mode of development and to build a social space which makes free time true wealth. It means that labourers recapture 'time-sovereignty' and become 'victors over time', developing themselves as 'social individuals'. 'Time-sovereignty' is the foundation of the social formation alternative to 'the mode of production based on capital'. It enables the mass of labouring individuals to control their labour themselves in 'the realm of physical necessity' and also offers the moral energy to strive for political power and to accomplish their complete development.

Fordism and the transformation of the wage relation

The core system in capitalism is the wage relation. It is a social relation that materialised historically in the struggle over the 'necessary labour time for producing surplus labour': that is, the sum of the terms and conditions which decide the mobilisation of the labour force and its reproduction. The capitalism of the 20th century evolved as Fordism by reforming the wage relation. This model of development was considered to have surmounted the economic crisis of the 30 years in the middle of the 20th century. The secret of its success was the 'Fordist compromise' as the structure which connected the increase in the productivity of labour and the distribution of the fruits of that increase. On one hand, the ordinary worker in society was mobilised in large numbers, and their labour was organised under the technological paradigm of 'Taylorism plus mechanisation'. This system of production raised productivity sharply. On the other hand, the rise of labour productivity was distributed to the workers in the form of increased wages, and the workers became the main force of effective demand. In the sense that this circular flow in the economic system created the consumer-oriented society and supported the dynamism of capital accumulation, Fordism as the evolution of capitalism. By contrast, for Britain in the 19th century (which Marx considered the model of capitalism), capitalism there did not have a 'consumer society' with unlimited multiplication of the desire for consumption. That is to say, it was a capitalism in which the basic contradiction of limited demand and unlimited supply was adjusted through violent panic. Michel Agrietta points out that 'the "consumer society" appears to have definitively resolved the contradictions of capitalism and abolished its crises' (Agrietta 1987: 161).

Marx said that the historical precondition of capitalism was the existence of 'the free labourer in a double meaning'. That is, on the one hand, labourers can dispose of the power of labour freely as free individuals. In other words, labourers are liberated from traditional restrictions of the community and become the subject of rights, for example, the right to choose an occupation or to move freely. On the other hand, labourers are separated from all the conditions that are necessary for the traditional realisation of labour. In other words, labourers lose the opportunity for labour assured by a traditional community and can only be engaged for labour as bearers of capital for the purpose of value-multiplication.

But in Fordism, labourers also develop a free existence as consumers in a double meaning. In the traditional community, various racial, religious and other restrictions controlled people's desire for consumption. Fordist labourers are free consumers in the sense of having been released from such traditional restrictions. As free subjects of a desire for consumption, labourers reproduce their labour power. However, on the other side, labourers lose the basis of a common life guaranteed by the community, and cannot satisfy their own desires simply by purchasing the goods on the market. Thus, labourers develop a free existence in a double meaning in both labour and consumption.

In the Fordist model of development, social forces of production not only expand with the change in the technological paradigm of labour organisation, but the realisation of surplus value which increases with expansion of productive powers is guaranteed by creation of the 'consumer society' as an infinite multiplication of an individual's desires. The creation of 'the consumer society' is a historical phenomenon peculiar to the 20th century. According to Baudrillard, the age of Fordism was a time when 'the myth of consumption' became 'customary' in the sense that ordinary labourers daily affirmed their society as a 'consumer society' (Baudrillard 1970). 'Consumption' is not simply the act of a human being to satisfy a material desire. People express their social prestige, gain consciousness as a member of a group, and identify themselves through consumption. In this way, they participate in the formation of 'the consumer society' actively through 'the consumption' of goods. Therefore, the more people abandon their right to self-control over labour and time and become the subjects of the 'consumer society', the more the life of the labourers is unified into the rhythm of the value multiplication of capital. In this way, the labour movement loses the power to conceive of an alternative society. Gorz points this out as follows:

> It became unnecessary for the labour movement to conceive of a different society, and the peculiar problem of lack of society in liberal capitalism was covered by the Fordist compromise. The labour movement delegated the power to control the social system to the welfare state.
>
> (Gorz 1988: 227)

Such a historical case as this can be seen in the fight for free time at the beginning of the 20th century. Schor points out that the conclusive issue in the labour movement of the 1920s was the choice between an increase in wage income and an increase in free time (Schor 1993: 120–1). Many trade unionists of those days regarded the exchange of time for money as 'a Faustian bargain' and rejected it. The unionists chose free time over high wages and supported a limit on private consumption and discouraging luxuries, and emphasised public goods such as education and culture. The activists of civil society criticised the logic of Fordism in stimulating wants as 'the most baneful assumption of the industrial society', and also emphasised the importance of free time rather than consumption.

At the beginning of Fordism, labour and radical social movements advocated the same path. They regarded free time as human wealth, and took growth in productivity in the form of an increase in free time rather than an expansion of income. Therefore, they took a joint step as a movement to form an alternative society. On the contrary, Charles Kettering, the general director of General Motor's research labs in those days, stated the matter baldly: business needed to create a 'dissatisfied consumer', but not a modest consumer, and the point of the sales strategy was 'the organised creation of dissatisfaction'. This was the strategy to expand sales based on advertisements and credit, and to make the consumer discontented with what he or she already had by introducing annual model changes, that is, planned obsolescence.

It is clear from the history of Fordism after that time which side had won the fight over free time. At the AFL-CIO's conference in 1956, one official claimed confidently that workers had become 'eager to increase their income, not to work fewer hours'. Unions jumped in on the banquet of economic growth and consumerism, too. The economy of the 19th century, which had been concerned with a lack of demand, was reversed in the economy of the 20th century, which was founded on excessive demand. Schor points out that the watershed was in the 1920s when Fordism was victorious in the fight over free time. The blossoming of consumerism and the extinction of the desire for free time are two sides of the same coin. In the Fordist model of development, people became locked into 'the insidious cycle of work-and-spend'. The desire for free time was pushed outside the loop. Then, as Fordism increased in power, a crack appeared between the labour movement and the radical social movement, though they had a joint struggle in the 1920s. The conflict and confrontation became remarkable in the 1970s between 'the people who fight for the higher wages' and 'the people who fight to work better' in the advanced countries.

Development of consumer society and crisis of the wage relation

Fordism offers a huge productive capacity. As such, the crucial point is not only the production of surplus value, but also how the demand conditions that enable its production are created. Paul A. Baran and Paul M. Sweezy once noted that the difficulty in producing surplus value appeared as the difficulty to create demand, and they considered the structure of the flow of surplus in 20th century capitalism (1966). Moreover, many theorists of the consumer-oriented society have analysed the social patterns of consumption. Material goods as a means of symbolic communication stimulate desire and then expand consumption. Fordism tends to solve the 'realization of surplus labour' by the creation of the 'consumer society' as a system which expands a free consumer's desire. However, as desire increases and surplus value is realised in consumer society, the labour employed in developing the expansion of desire becomes the dominant form of labour. Labour produces goods not only materially, but also as symbols. That is:

> Commodities in capitalist society have come to be less material, that is, more defined by cultural, informational, or knowledge components or qualities of service and care. The labour that produces these commodities has also changed in a corresponding way. Immaterial labour might thus be conceived as the labour that produces the informational, cultural, or affective element of the commodity.
>
> (Lazzarato 1996: 262)

The more Fordism secures the driving force of development by creating consumer society, the more the added value of goods strengthens the cultural and informational elements of society. The labour that produces goods is also transformed in a corresponding way. Lazzarato defines it as 'immaterial labour' (1996: 133–47). That is, consumer society has promoted such a transformation of labour.

In this labour, full use of the techniques that develop desire is made. These are the techniques of sending goods into a market so that dormant desire may be stirred up and profit can be taken. The greatest component parts in the price of goods today are the expenses of marketing, development, advertisement and sales promotion. These activities consist in the labour mobilised for building the space in which goods are consumed as symbols. In other words, the system of production and circulation sensitive to the different and uncertain desires of the consumer is built up, and the overwhelming part of the social labour is mobilised to maintain the system. A huge investment is required for the construction of such a system, and surplus value is turned to this investment.

Moreover, corresponding to such changes, labour in the direct process of production is also converted into flexible labour. In order for Fordism to gain its dynamism through the creation of a consumer society, reconstruction of the production system corresponding to it is indispensable. That is, in this system, a process of production is reorganised for the flow of market information that changes quickly. In this way, the system of production is converted into the system of 'just in time' known as 'Toyotas'. It is requested that labourers should also turn into flexible labourers who can adapt themselves to all kinds of information, corresponding to the conversion of production into a flexible system.

Fordism develops the productive force of labour, and reduces the proportion of direct labour in the production of material wealth, producing a huge amount of disposable time. Capital, as Marx said, produces disposable time, and converts it into surplus labour. But the overwhelming portion of this surplus labour is mobilised as labour for building the consumer-oriented spaces where wage labourers satisfy their desires as a free consumer, unlike in the era of Marx. That is, disposable time is mobilised as labour to create the environment in which people can devote themselves to consumption. This form of labour serves as the new source of surplus value for capital. Now, surplus value is not only produced in a direct process of production but has also expanded to all the processes of the social space.

Generally, as a tendency of post-Fordism, the proportion of manufacturing industries in the economy declines, and the share of service industries expands. It is also said that, after the 1970s, Fordism was converted into post-Fordism. However, the Fordist model of development has been maintained in the sense that the fruits of the rise in productivity are used up by the increase in income and expansion of consumption, and are not utilised for the reduction of labour time and the increase of free time. Fordism, which started in the mass production of a standardised 'Model T' car, created a consumer society which left it behind and developed dynamically. In this development, 'immaterial labour which produces informational, cultural, or affective elements of the commodity' becomes the dominant form of labour in the production of commodities. In short, Fordism completes itself by a conversion into post-Fordism, just as modernism converts itself into post-modernism.

Alternative pathways in an era of post-Fordism

However, the crisis involving labour and consumption becomes much more serious with this conversion. In the first place, a serious crisis of labour organisation takes place, and a split in society occurs. Labour in consumer society creates transient desires for consumption and accelerates the turnover of goods and, in a corresponding way, the market environment changes quickly. So, capital tends to build a system of production and circulation that can avoid overproduction when there is a change of market environment. That is, although capital mobilises social labour in large quantities, as consumption accelerates, it also reorganises labour, so that it can respond to rapid changes of market or technology immediately. In this way, the labour which bears the core business of capital circulation and the labour which bears subordinate or secondary business are classified, and if needed, the latter labour is mobilised as required. Labour in society polarises to the core and the periphery. The polarisation of labour produces a crisis of social integration.

Next, Fordism is faced with the more fundamental problem of ecological crisis. By securing the rise of income in the working class corresponding to the rise of productivity, Fordism surmounted the economic crisis of the 19th century, and evolved as sustainable capitalism. This capitalism reconstructed itself as a flexible system of accumulation, creating the consumer society of post-modernism. However, the more dynamic Fordism tends to become through this conversion, the more 'the insidious cycle of work-and-spend' supporting this dynamism amplifies an ecological crisis. It is a serious contradiction between the infiniteness of the desire of a consumer society and the finitude of the resources of the earth, and this appears as a set of environmental problems. The cycle of labour and consumption that Fordism generated is not sustainable ecologically, and it is vital for human beings to question this development model.

So, a new long-term compromise to promote the conversion of the Fordist model into an alternative model of development based on the increase of free time is very important. The challenge is to convert the labour which Fordism has mobilised towards the creation of a consumer society into the labour for the creation of an ecologist economy and a new 'welfare community' that aims to conquer the ecological crisis caused by overconsumption as well as the crisis of social integration. Lipietz calls a society in the process of this conversion an 'ecologist economy'. He explains as follows: 'Labour itself will be transformed into labour for the community, by the community, of the community in an ecologist economy' (Lipietz 1999: 106).

'The ecologist economy' is not limited to environmental problems in a narrow meaning. It is an alternative community that conquers the opposition of the 'state-market' of the 20th century. The labour that creates this community is guided by the value of autonomy from the state, by the value of solidarity against the market, and by the value of responsibility to nature. The 'welfare community' created with the conversion of such labour is an alternative path of post-capitalism. And in order for us to make this choice, as Marx also stated in the conclusion of *Capital*, 'the reduction of labour time is its basic prerequisite'.

The reduction of labour time converts the meaning of labour and consumption for every person. One of the most serious problems in a consumption society is a deficit in 'being' and an excess of the superfluous. An individual's identity is absorbed in the huge flow of goods, and people are not fulfilled even if they own many things. It is important to create 'consumption' in the sense of enjoying time peculiar to oneself that cannot be transferred, but not 'consumption' in the sense of shopping and spending. The reduction of labour time serves as the first step to convert the meaning of 'consumption' (Schor 1993: 138).

Second, the reduction of labour time serves as an opportunity for release from modern labour that makes labour 'the only well-spring of wealth'. In the same way that 'consumption' has served as the main value that unifies people socially, 'labour' has been the value by which the social identity has been realised. That a person is a wage earner is almost equal in meaning to his or her participation in society. So, unemployment means the decisive exclusion from society. While driving oneself to wage-labour because of the threat of unemployment, everyone embodies labour civilisation. The 'consumer-oriented society' where consumption is located at the centre of a social mechanism is 'labour-oriented society'. So, if we conceive of post-Fordism as the conquest of the consumption civilisation, post-capitalism has to be the end of labour civilisation, too. Also in this sense, the reduction of labour time is an indispensable condition: 'What is brought to the ensemble of individuals by loosening the restraints of labour is the epoch-making individual and collective value of the new relation to time' (Méda 1995: 310).

We should understand work-sharing in this context. It is not mere unemployment policy. It is one of the trial-runs for building a structure to conquer the ecological crisis and polarisation of labour. Of the many trial-runs for work-sharing, the case of the Netherlands offers the best example. The Netherlands has legislated work-sharing through the introduction of part-time labour. It is one of the features of the Netherlands model designed to prevent social fracturing and exclusion by dealing with part-time and full-time employment equally.

However, the real value of this model is the point of not simply achieving equal treatment within paid work, but also of including unpaid work-sharing into the policy. That is, the reduction of labour time in the Netherlands is done in the 'combination scenario' which aims at balancing care work in a family (unpaid-work) and wage earning (paid-work). In this model, paid-work time is reduced, and men and women share unpaid work equally. Unpaid work is borne by the citizen under the values of solidarity and autonomy, not externalised to the market economy, nor left to the welfare state.

In the current US system, when unpaid work is left to the market economy, prolonged labour is needed, for example, in order to purchase childcare. Men lose free time by extended labour to earn high income, and women also lose free time by working the same hours as men. This is the way of life that carries out the premise of the conventional masculine way of work. In this lifestyle, there is a division between the high profit class which purchases care labour, whereas the low income bracket must provide the care. This division constantly increases. The high income bracket strives for overconsumption, and the low, which serves it, enjoys the partial benefits of a consumer society. In this way, US consumer-oriented society is increasingly strengthened.

However, a movement which aims to be an alternative to the fracturing of society due to overconsumption is developing, and it is also permeating the labour movement in the US. This labour movement is reviving as a 'social labour movement' that pursues not only 'bread and butter' but 'dignity and justice' (Mantisios 1998). The labour movement and radical social movement that were divided in Fordism are beginning to move towards a new solidarity. In this way, the labour movement has begun to seek co-operation with social movements aiming to offer an alternative to Fordism.

Conclusion

When putting such a movement into perspective, we need to reconsider Marx's concept of 'association' with respect to post-capitalism in the 21st century. Marx developed this concept as a network of co-operatives for labourers. According to Marx, in the machine system of large industry, the process of production of capital transformed itself from a simple labour process into a scientific process, and the social co-operative power of wage labour was materialised there along with the form of the productive force of capital. Marx developed the concept 'association' as a network to control these social productive forces through the labourer's own autonomy and solidarity in consciousness. But the association must not be labour-oriented. This network is not enclosed within labour but should be opened up towards civil society. That is, the subject of post-capitalism is to reorganise the network of associations in civil society for the purpose of creating a new social space, where free time is considered to be the true wealth of human existence.

In this network, a social individual identifies himself or herself not only as a subject of work or 'consumption', but also as a pluralised complex existence by sex, race, culture, language, etc. Therefore, the important point is to reconstruct the social space of autonomy and solidarity by reflecting upon the oppression and discrimination that developed in this formation of pluralised identity. While the reduction of labour time and the introduction of work-sharing are the foundation which creates such a social space, the latter serves as a social safety net supporting the different associations in civil society. The reduction of labour time is the first step for a social individual in order to convert the historical meaning of labour and consumption, and to become the 'victors over time'. Marx's free time theory has offered us the key for conceiving post-capitalism in the 21st century.

References

Agrietta, M. (1987) *A Theory of Capitalist Regulation: The US Experience.* London: Verso.

Baran, P.A. and Sweezy, P.M. (1966) *Monopoly Capital.* New York: Monthly Review Press.

Baudrillard, J. (1970) *La Société de Consummation: ses mythes, ses structures.* Paris: Gallimard.

Gorz, A. (1988) *Métamorphoses du travail.* Paris: Galilée.

Hirata, K. (1993) *Civil Society and Regulation.* Tokyo: Iwanami Shoten.

Lazzarato, M. (1996) 'Immaterial labour', in *Radical Thought in Italy*, P. Virgo and M. Hard (eds). Minneapolis: University of Minnesota Press, 133–47, 262.

Lipietz, A. (1999) *Qu'est-ce que l'ecologie politique?* Paris: Editions La Decouverte.

Mantisios, G. (ed.) (1998) *A New Labour Movement for the New Century.* New York: Monthly Review Press.

Marx, K. (1977) *Grundrisse: Foundations of the Critique of Political Economy.* Harmondsworth: Penguin Books.

Méda, D. (1995) *Le travail.* Paris: Alto Aubier.

Schor, J.B. (1993) *Overworked American: The Unexpected Decline of Leisure.* New York: Basic Books.

5 Marx and distributive justice

Daisuke Arie

Introduction

The word 'justice' has an ambiguity in its meaning (Westphal 1996: xi). On the one hand, justice usually means fair and equal application of the law with a legal or a moral sense. On the other hand, justice often represents the appropriate distribution of goods, benefits, income, and sometimes even opportunities for political participation, within a certain value standard. It was the latter sense that occupied Marx. For him, it was almost a self-evident truth that capitalist society is an unjust society, because of the way that the capitalist's profit derives from the unpaid labour of the working class.

However, there are some difficulties involved in reviewing Marx's idea of justice. First, Marx himself did not seem to think much of justice as a concept in his writings, including letters. Marx scholars, therefore, have been quite prone to neglect it, or to interpret it freely and often improperly by reading only limited texts. For instance, popular dictionaries covering Marx's terms, such as Masset (1970) and Carver (1987), have an entry for neither 'justice' nor 'distributive justice'. Moseley (1993) does not discuss justice. The academic situation in this matter seems almost as Wesphal puts it: 'there is disagreement among scholars and commentators about whether Marx is *for* true justice . . . or *against* justice' (1996: xxiii). A comparatively old but well-known controversy on this point is that between Wood (1972), Husami (1978), Lukes (1982), Geras (1985) and Cohen (1988); see also Kain (1988: 135–8) and Sayers (1998: 113–19). In fact, Marx mentions the ideal principle of distribution for future society just once, in his *Critique of the Gotha Program*. He mentions justice in passing when he scorns Proudhon's ideal of justice. Marx is only concerned with making a fool of Proudhon, saying his argument about 'eternal justice' is overly abstract (Marx 2001b: 96). Therefore, this chapter will examine the *Program* in order to establish how Marx proposed a new principle that worked against the bourgeois standard for distribution in capitalist society.

Second, scholarly neglect of Marx's appropriation of Aristotle in his idea of justice raises difficulties for us. Scholars have often misinterpreted Marx's intention or overlooked the form of justice Marx tried to attack, though they have characterised him as one of the most radical critics of the problem of unequal distribution of income or goods in capitalist society. Elster finds Marx 'self-contradictory' in the *Critique of the Gotha Program*, but makes no comment on the relationship between Aristotle and Marx (1997: 37). In addition, Nielsen and Ware (1997), commenting on exploitation, which Elster (1997) also does, has no reference to Aristotle. This chapter, then, will trace the Aristotelian tradition of justice in Western scholarship and confirm that the target for Marx's critique was negative justice, or commutative justice.

The third reason for our difficulties is that the historical collapse of the Berlin Wall and the decline of Europe's communist states have accelerated a chaotic situation in Marx scholarship, particularly in Marxist political theory and economics. For a long time these studies focused on Marx's radical critique of liberalism, individualism, utilitarianism and bourgeois right through his labour-oriented philosophy. Further, pre-1989 representative works related to this critique of Marx's idea of justice are Miller (1975), Cohen *et al.* (1980) and Buchanan (1982). Lukes (1982) introduced some positive factors in his analysis of Marx's moral system, such as self-realisation in the community, freedom over alienation and the maximisation of welfare, though he also questioned the plausibility of Marx's account. Kain (1988), from the viewpoint of Kantian and Aristotelian ethical theory, carefully but optimistically traced the development of Marx's ethical thought towards a spontaneously transcendent morality, though he also pointed out a certain logical inconsistency between individual and community. However, a recent and newly emerged stream of analytical Marxism excludes the labour theory of value from consideration in discussing a proof of 'exploitation'. Since 1989, post-modernism and analytical Marxism have been two major disciplines that feature in publications on Marx. Some of these works are O'Neill (1995), Aronson (1995), Gamble *et al.* (1999), Callari and Ruccio (1996), Carver (1998) and Ware and Nielsen (1989).

Moreover, some apologetic Althusserian attempts at revitalising Marxism, for instance, do not yet seem successful in providing a new and plausible agenda. We can even find a declaration of 'the end of Marxism' (Aronson 1995: vii) or a commitment to 'multiple Marxes' (Carver 1998: 234), after the years of 'crisis'. The situation is worse in Japan where there was, and still is, the world's largest concentration of traditional Marxists who have been reading *Capital* like the Bible. Japan is the only developed country where an introduction to Marxian economics is taught as a prerequisite subject in the majority of universities. Its content is still a catechism-like reading of *Capital*, though Arie (1990) is an exception. It is not an easy task to extract something plausible and consistent concerning Marx's idea of justice from the Marx scholarship of last two decades. This chapter, then, will try to find a clue to contemporary social questions of distribution mainly by reading Marx's original texts from the viewpoint of the history of social science.

Concepts of justice in Western social science

Before entering directly into Marx's work, it will be instructive to consider how scholarship on justice has proceeded in the history of Western social science. The idea of justice has been discussed in an Aristotelian manner, deriving originally from book five of the *Nicomachean Ethics* (Aristotle 1934: 253–323). Aristotle introduces three kinds of justice concerning distribution and transactions in a community. The first is distributive justice. This is a principle according to which an apportionment of public goods can be made in accordance with each member's different personal valuation or degree of contribution to a community. He calls this result a 'geometrical proportion', acting as a qualitative standard for the distribution of public or common goods. The second is corrective justice, which operates in private transactions or contract. Aristotle offers a quantitative standard for this justice in the sense of an 'arithmetical proportion', which means the exchange of equivalent for equivalent. Then he introduces the third form, retributive justice, concerning the more practical cases of private transaction, such as barter for different kinds of commodities, requiring a 'geometrical proportion'. Thus the exchange-ratio of commodity A to commodity B is to be determined, first, in accordance with each maker's different valuation or contribution to the community, in accordance with distributive justice. Second, commodity A might be exchanged for commodity B in terms of equal value, following the case of corrective justice. Consequently, for both forms of justice, personal return is realised in accordance with the relevant values or grade of contribution. In this exchange of equal value, the quantity of each commodity is different, for example, one hundred shoes might be equal to one house, hence the value of a carpenter is one hundred times that of a shoemaker. See Rackham's account in Aristotle (1934: 282). In other words, 'geometrical proportion' in a person-to-person relation is completed through a process of realising an 'arithmetical proportion' in a commodity-to-commodity relation.

After the time of Albertus Magnus's and Thomas Aquinas's commentaries on this theme, justice has usually been divided into distributive justice and commutative justice, although Aristotle himself wrote of retributive or corrective justice instead of commutative justice. On the problem of the Latin translation of subdivided particular forms of justice in the *Nicomachean Ethics*, see Ritchie (1894: 188) and Baldwin (1959: 11, 62). While distributive justice is applied to public goods, commutative justice, on the contrary, is taken to be a fair exchange in private contract or commercial transactions, which has nothing to do with the personal worth of the individual agents concerned. In addition, it should be noted that distributive justice implies a positive value judgment with a fixed or sometimes absolute measure under the authority of a community, while commutative justice requires only formal propriety or 'fairness' in the context of a human rule (Baldwin 1959; Arie 1990: 19–104).

In the Continental tradition of natural jurisprudence, based on Roman law, it was not distributive, but commutative justice that became one of the key concepts of civil law by the beginning of the 17th century. Both Grotius and Pufendorf had posited the principles of contract law as the foundation of a system of positive law, implying a fundamental role for commutative justice in society. The important thing is that both tried to distinguish between legal and moral propriety by relegating distributive or attributive justice to the category of 'imperfect right', which was not commanded by law. In other words, the subject of distributive justice (i.e. property transfer from the rich to the poor) was removed to a moral world outside the scope of the law (Hont and Ignatieff 1983: 29–34).

In the 18th century, Scottish thinkers such as Hutcheson, Hume and Reid also treated commutative justice as a fundamental rule for property-based civil society, thought to be composed of people possessing equal rights – or as Reid said: 'Commutative Justice is employed in the Ordinary affairs between Man & Man considered as on a footing of equality' (Haakonssen 1990: 138). Following this tradition, Smith assumed a distinction between distributive and commutative justice and also regarded justice, not as a kind of positive virtue like beneficence, but rather as the foundation of society. He said: 'Justice ... is the main pillar that upholds the whole edifice. If it is removed, the great, the immense fabric of human society ... must in a moment crumble into atoms' (Smith 1976: 86). This justice undoubtedly has a *negative* virtue, and 'has traditionally been called *commutative* justice' (Haakonssen 1981: 99). Smith expressed this more clearly:

> There is, no doubt, propriety in the practice of justice, and it merits, upon that account, all the approbation, which is due to propriety. However, as it does no real positive good, it is entitled to very little gratitude. Mere justice is, upon most occasions, but a negative virtue, and only hinders us from hurting our neighbour.
>
> (Smith 1976: 82)

The quotation above, in a sense, is a typical expression of liberal individualism, linked with J.S. Mill's 'harm principle' or the Nozickean concept of the minimal state (Nozick 1974). For Smith, the less justice was required to function, the better the state of society became. This point of view was symbolised in the following famous phrase: 'We often fulfil all the rules of justice by sitting still and doing nothing' (Smith 1976: 82). In other words, Smith considered that modern commercial society could be sustained, on the condition that only a minimum of negative virtue, or commutative justice as a social rule, is exercised. In this sense, it could be said that commutative justice had almost lost its normative character. It was this bourgeois justice that confronted Marx. It is useful to add the comment that after the rise of the civic humanist paradigm in the 1970s, Smith often came to be characterised as a moral philosopher or even as a severe critic of the free market economy, rather than as a founder of economic liberalism. Typical works representing this point of view are Winch (1978), Dwyer (1987) and Pack (1991). As for economic justice, Witztum challenges the received interpretation of Smith's negative/commutative justice. He insists: 'Separating distributional considerations from Smith's idea of justice is not an appropriate interpretation of his work' (1997: 259). Needless to say, the civic interpretation above fails to grasp the essence of Smith's idea of the autonomous world of the economy portrayed in the *Wealth of Nations*, according to my account.

Capitalism as an unjust economic system

The subtitle of *Capital* is 'A critique of political economy'. Its implication is an attack on 'The Trinity Formula' (Marx 2001f: 801), symbolising the claimed harmonious existence of three classes, that is, capitalists, landowners and labourers, as portrayed in classical political economy. The three of them were said to live peacefully together by receiving profit, rent and wages as compensation for each other's contribution to the production of commodities. According to Marx's contrary account, the wage-relation between capitalists and workers hides the exploitation of working time without any compensation in reality to the workers. Marx, then, absolutely insists that he has thus revealed the 'secret' of the capitalist mode of expansion in *Capital*. His declaration is located at the very end of part five of *Capital* entitled 'The production of absolute and of relative value', where he completes his account of the 'secret' of capitalist production. Capital is therefore not only, as Adam Smith says, command over labour. It is essentially command over unpaid labour. All surplus value, whatever its particular form (profit, interest or rent) may subsequently crystallise into, is in substance the materialisation of unpaid labour. The secret of the self-expansion of capital resolves itself into having a power of disposal over a definite quantity of other people's unpaid labour (Marx 2001e: 534).

We can find another mode of critique in Marx, in that he clearly wants to argue that the system is deceptive by impeaching 'Freedom, Equality, Property and Bentham'. Marx indicates four major characteristics of the world where 'the sale and purchase of labour power goes on' (Marx 2001e: 186). Freedom there means the fact that both agents with free will in the wage-contract are just a buyer and a seller of a commodity, or labour power. Equality implies that they confront each other simply as commodity owners and so exchange equivalent for equivalent, that is, a realisation of commutative justice, as indicated above. Property means that everybody can 'dispose only of what is his own' (Marx 2001e: 186). Bentham is thought to be responsible for the identification of private interest with the general interest through his utilitarian felicific calculus. He is also used by Marx symbolically as a protagonist of an eternally harmonised bourgeois society based on transactions motivated by self-interest.

To put the assertion above more theoretically, I would say that Marx tries to characterise the capitalist economy by analysing it in abstract form as a process of simple commodity circulation founded on the private property system. In this situation, there are socially equal individual economic agents who can buy and sell their commodities freely amongst themselves under contracts of exchange. Individuals in this process are motivated by selfishness. It would be natural to assume that Marx thinks that there should be something wrong or unjust going on in the ordinary social process where there is an appearance of harmony, produced by a 'free and equal contract' between labourers and capitalists. The point of Marx's core critique of capitalism is that there is an unequal exchange in the quantity of labour, albeit under the veil of an equal exchange of labour power and the wages paid for it. This is the exploitation problem. To use Aristotelian terminology, distributive justice, or the exchange in accordance with an endowed labour-quantity, does not realise itself under commutative justice, or the appearance of the exchange of equivalents, that is, labour and wages. I think that putting Marx's idea of justice in the Aristotelian tradition is the only path to a consistent and plausible interpretation. If I am right, some past controversies mentioned above were unnecessary. Marx himself characterised the unjust situation as follows: 'capital obtains this surplus labour without an equivalent, and in essence it always remains forced labour, no matter how much it may seem to result from free contractual agreement' (Marx 2001f: 806). All these things so far make it clear that Marx judged capitalism to be unjust.

On the other hand, it is well known that when Marx applies the theory of historical materialism derived from a Hegelian philosophy of history, he puts a positive value on capitalist economic development. In this theory, capitalist development itself creates the conditions that emerge to form the new, higher and developed stage. It is worth mentioning, in passing, that some of Marx's historical views stemmed from this idea. This includes his view on development as the result of 'the great civilizing influence of capital' (Marx 2001d: 336). However, it also includes his view that the existing social system is not stable and comes to be an obstacle to human development. This is the case for capitalist society. Theoretically Marx also argues that not only the capitalist–labourer relation but also present-day human nature, culture and even law, on the whole, are relative or progressively changeable, depending on newly created conditions, or on the mode of production. There is space here for no more than this brief indication of the relationship between Marx's philosophy of history and justice.

In addition, it is useful to say here that Marx's claim above implies certain criticisms of contemporary theories of justice. In this discussion I owe a great deal to Sayers (1998) and to Gamble *et al.* (1999). First, Marx opposes universalism not only with respect to capitalist society but also with respect to human nature. Marx writes about malleable human nature, noting that: 'By ... acting on the external world and changing it, he [man] at the same time changes his own nature' (Marx 2001e: 187). Second, Marx separates himself from liberal individualism by emphasising the communal nature of the production process. He writes: 'In order to produce, they [men] enter into definite connections and relations with one another and only within these social connections and relations does their relation with nature, does production, take place' (Marx 2001b: 211). Third, Marx is not allied to the scholarship of mere perception, but claims instead the necessity of practical action, which makes subjective and social factors indispensable for social science. As Marx's famous aphorism puts it: 'The philosophers have only interpreted the world in various ways; the point is to change it' (Marx 2001a: 5).

Thus Marxism provides a radical critique of the utilitarian neo-classical assumption of the eternal human being as *homo economicus*. It also lodges certain objections to oversimplifications in Rawlsian theory concerning consumer utilities in the market place whilst neglecting the sphere of production. That position overlooks the existence of class-relative judgments that ignore other members of society with value standards that are incommensurable. Moreover it does not theorise any mechanisms of transition from current society to an expected well-ordered society. I have extracted some of these objections to Rawlsian theory from Buchanan (1982: 122).

Having made the point that Marx has put a negative value on the capitalist economy in these respects, we must return to the main subject: how Marx proposes a new principle of distributive justice.

Marx's ideal principle of distributive justice

Exceptionally in his work, Marx's *Critique of the Gotha Program* tries to speak to the distribution problem in future society. First, Marx discusses a distribution principle for the first stage of communist society – 'to each according to his contribution' – and then proceeds to the higher stage – 'to each according to his need' (Marx 2001c: 87). I will show a plausible and consistent interpretation of Marx's idea by applying the Aristotelian terminology of justice discussed above, making reference to Aristotle and thus avoiding some scholarly confusions. Let us consider the following quotation:

What we are dealing with here is a communist society, not as it has developed on its own foundations, but on the contrary, just as it emerges from capitalist society, which is thus in every respect, economically, morally and intellectually, still stamped with the birth-marks of the old society from whose womb it emerges.

Accordingly, the individual producer receives back from society – after the deductions have been made – exactly what he gives to it ... he draws from the social stock of means of consumption as much as the same amount of labour costs. The same amount of labour that he has given to society in one form he receives back in another.

(Marx 2001c: 85–6)

The essence of the distribution principle here, as Marx himself says, is this: 'the same principle prevails as in the exchange of commodity-equivalents: a given amount of labour in one form is exchanged for an equal amount of labour in another form' (Marx 2001c: 86). From the Aristotelian viewpoint, it is almost self-evident that the lower level principle of distribution, to a certain extent, is considered as retributive justice. If we think of it as the exchange of the quantity of labour in a commodity, this is then the simultaneous realisation of both equal quantitative exchange and exchange in proportion to each person's value. Therefore, both the 'arithmetical proportion' based on the equal exchange of commodities and the 'geometrical proportion' based on different personal values are properly realised at the same time. In other words, the latter indicates the compensatory return from society in proportion to each personal contribution. Some Marx scholars' confusion or misunderstanding is due to their neglect of Aristotelian language in Marx, or due to confusion between the classical conception of distributive justice and that of today. The former is unequal distribution by authority based on an imposed standard, while the latter definition of distributive justice does not always assume inequality.

Marx opposes the contribution principle, or 'geometrical proportion', because it does not meet the real life necessities of contributors whose living conditions are different. Marx evaluates this situation as still unequal and therefore unjust by saying that 'equal right here is still in principle – bourgeois right' (Marx 2001c: 86). As far as the claim of each individual for consumption goods is validated by means of unequal contributions in terms of different quantities of labour, there remains a real inequality in spite of the realisation of 'equal exchange', or the establishment of an 'arithmetical proportion'.

Marx then ascends to the higher stage of the communist society. He shows the final principle of distribution:

After the enslaving subordination of the individual to the division of labour, and thereby also the antithesis between mental and physical labour, has vanished; after labour has become not only a means of life but life's prime want; after the productive forces have also increased with the all-round development of the individual, and all the springs of common wealth flow more abundantly, only then can the narrow horizon of bourgeois right be crossed in its entirety and society inscribe on its banners: From each according to his abilities, to each according to his needs!

(Marx 2001c: 87)

Here Marx rejects the former principle that each individual producer receives back an equivalent from society in proportion to what is contributed or supplied in the form of labour. Instead, each individual receives in proportion to his/her needs, not in proportion to his/her contribution. The quantity of contributed labour, then, has nothing to do with distribution process. The contribution principle has been transformed into the needs principle. This situation is very similar to the Aristotelian principle of distributive justice for the distribution of public goods, that is, the 'geometrical proportion', but without the 'arithmetical proportion'. Marx seems to think it to be the establishment of true equality. This 'needs principle' excludes a nominal equality based on commodity exchange. That is why Castoriadis says: 'In fact, essentially, his [Marx's] response in the *Critique of the Gotha Program* is only a paraphrase of a certain passage in the fifth book [of Aristotle's *Nicomachaean Ethics*, but] twenty-two centuries later' (1978: 718). On Marx in Aristotelian tradition, see Dognin (1958).

The point here is that the higher stage of the communist society is an 'unequal society' presuming various differences between persons, such as the need for goods, the capacity for activity, the strength of desire, and so on. However, what kind of society is this higher stage in terms of its economy? Logically, this is a society where there is no restriction on the consumption of goods or resources with respect to all members' needs or necessity, and where labour seems to be unrelated to distribution. Singer comments on this vision as 'optimistic' and remarks: 'Everything Marx says about communism is premised on material abundance' (1980: 64, 65). Nevertheless, Marx maintains a reciprocal relation between labour and goods, while rejecting a quantitative relation between them. Each individual member is still required to make a labour contribution in order to claim the right to a supply of necessities. The higher stage of communism is surely a kingdom of labourers. We have returned to the problem of labour in Marx's whole system.

It is not unreasonable to suppose that Marx's concept of the principle of distributive justice implies the following. First, his image of future productive power is quite optimistic and seems limitless. Second, a labour contribution that entitles a member of society to make a claim on distribution reflects Marx's particularly positive evaluation of labour as such, which has ethical and philosophical significance. Third, Marx's labour-based principle of distributive justice seems to have a close relationship with his basic idea of labour as the substance of value in his labour theory of value. This evaluation may well be common knowledge in the historical scholarship of economic theory. Blaug concluded that the whole system of Marx's economics depends on 'the philosophical significance of labour cost' (1958: 38), and Backhouse says that Marx's labour theory really resides in its 'ideological' and 'ethical' implications (1985: 122).

Conclusion

The increasingly complex character of contemporary capitalism, together with globalisation, has led us to re-examine classical ideas of society, economy and humanity. The question of distributive justice is one of the fundamental issues that all countries face today. Reviewing Marx's idea of distributive justice certainly gives us an opportunity to rethink contemporary problems. What then can we learn from it? We see first, that distributive justice, whether classical or contemporary, requires by definition a certain kind of commonly acceptable moral criterion, and may also require an authority to implement it. Second, for Marx, labour is always indispensable in his social theory, and so plays an important role in the distributive principle for his predicted communist society. Needless to say, labour-based Marxian human nature is too simple to cope with our contemporary world. Finally, if distribution is the economic issue of critical importance, then a new principle of distributive justice should be a combination of economics and ethics, following Sen's warning that 'modern economics has been substantially impoverished by the distance that has grown between economics and ethics' (1992: 8).

References

Arie, D. (1990) *Labour and Justice: A History of Socio-Economic Ideas from Aristotle to Roemer* (Japanese). Tokyo: Sofusha Press.

Aristotle (1934) *The Nicomachean Ethics*, trans. by H. Rackham. Cambridge: Harvard University Press.

Aronson, R. (1995) *After Marxism*. New York: Guildford Press.

Backhouse, R. (1985) *A History of Modern Economic Analysis*. Oxford: Blackwell.

Baldwin, J.W. (1959) 'The medieval theory of the just price: Romanists, Canonists, and theologians in the twelfth and thirteenth centuries', *Transactions of the American Philosophical Society*, New Series, 49: 1–92.

Blaug, M. (1958) *Ricardian Economics: A Historical Study*. New Haven: Yale University Press.

Buchanan, A.E. (1982) *Marx and Justice: The Radical Critique of Liberalism*. Totowa: Rowman & Allanheld.

Callari, A. and Ruccio, D.F. (1996) *Postmodern Materialism and the Future of Marxist Theory: Essays in the Althusserian Tradition*. Hanover: Wesleyan University Press.

Carver, T. (1987) *A Marx Dictionary*. Cambridge: Polity Press.

Carver, T. (1998) *The Postmodern Marx*. Manchester: Manchester University Press.

Castoriadis, C. (1978) 'From Marx to Aristotle, from Aristotle to us', *Social Research* 45: 667–738.

Cohen, G.A. (1988) 'Freedom, justice and capitalism', *New Left Review* 126: 3–16.

Cohen, M., Nagel, T. and Scanlon, T. (eds) (1980) *Marx, Justice and History*. Princeton: Princeton University Press.

Dognin, P.D. (1958) 'Aristote, Saint Thomas et Karl Marx', *Revue des Sciences Philosophique et Theologiques* Tome XLII: 726–35.

Dwyer, J. (1987) *Virtuous Discourses: Sensibility and Community in Late Eighteenth Century Scotland*. Edinburgh: John Donald.

Elster, J. (1997) 'Exploitation, freedom, and justice', in K. Nielsen and R. Ware (eds) (1997) *Exploitation*. Atlantic Highlands: Humanities Press, 27–48.

Gamble, A., Marsh, D. and Tant, T. (eds) (1999) *Marxism and Social Science*. Basingstoke: Macmillan.

Geras, N. (1985) 'The controversy about Marx and justice', *New Left Review* 150: 47–85.

Haakonssen, K. (1981) *The Science of a Legislator: The Natural Jurisprudence of David Hume and Adam Smith*. Cambridge: Cambridge University Press.

Haakonssen, K. (ed.) (1990) *Thomas Reid, Practical Ethics: Being Lectures and Papers on Natural Religion, Self-Government, Natural Jurisprudence, and the Law of Nations*. Princeton: Princeton University Press.

Haakonssen, K. (1996) *Natural Law and Moral Philosophy: From Grotius to the Scottish Enlightenment*. Cambridge: Cambridge University Press.

Hont, I. and Ignatieff, M. (1983) 'Needs and justice in the wealth of nations: An introductory essay', in I. Hont and M. Ignatieff (eds) (1983) *Wealth and Virtue: The Shaping of Political Economy in the Scottish Enlightenment*. Cambridge: Cambridge University Press, 1–44.

Husami, Z. (1978) 'Marx on distributive justice', *Philosophy and Public Affairs* 8: 27–64.

Kain, P.J. (1988) *Marx and Ethics*. Oxford: Clarendon Press.

Lukes, S. (1982) 'Marxism, morality and justice', in G.H.R. Parkinson (ed.) (1982) *Marx and Marxisms*. Cambridge: Cambridge University Press.

Marx, K. (2001a) *Theses on Feuerbach*, in K. Marx and F. Engels, *Collected Works*, electronic edn, vol. 9. Charlottesville: InteLex Corporation.

Marx, K. (2001b) *Wage Labour and Capital*, in K. Marx and F. Engels, *Collected Works*, electronic edn, vol. 9. Charlottesville: InteLex Corporation.

Marx, K. (2001c) *Critique of the Gotha Program*, in K. Marx and F. Engels, *Collected Works*, electronic edn, vol. 24. Charlottesville: InteLex Corporation.

Marx, K. (2001d) *Outline of the Critique of Political Economy (Rough Draft of 1857–58)*, in K. Marx and F. Engels, *Collected Works*, electronic edn, vol. 28. Charlottesville: InteLex Corporation.

Marx, K. (2001e) *Capital* I, in K. Marx and F. Engels, *Collected Works*, electronic edn, vol. 35. Charlottesville: InteLex Corporation.

Marx, K. (2001f) *Capital* III, in K. Marx and F. Engels, *Collected Works*, electronic edn, vol. 37. Charlottesville: InteLex Corporation.

Masset, P. (1970) *Les 50 mots-cles du marxisme*. Toulouse: Edouardo Privat.

Miller, R. (1975) 'Rawls and Marxism', in N. Daniels (ed.) *Reading Rawls: Critical Studies on Rawls' 'Theory of Justice'*. New York: Basic Books, 206–29.

Moseley, F. (ed.) (1993) *Marx's Method in Capital: A Reexamination*. Atlantic Highlands: Humanities Press.

Nielsen, K. and Ware, R. (eds) (1997) *Exploitation*. Atlantic Highlands: Humanities Press.

Nozick, R. (1974) *Anarchy, State, and Utopia*. Oxford: Blackwell.

O'Neill, J. (1995) *The Poverty of Postmodernism*. London: Routledge.

Pack, S.P. (1991) *Capitalism as a Moral System: Adam Smith's Critique of the Free Market Economy*. Basingstoke: Edward Elgar.

Sayers, S. (1998) *Marxism and Human Nature*. London: Routledge.

Sen, A. (1992) *On Ethics and Economics*. Oxford: Blackwell.

Singer, P. (1980) *Marx*. Oxford: Oxford University Press.

Smith, A. (1976) *The Theory of Moral Sentiments*, edited by D.D. Raphael and A.L. Macfie. Oxford: Oxford University Press.

Ware, R. and Nielsen, K. (eds) (1989) *Analyzing Marxism, Canadian Journal of Philosophy*, supplementary vol. 15. Calgary: The University of Calgary Press.

Westphal, J. (ed.) (1996) *Justice: Readings in Philosophy*. Indianapolis: Hackett.

Winch, D. (1978) *Adam Smith's Politics: An Essay in Historigraphic Revision*. Cambridge: Cambridge University Press.

Witztum, A. (1997) 'Distributive considerations in Smith's conception of economic justice', *Economics and Philosophy* 13: 241–59.

Wood, A. (1972) 'The Marxian critique of justice,' *Philosophy and Public Affairs* 1: 244–82.

6 Marx and the environmental problem

Hideaki Kudo

Introduction

The 20th century brought unprecedented economic prosperity, and it has been called 'the century of the economy'. In the middle of the century, mainstream economics prospered as 'the queen of social sciences'. However, there were dark sides to prosperity. In particular, environmental problems became acute towards end of the century. Economics was unable to present a fundamental solution. Has Marxian economics demonstrated its power as a critique of economics in this situation? Regrettably, it lapsed into a crisis over problems concerned with increasing economic growth, even before mainstream economics did so too.

The 21st century is working towards a solution to the environmental problem, the greatest negative inheritance of modern industrial society. It is said that 'the century of ecology' has arrived. In order for Marxian economics to revive, it has to be rediscovered and reconstructed as a system which can tackle this problem upfront. This chapter explores this possibility in Marx's own works.

The environmental problem

The affluence attained in 'the golden 30 years' of the 20th century seemed wonderful. It is estimated that the quantity of goods produced and consumed in those years rose by four times the quantity of goods produced and consumed since the dawn of history up to that time (Brown 1989). It was considered that mainstream economics was the science that had facilitated such high growth. And it was assumed that if there were any problems, they were solvable with application of the principles and frameworks of economics. Therefore, such applications began to be tried when environmental problems appeared. Soon these trials developed into the newest field in applied economics. According to this view, environmental problems are an 'external diseconomy' that is brought about by the act of a certain economic subject on other subjects without passing through a market, and is therefore 'market failure'. Through taxation etc., the government should then reflect this diseconomy in a price, and thus put it into the market. In that way, environmental economic theory aimed to solve environmental problems through realising the optimal distribution of resources.

However, the environmental problem itself gradually expanded from a local problem to a national one, an international one and, finally, a global one. Global environmental problems arose, such as desertification, pollution of the seas, acid rain, ozone holes, climatic warming and abnormal weather (Brown 2001). Thus, as environmental problems became more severe, another view developed, which was that the environmental problem itself is a criticism of conventional economics and thus demands an alternative new economics. The main researchers who started this movement are the following: Boulding (1968) advocated 'the economics of spaceship earth', which replaces an old, cowboy-like view of the economy and instead positions it in a cyclical, closed ecosystem. In addition Georgescu-Roegen (1971) pointed out the irreversibility of the economic process, and advocated an economics based on the law of entropy. Schumacher (1973) introduced 'Small is Beautiful', instead of large-scale planning, and conceived of the human economy on the basis of regional ecosystems. Daly (1974) advocated the shift to a steady-state, in which material wealth and population are maintained by the throughput of a fixed scale, from the present condition governed by growth mania. And Tamanoi (1974) called for a conversion of economics, in the wider sense, considering a 'social economy' in an open yet steady system, moving away from economics in the narrow sense, always centring on the analysis of capitalist markets and industry.

While sympathy for these opinions has been spreading, there has also been a re-examination of the history of economics based on the recognition of ecology (Immler 1985; Martinez-Alier 1987). Moreover, the network of cooperation centring on the above-mentioned economists began to spread interdisciplinarily and internationally. For example, in Japan, the Society for Studies on Entropy (SSE) was founded in 1983 by researchers in economics, physics, biology and so on, and by activists in citizens' campaigns. Tamanoi was elected chairman. Moreover, The Other Economic Summit (TOES) was formed in Britain in 1984 by various researchers, engineers and practitioners who sympathised with Schumacher. Moreover the New Economics Foundation was established on that basis in 1986. In the United States, the International Society for Ecological Economics (ISEE) was organised by Daly, Martinez-Alier and others in 1989. It aims at the realisation of an ecologically and economically sustainable world. In Italy, The European Association for Bioeconomic Studies (EABS) was founded in 1990, and subsequently elected Georgescu-Roegen honorary chairman. It promotes research into bioeconomics in connection with his entropy theory.

The common goal of these movements aiming at a new economics is to convert the theory that 'the social economy consisting mainly of a market and industry is primary and the environment is merely secondary' into an alternative way of thinking such 'that the natural ecosystem is a basis for sustainability of the social economy' which should adhere to the laws of natural ecosystem. Such movements were criticised for weak analysis of the history and structure of the capitalist social economic system. However, support for the goal spread quickly. Also, some typical researchers in conventional economics began to share these intentions. For example, Kenichi Miyamoto, the Japanese Marxian economics group's environmental economist, declared his agreement with ecological intentions in his masterpiece, *Environmental Economics* (1989). Moreover, Hirofumi Uzawa, a mainstream but environmental economist, also approved of Miyamoto's declaration (1989).

However, such movements do not limit themselves to economics as an individual science concerned with environmental problems. Rather they bear a more fundamental and comprehensive task in the long-term historical context. According to Worster (1989), a leader in the study of environmental history, the situation is as follows. In modern thought and science, two kinds of views have repeatedly confronted each other concerning the relationship between man and nature. One of them is a dualism with a mechanistic outlook on nature. This considers nature to be what was made for man, and other existence to be worthless in itself. Nature is thus the object which should be governed, developed and used by man. Another view is a monism with an organicist outlook on nature. This considers nature to be a united whole which has subjective value and a rational order in itself. It is considered that man should aim at peaceful coexistence with other living things as a part of nature. Perhaps we can term the former 'mancentrism' and call the latter 'naturalism or naturalistic humanism'. Both of these have permeated all thought and science, and have fought each other over several centuries. The former has taken pride in its dominant influence, and mainstream economics has also always been based on it. However, according to Worster, the urgent task of the present age is to dissolve the dualism of the former view that divides man from nature, and instead to develop extensively the latter outlook on nature that includes society and human beings.

In fact, the above-mentioned new movement in economics is bearing this historical and theoretical task in the present age. Economics reigned over 'the century of the economy' and must now tackle this difficult task as a matter of priority in order to play a significant role in the 21st century, 'the century of ecology' (Weizsäecker 1992). Great pioneers in the history of economics have suggested a solution to the difficult problem imposed on present-day economics. Moreover, searching for the solution will be one of the main subjects of research in the history of economics. However, if mainstream economics has always been based on the former outlook on nature, how can an alternative be derived from its history?

'Naturalism' in Marx's works

Some currents of economics have their origins in a utility theory of value, and others in a labour theory of value. To be sure, each of these may have a dualistic view of man's divided nature. For all of them, though, man is the one subject who might give value and order to all existence, and govern and freely use these resources. Various kinds of economics have stood on this man-centric premise. On this premise, they have analysed the capitalist economic system on a market equilibrium basis or on a historical structuralist basis. None of the pioneers in the history of economics seem to have understood nature as a subjective existence with a peculiar value and rational order, and as a monistic and organic united whole which contains man as a part. Has anyone in the history of economics ever taken this view? In my view there is one exceptional person who had such an understanding. It is Marx who made such a critique of economics his life-work. Two of his early works show this clearly. One is his doctoral dissertation 'Difference between the Democritean and the Epicurean philosophy of nature', and the other is *Economic and Philosophical Manuscripts* (1844). The former was a starting point for his whole intellectual development, and the latter was the starting point for his critique of economics. In order to confirm the matter mentioned above, I will examine these works here, focusing on his view of nature, i.e. his conception of nature–human relations. Although they are philosophical and very difficult to understand, we cannot pass them by.

Marx's doctoral dissertation

This thesis treats the philosophy developed in the ancient Greek *polis* in its decline. This decline of civil society was accompanied by the destruction of its natural basis. The cosmopolis which Alexander the Great brought about continued this confusion and disorder. In such a general collapse, the philosophy of 'abstract individuality' in Epicurus pursued the independence and *ataraxia* of man returning to an individual existence. This philosophy aims at 'freedom from existence', abstracting from natural attributes as 'restrictive existence', and escaping from reality. It states that man exists without mediation, and that the relation of friendship with many individuals who have freed themselves from natural restrictions and become independent is important.

A philosophy of 'concrete individuality, i.e. universality' in Marx is developed through a critical examination of this Epicurean philosophy. According to it, man is an existence united with nature and inside nature, and so shares the subjectivity of nature. Man exists as part of the process in which nature changes itself repeatedly and forms the world. His sensitivity is precisely 'the reflection in self' of nature. Marx's description of this is as follows:

Nature is hearing itself in man's work of hearing and smells itself in man's work of smelling and is looking at itself in man's work of looking. Therefore, man's sensuousness is mediation in which natural processes are reflected as in a focus and are ignited into the light of appearance

(MEGA Series 2 (1975): 50)

So, it is important for human beings to accept various restrictions of nature, and to be active in internalising them. It is also important to form a society that realises 'freedom in existence' and can shine 'in the light of existence'. Man is the existence that can affirm itself only by affirming nature in nature. Such ontological naturalism (naturalistic humanism) is fundamental to Marx. It is his viewpoint that orients the theory towards social change and reconstruction in a crisis. This comprehension was gained at the starting point of his intellectual development and serves as a basis for his critique of economics, which he began soon afterwards.

Economic and philosophical manuscripts of 1844

'The first manuscript' is the first systematic attempt at the critique of economics by Marx. The existence and general collapse of modern capitalist society are analysed through a critique of economy at the national level. The essential meaning of 'alienated labour' is considered, down to the most basic dimensions. Natural beings and things form parts of the life of man materially as objects which satisfy desires in his life. Moreover, they form parts of man's consciousness intellectually as objects of science or art. However, 'the corporal and mental life of man being connected with nature is exactly that nature is connected with nature itself. It is because man is a part of nature' *(MEW* 1968: 515f.). This shows that Marx has gained a naturalistic comprehension of human life. But it is important that the specific way that human beings are a part of nature is understood. That is, since man is conscious of natural existence *(Gattungswesen)*, he performs life-activity relationally. Man can connect with natural beings and things mutually, receiving and respecting the character and basis of each of them. The essential meaning of 'alienated labour' is that this relational life activity is developed by reversing ends and means.

Marx plans to make a genetic description of many categories of national economy from this dimension, making the alienated relations between man and man (his fourth distinction) a starting point from which to step up to more concrete dimensions. When it is achieved, it means that estranged and established categories in everyday consciousness are grasped conceptually as self-alienated forms of the relational life activity of man. So, when this genetic description is attained, the possibility of rebuilding human (that is, natural) society through acts that reverse ends and means once more can be pursued immediately.

Marx's 'Comments on James Mill'

These 'Comments' were written when Marx was studying James Mill's *Elements of Political Economy*. He read the passage that resonates strongly with the fourth distinction mentioned above, and got a new idea. According to this new idea, 'the relation of a private owner with another private owner' is the systematic starting point of a genetic description of the economic categories. In an exchange relation, private property is converted qualitatively, and is alienated. Then value, money, etc. are brought forth and, finally, a general collapse takes place. However, because exchange, which is one form of the social relationship between man and man, was the starting point here, this does not mean that the most critical viewpoint of the nature–human relationship, developed in the fourth distinction in 'the first manuscript', has been eliminated. Rather that view became the most fundamental premise supporting Marx's system as a whole. For him, the human–human correlation was the realistic and actual form for essential and potential nature–human relations. Two important propositions are included here.

The first is that in exchange, private property is converted qualitatively and alienated, after which a general collapse ensues. This genetic deployment clarifies Marx's view that the alienation of man is also the process that completes the alienation of nature, and so private property will form the world which deviates from nature. He develops this further in his 'second manuscript'.

The second is that the most fundamental premise for sublating the alienation of man as a private owner in exchange is sublating 'the potential form (germ)' of the exchange of labour for labour products between man and nature. In other words, the famous 'double affirmation (between you and me)' comes to fruition only in the human–human correlation whose potential form (germ) is the 'exchange of courtesies' between man and nature. Marx discusses this at length in 'the third manuscript'.

The final part of 'the second manuscript'

Marx's critique systematically reveals the process in which the relation between private owners (citizens) develops into a confrontational relation between classes. On the one hand, human activity is produced there as 'labour', which is a completely estranged activity for man and nature. On the other hand, the object loses its natural and social quality when it is held as private property, and is produced as 'capital', which is completely indifferent to natural and social existence. Thus the process in which the relation between citizens develops as the labour–capital relation is a process that completes the alienation of man and nature. There, labour and capital deviate from a natural cycle and thus form a world independent from nature. So, when this process proceeds to the limit, it is also the limit of denaturalisation. Therefore, all relations cannot but go to ruin. Such a situation is potentially included in the relation between private owners at the starting point. The human–human correlation at that point is thus the actualisation of what is latent in the relation between man and nature. The ultimate focus is then the state of the relationship between man and nature in the private property of the individual citizen. Therefore, the new relation, which will replace all the relations that went to ruin, must be, and can be, reconstructed on the basis of realising an alternative state of the essential relation between man and nature.

In that way, the final part of 'the second manuscript' forms the conclusion of the critique of economics. The theory of change developed after that is the theme of 'the third manuscript'.

Gesellschaft theory in 'the third manuscript'

'The third manuscript' tends to clarify features of sublation of private property and human *Gesellschaft* as a goal. It mentions the relation between male and female as an index measuring the degree of maturity of social change. In this relation, the human–human correlation is at one directly with the man–nature relation. So, we can judge from this relation to what extent the human–human correlation and the man–nature relationship have been released from one-sided evaluation and domination. Marx's view is as follows. The female is subjective existence which should not be evaluated and dominated by the male one-sidedly, but rather it has differing values. In the same way, natural beings are subjective existences that should not be evaluated and dominated by man one-sidedly, but have respectively differing values. Rather, the degree of maturity and training of man can be measured by his ability to properly form his relationship with nature as subjective existence.

Therefore, completed communism is specified as 'completed naturalism = humanism'. Moreover, the *Gesellschaft* that shows the characteristics of a communist movement is the state in which the essential oneness of man with nature is realised, and nature is truly revitalised. In this *Gesellschaft*, nature and natural beings are neither merely use value, which has utility for man, nor merely exchange value, as the alienated form of use value. Rather nature and natural beings are received, respected and related to by man as things which have their peculiar and independent values (that is, existence values or natural values). In other words, man and his senses relate to them, being released from a one-sided sense of possession and activity under private property and appropriating a fully-rounded human existence in an all-round way.

'Naturalism' and world history in Marx's critique of Hegel

In the critique of Hegel planned for 'the last chapter' of Marx's book, the fundamental nature–man conception, which underpins this whole early work, is summarised in the recognition of history. According to this, nature is a subject in itself and is constituted through various forms of existence. Among these are living natural beings (animals and plants etc.), which are active existences demonstrating subjectively their essential life powers based on desires. However, their existences are produced and restricted by various others. Moreover, their desires and objective activities cannot be realised if they lack various other objective existences. That is, there are also passive existences that are restrained and restricted by many other active ones, and are thus made into objects of those activities. While all natural existences are subjects, they are also objects in this way. Among them, activity and passivity are each interwoven with the other in many directions, and thus overlap. In this way, nature as a whole and its individual existences are changing and regenerating through mutual influence.

Man is also one of these existences. The specific difference between man and other forms of life is that he is conscious of himself and so his existence is accompanied by consciousness. This means that man can recognise himself and objects as individuals from a universal viewpoint that exceeds them. Man can work on himself in a relationship with others from such a viewpoint. Therefore, man can be conscious of deviations in his desires from objects and of the alienation of his essential powers as various negative states, and he can recognise these states as tasks that must be overcome (the negation of the negation). History is a generative act common to living natural beings. However, since man has such a specific kind of existence, history turns into 'man's true history of nature' or 'world history' as an accumulation of 'negation' and 'negation of negation' from the mere 'history of nature'.

Marx understands that man's history is formed as a part of generative process of nature out of nature in nature. He then recognises the peculiar dynamism produced here by conceptualising history as 'a relational act' accompanied by consciousness. He calls his position 'naturalism'. According to him, only in this way can the act of world history be grasped conceptually.

Thus ontological 'naturalism', as a fundamental conception of the nature–human relationship, was acquired in Marx's early critique of economics as his most fundamental premise for systematising his critique. It serves as a potential and essential motive supporting his starting point for the systematic development of economic categories, such as value, money etc. Moreover, the 'ruin of all relations' described in the concluding part of his systematic development (that is, in the final part of his second manuscript of 1844) is founded on this understanding. Furthermore, in the theory of transformation developed following that concluding part, this naturalism is materialised as an important substance of the movement of sublation. Marx declares this to be the only position from which world history can be grasped conceptually.

Marx's 'naturalism' was structured systematically in his first critique of economics in this way. Moreover, systematisation of his critique of economics was pushed forward and accomplished through this kind of 'naturalism'. To be sure, in his early works Marx was dependent on the latter (that is, the monistic and organicist one of two views on nature), classified only recently by Worster. It is clear that Marx's critique of economics set out from the position at the opposite pole from that of mainstream economics (Kudo 1997).

'Naturalism' in the later Marx

How was 'naturalism' transmitted through Marx's subsequent process of research? Surely 'naturalism' disappears from Marx's language, at least on the surface. However, the manifestation of his understanding that the connection between man and nature and the connection between man and man are both just a connection of nature with itself is repeated in important writings from *The German Ideology* and the *Grundrisse* to the *Critique of Gotha Programme*. The view that nature and human beings are essentially at one is consistently invoked during Marx's whole intellectual life. It is demonstrated directly in the passage concerning 'reconstruction' at two key points in the first volume of *Capital*, which he continued polishing through his later years (*MEW* 1962: 528, 791). In section 10 of Chapter 13 of part IV (the substantial closing section on the process of production), which is the first key point, the most important task of the mode of production that should succeed the capitalist system is presented as the reconstruction of the metabolism between man and nature systematically as a regulative law of social production. In section 7 of Chapter 24 of part VII (the substantial closing section on the accumulation of capital), which is the second key point, the reconstruction of individual property is regarded as a task united with the one mentioned above. The metabolism of man and nature has been disturbed by the capitalist mode of production, which pursues infinitely an increase in value and use value, and therefore destroys the external and natural conditions for the sustainable fertility of land. The former reconstruction calls for an understanding of the logic of subjective life activity or the movement of natural existence, and for an evaluation of the existence values (natural values) peculiar to them, and for carrying out qualitative and structural changes in social production which respect and observe those original existence conditions and laws. The latter reconstruction is exactly the process through which individuals, who are going to be free, carry out such changes systematically in a form suitable for human development. Marx's 'naturalism' thus fulfils his life-long and most important work.

Marx in 'the century of ecology'

Early in the second half of the 20th century, Alfred Schmidt, the standard-bearer of the Frankfurt school, had a sense of an impending crisis that would lead to the destruction of the natural foundation of society. He tackled this with Marx's concept of nature, which had hardly been researched until then (Schmidt 1962). This is an excellent pioneering study, taking up the environmental problem as one way of rereading Marx's writings. However, in the postscript to the new edition in 1971, Schmidt points out that Marx later shifted to the critique of economics, with great theoretical sacrifice, and so he evaluated the later Marx negatively. The environmental problem at that time in 'the century of the economy' did not allow for a rehabilitation of the early Marx through the later Marx's critique of economics.

However, the environmental problem, aggravated as the century drew to its close, has fostered not only innovations in mainstream economics down to its fundamentals (or the possibility to create a new economics), but also re-examinations of the entire work of Marx as a thinker who made the critique of economics his life-work. There is a good example to demonstrate this. Foster, the noted environmental sociologist, reflects on the environmental destruction which advances on a global scale, and presents a sharp analysis of the present situation (Foster 1994). He has published a very substantial work at the beginning of 'the century of ecology' (Foster 2000). This will certainly serve as a forerunner for a re-examination of Marx's writings. According to Forster, Marx tackled the natural philosophy of Epicurus and others in his dissertation, and found the origin of the problems of modern society in the alienation of human beings from nature in the *Economic and Philosophical Manuscripts* of 1844. He continued during his lifetime to develop his materialist conception of nature and materialist conception of history in order to conquer this alienation. It was *Capital* that unified these two conceptions. It conceptualised the declining fertitlity in farms and the pollution and contamination of the towns, arising from a confrontation between town and country, in terms of a division in the human–nature metabolism, and positioned this view at the core of a critique of economics. In *Capital* Marx precisely grappled with the subject from the beginning of his intellectual life (that is, the conquest of natural alienation and labour alienation together). Foster calls the thought of Marx 'dialectic naturalism', and criticises Western Marxism for limiting dialectic to the social dimension, and missing this 'naturalism'. Furthermore, he indicates that the cause of this is both in the failure to understand the philosophies of Epicurus and others, and in neglecting the analysis of natural alienation. He argues that it is necessary to re-examine Marx fundamentally, facing up to the environmental problem as the biggest problem in the modern age.

As seen previously, 'naturalism' carries through Marx's whole system in his early manuscripts. Thereafter Marx concentrated his power on a certain portion of his critique of economics, which became the text of *Capital*. However, this does not mean that his earlier premises had became unnecessary. Rather, his critique of economics can be fully understood only on the basis of his 'naturalism'.

Various movements that aim at a new economics, proceeding from a critique of mainstream economics undertaken with respect to the environmental problem, will pick up speed in systematising results hitherto accumulated in 'the century of ecology'. Their efforts toward such systematisation will probably be in sympathy with the attempt to re-examine and reconstruct Marx's entire critique of economics, containing not only the portions he worked out but the portions developed only in potential. In other words, these efforts are resonant with the attempt to complete the critique of economics by developing its potential. For example, Marx, who thought much of existence value is different from exchange value or use value, would probably be in line with efforts by ISEE and TOES, which distinguish primary value from secondary value and then, using methodological pluralism, explore multi-criteria evaluations, different from money-evaluations (Norgaard 1989; Turner and Pearce 1993; Gren *et al.* 1994; Daly 1996; Martinez-Aliez *et al.* 1998), and so resonate with each other. Moreover, Marx pursued the conquest of natural alienation in modern society and the reconstruction of the metabolism of man with nature as a subject all throughout his lifetime. SSE and EABS emphasise 'the entropy disposal ability' of the earth as damaged by modern industry, which draws underground resources to excess, compared with material cycles of cleansing, and they aim at the reactivation of the ecocycle by developing human alternative economic activities (Pillet and Murota 1987; Murota 2001; Mayumi 2001). From these points, too, Marx and social movements aiming at a new economics share this intention widely and deeply.

Conclusion

In Japan it is often said that 'the great thinker completes his thought out of his early work'. Marx did not actually do this, because along the way he concentrated his effort on one portion of his critique. The above mentioned attempt takes over Marx's work to 'complete his thought out of his early work'. It is this attempt that will pave the way for unifying Marxian economics, which has produced historical and structural analysis of the internal system of social economy, with ecologism, which has prioritised the human–natural relation as important and has developed radical social criticism in a new dimension.

References

Boulding, K.E. (1968) *Beyond Economics.* Ann Arbor: University of Michigan.
Brown, L.R. (1989) *State of the World.* New York: W.W. Norton.

Brown, L.R. (2001) *Eco-economy*. London: Earthscan.

Daly, H. (1974) 'The economics of steady state', *American Economic Review* 15–21 May.

Daly, H. (1996) *Beyond Growth*. Boston: Beacon Press.

Foster, J.B. (1994) *The Vulnerable Planet*. New York: Monthly Review Press.

Foster, J.B. (2000) *Marx's Ecology: Materialism and Nature*. New York: Monthly Review Press.

Georgescu-Roegen, N. (1971) *The Entropy Law and Economic Process*. Cambridge: Harvard University Press.

Gren, I.-M., Forke, C., Turner, R.K. and Bateman, I. (1994) 'Primary and second values of wetland ecosystems', *Environmental and Resource Economics* 4: 55–74.

Immler, H. (1985) *Natur in der Ökonomischen Theorie*. Opladen: Westdeutscher Verlag.

Kudo, Hideaki (1997) *First Critique of Political Economy and Naturalism*. Economic Study Series of Chiba University, no.1 (in Japanese).

Martinez-Alier, J. (1987) *Ecological Economics*. Oxford: Blackwell.

Martinez-Alier, J., Munda, G. and O'Neill, J. (1998) 'Weak comparability of values as a foundation for ecological economics', *Ecological Economics* 26: 277–86.

Mayumi, Kozo (2001) *The Origins of Ecological Economics: The Bioeconomics of Georgescu-Roegen*. London: Routledge.

MEGA Series 2 (1975) *Karl Marx/Friedrich Engels, Gesamtausgabe*, Erste Abteilung, Werke-Artikel-Entwürfe, I/1:1. Berlin: Dietz Verlag.

MEW (1962) *Karl Marx-Friedrich Engels Werke*, 23. Berlin: Dietz Verlag.

MEW (1968) *Karl Marx-Friedrich Engels Werke*, Ergänzungband, Erster Teil. Berlin: Dietz Verlag.

Miyamoto, Kennichi (1989) *Environmental Economics*. Tokyo: Iwanamishoten (in Japanese).

Murota, Takeshi (2001) *The Ecology of Material Cycle*. Tokyo: Koyoshyobo (in Japanese).

Norgaard, R. (1989) 'The case for methodological pluralism', *Ecological Economics* 1: 37–57.

Pillet, G. and Murota, T. (1987) *Environmental Economics*. Geneva: Roland Leimgruber.

Schmidt, A. (1962) *Der Begriff der Natur in der Lehre von Marx*. Frankfurt: Europäische Verlagsanstalt.

Schumacher, E.F. (1973) *Small is Beautiful*. London: Blond & Briggs.

Tamanoi, Yoshiro (1974) 'Toward the economics in a broad sense on metabolism', *KEIZAI-Seminar*, November (in Japanese).

Turner, R.K. and Pearce, D.W. (1993) 'Sustainable economic development: economic and ethical principles', in E.B. Barbier (ed.) *Economics and Ecology*. London: Chapman and Hall.

Weizsäecker, E.U. von (1992) *Erdpolitik: Ölologische Realpolotik an der Sohwelle zum Jahrhundert der Umwelt*, 3rd edn. Darmstadt: Wissenschaftiche Buchgesellschaft.

Worster, D. (1989) *Nature's Economy: A History of Ecological Ideas*. Cambridge: Cambridge University Press.

7 The theory of labour money

Implications of Marx's critique for the Local Exchange Trading System (LETS)

Makoto Nishibe

Introduction

In this chapter I will examine Marx's critique of the theory of labour money, and present his own vision of communism. Based on the results thus obtained, I will then evaluate the significance of the Local Exchange Trading System (LETS). Proudhon, Owen and Ricardian socialists, in common, claim that labour money should be introduced in order to correct the unfairness of capitalism and to establish their ideal societies. They argue that labour is the true measure of value, which they define as the labour necessary to produce products. This presumes that the labour theory of value holds valid constantly over time, not only in the long run but also in the short run. All of them view the market as static in stationary equilibrium, and regard money merely as the medium of exchange. Marx criticises the theory of labour money because it ignores disequilibrating or dynamic factors intrinsic to the market economy where anarchical commodity production prevails, and where value is only revealed *a posteriori* as a social average of oscillating market prices determined by the relation between demand and supply.

Marx visualises communist society, on the one hand, as an association of free individuals, as Proudhon does, and, on the other hand, as a co-operative society with common ownership of the means of production, as Owen and Ricardian socialists do. I think that it is possible and desirable to synthesise these visions into one: an associative and co-operative market economy consisting of free individuals and freely formed organisations, using some form of 'alternative money'. LETS would be an alternative form of money constituting such an economy, immune to Marx's critique of labour money. It is individually created and multilaterally settled as credits or debit of account. Associative money with zero interest helps non-profit organisations to propagate more easily than in a capitalist economy, and its zero-sum principle prevents the self-expansion of capital. Thus LETS has the immanent potential to transform a capitalist market economy gradually into an associational one.

Marx's critique of the theory of labour money

Marx began his critique of the theory of labour money in *The Poverty of Philosophy*, in which he attacks Pierre-Joseph Proudhon's concept 'constitutive value' or 'synthetic value', the cornerstone of Proudhon's work generally known in English as *The Philosophy of Poverty* (Proudhon 1888). Proudhon explains that value in use (utility) and value in exchange (scarcity) mutually contradict each other if we need a great variety of products and must therefore produce them by means of labour. If liberty for producers and consumers is granted, the price of merchandise will always fluctuate and stagnation will develop; equilibrium in the market will be destroyed. On the other hand, Proudhon sees communism as an attempt ideally to realise equality, but eventually to violate individual liberty. He argues that justice is a necessary condition of fraternity if labour has to be done in an associative society in order for people to live, and that justice will be imperfect without a fair measure of value. He then introduces the concept of 'constitutive value', which registers absolute value conceived in terms of the proportionality of products.

Marx criticises Proudhon for his unaccountable neglect of an important predecessor, Ricardo, who had explained a concept equivalent to Proudhon's 'constituted value', but in more precise terms as the relative labour time needed to produce a product. However, regardless of any outward similarity in their doctrines, when considering their implications, there is a big difference between Proudhon and Ricardo (Marx 1976: 120–44). While Ricardo's theory of value is descriptive in the sense that it explains the laws prevailing in the existing capitalist economy, Proudhon's concept of 'constituted value' presents instead a set of normative criteria for judging the fairness of exchanges in society. Marx concludes that Ricardo is right because the equality of labour is already realised, for example, in an automated workshop where simple labour, reducible from compound labour, has already become the measure of value.

Marx also demonstrates the erroneous character of Proudhon's thesis. The value of what is produced is only shown as a gravitating point through the fluctuation of market prices caused by incessant changes of supply and demand. Later on, in Chapter 10 of *Capital*, volume three (Marx 1998: 171–98), Marx explained more accurately that this relationship should be realised not between value and market prices, but between prices of production and market prices. Proudhon inverts the order of cause and effect, and argues that value itself could assure the balance of supply and demand in the market. As far as the industrial stage of capitalist economy is concerned, the law of proportion (or equilibrium in the market) cannot be continuously maintained, but rather disproportion prevails in most cases, because of the anarchic character of production in a capitalist economy. There is also another reason why the proportional relation is not stable. Value tends to decrease as labour productivity increases in some cases.

The continual diminution of value caused by inventions brings about the realisation of minimum labour time as value through competition among capitalists, and the formation of monopoly or dominance of particular products with the lowest price owing to new inventions. The reduction of value is countervailing to a tendency towards proportional relations.

Furthermore, Proudhon's application of the concept 'constituted value' to an ideal society was neither new, nor unique. Marx knew that many Ricardian socialists in England, such as Hodgskin, Thompson, Edmonds and Bray, had already re-interpreted Ricardo's economic theory as 'the right to the whole produce of labour' and by the 1830s had applied it theoretically and practically to an egalitarian co-operative society in the form of 'labour money' or a 'labour-chip'. Anton Menger later characterised the basic claim against capitalism made by Ricardian socialists as the legal expression of a property right to the products of labour held by their producers. In fact, there is some divergence of opinion, and their claim is not necessarily on the level of the 'legal' but rather that of the 'social', in the sense that many of them seek to realise this claim by changing society, rather than law. However, as this expression is convenient for indicating the common feature of their claim, we will continue to use it in this chapter. Marx recognised that Proudhon's idea was only a modified repetition of the one developed by Ricardian socialists, in particular, Bray.

Marx, in *Capital*, volume one, attacks Proudhon for seeing the juridical relations of the commodity economy as expressing an ideal, '*justice éternelle* (eternal justice)', and, in order to realise it fully, for seeking to reform the production of commodities (Marx 1996: 68, 84). Although this criticism is true, we should not regard Proudhon's anarchism as mere petit bourgeois ideology and simply reject it, but should rather appreciate the positive sides of his thought: the primacy of freedom and individual independence. His problem is not that he seeks to realise liberty and justice in exchange, but that he assumes that he can realise justice with labour money. He surely denied such collective authority as the state or parliament, and insisted instead that such institutions should be replaced by associations of independent producers. However, his blueprint for 'The Exchange Bank' presented subsequently is incompatible with this anarchism or 'mutualism'.

In 1849, Proudhon applied his principle of *crédit gratuit* (free credit), according to which individuals or banks should provide credit with extremely low, or no, interest. He proposed to establish The Exchange Bank as an institution for circulation and credit in order to correct inequalities in exchange. According to his plan, workers would become members, without holding shares, of a commercial union called The National Exchange Bank, so that they could mutually exchange their products, both as producers and consumers, at equitable prices calculated on the basis of labour time and cost of production. The National Exchange Bank was supposed to determine the prices of products, to be in charge of buying and selling the products of its members, and to issue four kinds of vouchers used in the trade of products. However, Proudhon's proposal was defeated in the assembly, and was not put into practice. In the end, it had not been tested by its success or failure, but the basic idea was the same as Owen's Labour Exchanges.

Proudhon had argued that, while all products in a modern society are the fruits of 'collective force' born of workers' co-operation and the division of labour, capitalists then deprive workers of this force and appropriate the products gratis. This is theft, which is by definition unjust. Proudhon attacked private ownership of property from this perspective. At the same time, he regards private property as ultimately ensuring individual liberty against the authoritative or coercive power of the state. In this respect it sounds as if his claim is self-contradicting, but this is not so. Rather, he recognised both sides, good and bad, of property. On the other hand, he criticised the National Workshops proposed by communists such as Louis Blanc, insisting that they would ultimately form state monopolies, and so threaten individual liberty. His anarchism directed against capitalism or state authoritarianism was not itself problematic, but there was rather a fundamental flaw in his theorising that equitable exchange could be immediately achieved by applying the concept of 'constitutive value', assuming that money is just a 'representative symbol of labour', and that the abolition of the 'sovereignty' of money would be sufficient in itself to produce an ideal society.

There is another essential problem. Despite Proudhon's denial of collective authority, The Exchange Bank as an equitable price fixer would really turn out to be a planner and practitioner of production. As a regulator it would need to command people to exchange their products according to the labour time necessary to produce them. Marx criticises John Gray's ideas on labour money for problems with a national central bank, and thereafter he attacks Proudhon as follows:

> *John Gray* was the first to set forth the theory that labour-time is the direct measure of money in a systematic way. He proposes that a national central bank should ascertain through its branches the labour-time expended in the production of various commodities. In exchange for the commodity, the producer would receive an official certificate of its value, i.e., a receipt for as much labour-time as his commodity contains, and this bank-note of one labour week, one labour day, one labour hour, etc., would serve at the same time as an order to the bank to hand over an equivalent in any of the other commodities stored in its warehouses ... Although Gray merely wants 'to reform' the money evolved by commodity exchange, he is compelled by the intrinsic logic of the subject-matter to repudiate one condition of bourgeois production after another. Thus he turns capital into national capital, and land into national property and if his bank is

examined carefully it will be seen that it not only receives commodities with one hand and issues certificates for labour supplied
with the other, but that it directs production itself ... But it was left to
M. *Proudhon* and his school to declare seriously that the degradation
of *money* and the exaltation of *commodities* was the essence of socialism and thereby to reduce socialism to an elementary misunderstanding of the inevitable correlation existing between commodities and
money.

(Marx 1987: 320–3)

This would consequently lead to collective economic planning, which
would deny market freedom and repress individual liberty. Hence, Proudhon's proposal would necessarily fall into self-contradiction. It is worth
noting that Proudhon regarded money as an indispensable medium for the
exchange of products, but we should not ourselves necessarily endorse his
centralised institutional structure, because it inevitably requires authoritative power.

Marx thus clarified the problems in Proudhon's conception of value and
money, as well as in his plan for labour money, arising out of his misunderstanding of political economy. Nonetheless, Marx never denied the ideal
of an association of free individuals expressed in Proudhon's anarchical
political philosophy. His evaluation of Proudhon varies, depending on the
field of study that he was engaged in.

Robert Owen and the Ricardian socialists

After considering Proudhon's idea of labour money, we now turn to Ricardian socialists. Above all, we cannot ignore the experiment of labour notes
in which Robert Owen and many Ricardian socialists, such as John Gray,
William Thompson and John Francis Bray, also participated. At present,
this is also regarded as the origin of modern local currencies. After the
failure of a co-operative village in New Harmony, in the United States,
Owen returned to England and played a leading part in the process
through which the workers' co-operative societies of the National Equitable Labour Exchange were established in London in September 1832.
Thereafter, similar systems were set up in Sheffield, Leeds and many other
towns in England. 'Labour notes' were to be issued by the Exchanges and
imprinted with the labour time expended on products. Workers
would receive them in exchange for their products, whereby they could
purchase other products of the same value. A labour note of 6*d* was
regarded as equivalent to one hour of labour, and a fee of 8.33 per cent
was charged on each transaction in order to cover operational costs. The
experiment sought to promote equitable exchanges of products based on
Ricardo's labor theory of value. Owen and others believed that if these
Labour Exchanges diffused throughout the nation, and if this occurred in

conjunction with the development of co-operative movements, a peaceful transformation of capitalism into communism would take place.

More than ten years before, Owen had insisted in his *Report to the County of Lanark of a Plan for relieving Public Distress* that a natural measure of value should be labour, not gold or silver, nor the notes of the Bank of England, and, that if labour money were introduced in co-operative villages, the demand for labour would be stabilised, which would then reduce unemployment and poverty, and workers would receive an 'equitable reward' for their labour. In this respect, Bray is theoretically clearer than Owen. He writes:

> From the very nature of labour and exchange, strict justice not only requires that all exchangers should be *mutually*, but that they should likewise be *equally*, benefited. Men have only two things which they can exchange with each other, namely, labour, and the produce of labour.
>
> (Bray 1839: 48)

Similarly, Ricardian socialists such as Hodgskin, Thompson, Bray and Gray, in line with the theory of value in Ricardo's *Principles of Political Economy and Taxation*, insisted that the whole produce of labour should be given to producers, because labourers create all the value of anything that is produced. This movement aimed at realising such an ideal, but it terminated in only two years because of intrinsic problems. One problem concerned the computation of the value of products by measuring average labour time. It required a proper appraisal of values in heterogeneous labour in various jobs and industries as well as in complex forms of labour related to skills and proficiency, but it was not successfully done, which caused inequality among producers. As a result, the Labour Exchange could not adjust the supply of, and the demand for, necessary goods. The other problem is that speculation spread, which made its operation difficult to sustain. The experiment in labour notes clearly demonstrated the fundamental defects in the direct use of labour time as the standard of value for equitable exchange.

It is true that Marx's theory of surplus value owed much theoretically to them, yet he repeated his criticisms against 'the right to the whole produce of labour', and to labour money as its application, in his successive critical studies on political economy: *Grundrisse, Contribution to Critique of Political Economy, Manuscripts of Capital* and *Capital* as published. Marx, for instance, rebutted the argument concerning bank reform proposed by Alfred Darimon, a Proudhonist, which was also advocated by Ricardian socialists:

> The replacement of metal money (and of paper or fiat money denominated in metal money) by labour money denominated in labour time

would therefore equate the *real value* (exchange value) of commodities with their *nominal value, price, money value*. Equation of *real value and nominal value, of value and price*. But such is by no means the case. The value of commodities as determined by labour time is only their *average value* ... Market value equates itself with real value by means of its constant oscillations, never by means of an equation with real value as if the latter were a third party, but rather by means of constant non-equation of itself (as Hegel would say, not by way of abstract identity, but by constant negation of the negation, i.e. of itself as negation of real value) ... The time-chit, representing *average labour time*, would never correspond to or be convertible into *actual labour time*; i.e. the amount of labour time objectified in a commodity would never command a quantity of labour time equal to itself, and vice versa, but would command, rather, either more or less, just as at present every oscillation of market values expresses itself in a rise or fall of the gold or silver prices of commodities ... The difference between price and value, between the commodity measured by the labour time whose product it is, and the product of the labour time against which it is exchanged, this difference calls for a third commodity to act as a measure in which the real exchange value of commodities is expressed. *Because price is not equal to value, therefore the value-determining element – labour time – cannot be the element in which prices are expressed, because labour time would then have to express itself simultaneously as the determining and the non-determining element, as the equivalent and non-equivalent of itself.* Because labour time as the measure of value exists only as an ideal, it cannot serve as the matter of price-comparisons.

(Marx 1986: 74–7)

In Marx's writings before *Capital* there are still confusing usages of concepts like value and price, but the point in Marx's argument is clear. Ricardian socialists believe that the labour embodied in products is in itself equal to social labour, or, to put it in Marx's terminology, 'nominal value, price, or money value' is always equal to 'real value' (exchange value) of commodities. However, this is not sustainable, because real value is only shown as an average of fluctuating nominal values or prices deriving from each transaction to buy and sell using money in the market. In short, 'labour time as the measure of value exists only as an ideal' of the ceaselessly moving real. Ricardian socialists had overlooked the necessity of money as a detour for ensuring social acceptance, and had postulated that ideal, social labour should become directly real, that is, money.

During his preparation for *Capital* Marx came to recognise that this is true not only for Ricardian socialists, but also for Ricardo himself, and that the fundamental defect in conventional political economy lay in the absence of an analysis of money as a general form of value, or an analysis of the inevitable asymmetry between commodities and money in a market economy. He did this in 'the theory of the form of value' in *Capital*. It is noteworthy that the critique of labour money gave rise to dichotomous concepts in Marx's *Capital*, in distinction from Ricardo's *Principles*, such as substance of value and form of value, value and price of production, and the price of production and market price. This needs to be pursued further in relation to the genesis of Marx's economic theory. If labour money were to express socially necessary labour time directly, it would be more than 'money', defined as direct exchangeability with commodities, because it would require not only an equilibrium of demand and supply but also a universal homogeneity and intensity of labour. However, this is not the function of money, but of competition, which would presumably establish such conditions in a capitalist market economy. That is why Marx rejected the idea of labour money as a flawed and unreal fantasy.

Marx's two visions of communism

Labour money is defective as an economic theory, but it was truly one of the major efforts in trying to develop a new co-operative society. In this respect, Marx evaluated Owen higher than Proudhon, even if they both advocated an almost identical plan for labour money. While the former tried to introduce it into co-operatives or co-operative societies in order to change the 'competitive' character of the market economy, the latter only did so in his contemporary market economy. Owen was more conscious of its partial and limited qualities. He knew that if labour money were the sole endeavour, and if it were not connected with the co-operative movement, it could not be successful. The difference between Owen and Proudhon is significant for our reconsideration of Marx's own view of communism. Although he barely described a future ideal society at all, we will find that there are two different visions of communism if we look through his writings.

The first vision depicts communist society as an association or community of free individuals, similar to Proudhonian anarchism. Marx defines it as: 'an association in which the free development of each is the condition for the free development of all' (Marx 1976: 506); 'a community of free individuals, carrying on their work with the means of production in common, in which the labour-power of all the different individuals is consciously applied as the combined labour-power of the community' (Marx 1996: 89); and 'a higher form of society, a society in which the full and free development of every individual forms the ruling principle' (Marx 1996: 588). The second quotation does not necessarily mean economic planning together with the national ownership of the means of production. Rather we should understand it as explaining the co-operative aspect of communism. By contrast, Proudhon writes: 'Free association, liberty – whose sole function is to maintain equality in the means of production and equivalence in exchanges – is the only possible, the only just, and the only true form of society' (Proudhon 1898: 272).

The term 'free' has two meanings here. One is that individuals are 'free' to form associations of their own free will based on spontaneous agreements, and the other meaning is that they are 'free' to develop their peculiar abilities to the full extent and in various directions without any social hindrance. The second vision defines communism in terms of a co-operative society composed of production–consumption co-operatives whose means of production are owned in common by the members. This vision has much in common with Owenite communism and Ricardian socialism. While the first vision focuses on 'freedom' and 'association', the second focuses on 'co-operation' and 'common ownership'.

In volume three of *Capital*, Marx explains that once credit has developed, it not only progresses all the way to bank credit, but also helps to create two different organisations for production – stock companies and co-operative factories. Marx writes:

> In stock companies the function is divorced from capital ownership, hence also labour is entirely divorced from ownership of means of production and surplus-labour. This result of the ultimate development of capitalist production is a necessary transitional phase towards the re-conversion of capital into the property of producers, although no longer as the private property of the individual producers, but rather as the property of associated producers, as outright social property.
>
> (Marx 1998: 434)

> The co-operative factories of the labourers themselves represent within the old form the first sprouts of the new, although they naturally reproduce, and must reproduce, everywhere in their actual organisation all the shortcomings of the prevailing system. But the antithesis between capital and labour is overcome within them, if at first only by way of making the associated labourers into their own capitalist, *i.e.*, by enabling them to use the means of production for the employment of their own labour ... The capitalist stock companies, as much as the co-operative factories, should be considered as transitional forms from the capitalist mode of production to the associated one, with the only distinction that the antagonism is resolved negatively in the one and positively in the other.
>
> (Marx 1998: 438)

Marx contends that these are two different 'transitional forms' in the movement from the capitalist mode of production to 'the associated mode of production'. For him, stock companies and co-operative factories are, respectively, negative and positive sublations (*Aufheben*) of a contradiction in the capitalist mode of production. Stock companies can transform private ownership of the means of production by individual capitalists into common ownership by many shareholders, and thus make a separation between ownership and administration of firms, which will change capitalist economy from within. But stock companies bring about 'private production without the control of private property', and so cause side effects such as monopolies, state interventions and financial aristocracy. This limitation of stock companies is a 'negative' factor for Marx, as they abolish capital as private property only 'within the framework of capitalist production itself'. Contrarily, Marx evaluates co-operative factories 'positively' because they 'present within the old form the first sprouts of the new', even though they reproduce 'all the shortcomings of the prevailing system'. He appreciates this potentiality in the sense that it shows that large-scale production can be conducted by 'co-operative labour' without the existence of managers and capitalists. Nevertheless, he was cautious not to overrate the experiment of the co-operative movement. For example, Marx writes:

> But there was in store a still greater victory of the political economy of labour over the political economy of property. We speak of the co-operative movement, especially the co-operative factories raised by the unassisted efforts of a few bold 'hands'. The value of these great social experiments cannot be overrated ... At the same time the experience of the period from 1848 to 1864 has proved beyond doubt that, however excellent in principle and however useful in practice, co-operative labour, if kept within the narrow circle of the casual efforts of private workmen, will never be able to arrest the growth in geometrical progression of monopoly, to free the masses, nor even to perceptibly lighten the burden of their miseries.
>
> (Marx 1985a: 11–12)

This is because he knew that if co-operative factories were scattered, they would never have the power to transform the capitalist economy, and that if they must compete with monopolised big companies, they would fail or degenerate into ordinary companies. Therefore, the co-operative movement needs, as external circumstances for their development, a type of market different from the present one, which, I believe, LETS can create. In order to examine Marx's evaluation of co-operative societies further, we need to consider his *Instructions for the Delegates of the Provisional General Council*. Marx writes:

> (a) We acknowledge the co-operative movement as one of the transforming forces of the present society based upon class antagonism. Its great merit is to practically show, that the present pauperising, and despotic system of the *subordination of labour* to capital can be super-

seded by the republican and beneficent system of *the association of free and equal producers*. (b) Restricted, however, to the dwarfish forms into which individual wages slaves can elaborate it by their private efforts, the co-operative system will never transform capitalist society. To convert social production into one large and harmonious system of free and co-operative labour, *general social changes* are wanted, *changes of the general conditions of society*, never to be realised save by the transfer of the organised forces of society, viz., the state power, from capitalists and landlords to the producers themselves. (c) We recommend to the working men to embark in *co-operative production* rather than in *co-operative stores*. The latter touch but the surface of the present economical system, the former attacks its groundwork.

(Marx 1985b: 190)

Marx explains in the section 'co-operative labour' that the co-operative movement is significant in so far as it is 'one of the transforming forces of the present society based upon class antagonism', since 'the republican and beneficent system of the association of free and equal producers' can supersede the subordination of labour to capital. His recommendation to the workers is 'to embark in co-operative production rather than in co-operative stores', because the former has the potential to change the groundwork of the capitalist system, transforming it into 'one large and harmonious system of free and co-operative labour', starting from the sphere of production. This corresponds to his second vision of communism. Although we admit that changes in the general conditions of society must occur, the added condition that 'the organised forces of society, namely, the state power' could only fulfil the transformation is not agreeable. Marx's claims concerning the primacy of producers' co-operatives and his concomitant requirement for a continuing state are deduced from his doctrine of historical materialism. But, as will be seen later, we should abandon these basic assumptions: one-way causality from the powers of production to the relations of production, as well as the primacy of production over circulation.

It is true that Marx sees that labour money is only valid in the first phase of communism, i.e. 'co-operative society based on common ownership of the means of production', where associated labour is conducted. Marx writes:

Owen's 'labour-money', for instance, is no more 'money' than a ticket for the theatre. Owen pre-supposes directly associated labour, a form of production that is entirely inconsistent with the production of commodities. The certificate of labour is merely evidence of the part taken by the individual in the common labour, and of his right to a certain portion of the common produce destined for consumption.

(Marx 1996: 104)

> Within the co-operative society based on common ownership of the
> means of production, the producers do not exchange their products;
> just as little does the labor employed on the products appear here as
> the *value* of these products, as a material quality possessed by them,
> since now, in contrast to capitalist society, individual labour no longer
> exists in an indirect fashion but directly as a component part of total
> labour ... What we have to deal with here is a communist society, not
> as it has *developed* on its own foundations, but, on the contrary, just as
> it *emerges* from capitalist society ... Accordingly, the individual pro-
> ducer receives back from society – after the deductions have been
> made – exactly what he gives to it. What he has given to it is his indi-
> vidual quantum of labour ... The same amount of labour which he has
> given to society in one form, he receives back in another.
>
> (Marx 1989: 85–6)

In such a condition, individual labour is directly regarded as social labour,
'as a component part of total labor'. Owen's labour notes are used for 'the
certificate of labour' which 'is merely evidence of the part taken by the
individual in the common labour, and of his right to a certain portion of
the common produce destined for consumption'. As it is not money but
'the certificate of labour' – like 'a ticket for the theatre' – 'the producers
do not exchange their products'. Rather they redistribute their products
using these labour certificates after socially necessary deductions are
made. In short, a co-operative society is not a market economy, because it
has no market where value is determined as an average of continuously
fluctuating market prices. However, it is uncertain that Marx believed that
there would be no need for money in a co-operative society, and whether
there would also be no market between co-operative societies. We could
at least say that co-operative society is not the same as the planned economic society in terms of state power, because Marx also criticised the
Lassallean idea of a producers' co-operative society with state aid in his
Critique of the Gotha Programme.

As already stated, despite his repetitive warning that the reality of the
market should not be dismissed easily, Marx was clearly inclined to the
second vision of communism. But, I think it fruitful not to take either of
these positions, but to synthesise them into one that emphasises both
freedom and co-operation. Communist society must be non-capitalistic,
but I do not believe that it would be either a traditional society based on
reciprocity in tribal communities with common ownership, or a construc-
tivist society based on central planning with national ownership, but rather
one that would instead maintain the existence of money and the market. If
so, the synthesised vision could be depicted not as a 'co-operative society'
(using 'certificates of labour') but as an 'associative market economy', in
which, using 'alternative money', individuals could freely trade products
on the basis of mutual trust and contracts, and in which individuals could

freely engage in various forms of organisation with common ownership: stock companies, producers' and consumers' co-operatives, or non-profit organisations.

However, this cannot be accomplished by means of labour money resting on labour as a value standard. It is not money that creates markets, but rather the certificate of labour. These certificates cannot take account of the difference between skilled labour (complex labour) and unskilled labour (simple labour), nor can they take into account the different qualities of output attained by individuals. If we simply ignore such differences and, in principle, regard all kinds of labour as equal, such egalitarianism would reduce the spontaneity and incentives of individuals, and indeed restrain individuals' freedom to develop their different abilities and needs. On the other hand, if we pursue a certain system of evaluation of various kinds of labour, it would inevitably require an authoritative power to determine the terms and conditions, and to put it into practice, which would then threaten individual freedom. In any event, we conclude by abandoning Marx's first vision of communism. To escape from this knotty problem, we need 'alternative money' that has the ability not only to create a market, but also to encourage co-operation more than competition.

When Marx, in *The Poverty of Philosophy*, criticises Bray's egalitarian idea of the individual exchange of equal labour, he bases his argument on the relation of the form of exchange of products to the form of production. Marx writes:

> In general, the form of exchange of products corresponds to the form of production. Change the latter, and the former will change in consequence. Thus in the history of society we see that the mode of exchanging products is regulated by the mode of producing them. Individual exchange corresponds also to a definite mode of production which itself corresponds to class antagonism. There is thus no individual exchange without the antagonism of classes.
>
> (Marx 1976: 143–4)

Here Marx postulates that 'the mode of exchanging products is regulated by the mode of producing them'. This might be regarded as a variation in the formula of historical materialism. But we cannot take it for granted, because, observing the upswing of electrical, informational and financial technologies like internet banking and electronic money in the present day, we need to recognise that these modern technologies are related to the production process as well as to the circulation or exchange of products. It thus follows not only that the mode of producing products determines the mode of exchanging them, but also that the latter determines the former. The relationship concerned involves, not one-way, but two-way causations; it is a relation of dual determination. By reconsidering this, we could see a possibility that an institutional change in the mode of exchange of products by means of some type of 'alternative money' could result in a change in the mode of producing them.

The potential of LETS as associational money

What medium of exchange should be used in order to actualise an association of free and equal individuals? I believe that LETS is the most likely form and has the most potential. LETS is a kind of local currency which has spread since the 1980s and has reportedly reached more than 3,000 venues over the world. It was initiated in Canada in 1983, but its core idea is much older. LETS has properties similar to those found both in 'money' and 'credit'. It is 'money' in the sense that it can function, like conventional national currencies, as a means of circulation to mediate exchange, as a measure of value to provide the standard for exchange, as a means of payment to settle deferred payment, and as a means of hoarding to store value. It is also 'credit' in the sense that it is a multilateral settlement system through balancing accounts. But, on the other hand, it is not conventional money or credit, because it bears no interest and prevents resources from draining out of communities as well as credit creation by the banking system, hence it would not turn into 'money in *perpetuum mobile*', i.e. capital. Hence LETS fulfils economic purposes such as stimulation of depressed local economies, elimination of unemployment, establishment of cyclic economy and prevention of capital accumulation. However, LETS is not just an economic medium; it is also a social, ethical and even cultural medium, whose purposes are to rebuild cooperative and mutual-aid human relationships, based on the idea of reciprocal exchange (Nishibe 2001a), to bring about trust in regions and communities, to share values and interests, and to encourage communication. Thus, in LETS, the economic, the social, the ethical and the cultural are closely interrelated, which itself embodies the principle of a new economic society. LETS is a synthetic medium of 'intercourse' (*Verkehr*), expanding the meaning of freedom and rebuilding a domain for cooperation (Nishibe 2001b).

LETS is not intended to re-embed the alienated capitalist market economy in society and to restore economically reciprocal relationships, but is rather an 'alternative money', which creates an associative market by forming society in terms of economic exchange. LETS is based on Marx's critique of labour money and is designed to overcome the shortcomings he specified. Accordingly, its standard of value is not defined in terms of labour time, but is rather a unit of account linked with a national currency, depending on location. If, for example, a certain LETS is formed in Canada and its unit is called the 'green dollar', one green dollar is assumed to be equivalent to one Canadian dollar. Its purpose is not to fulfil egalitarianism in terms of labour as labour money was intended to do, but rather to coexist initially with national currencies and to function as a 'supplementary' to them, and so gradually as 'alternative money' to create associative markets.

In LETS, participants:

1 start with zero accounts;
2 publicise their intentions to offer and to buy products and services with specific terms of price and quantities;
3 make contracts and transactions on a peer-to-peer basis.

It adopts an accounting system that credits 'black' to a seller and debits 'red' to a buyer on each transaction, so that the sum of all participants' accounts constantly equal zero. Because of this 'associative counterbalance (zero–sum) principle', money exists only in the accounts with credit as 'black' on the micro-level, but does not exist in the association as a whole, on the macro-level. Hence LETS is regarded as 'associative credit system', since participants mutually provide 'credit' through the association that they belong to. Accordingly, participants can purchase products and services whenever they want, even without prior possession of 'credit', because, if necessary, they can freely create 'debit' their accounts with no interest. They only have to promise to return their 'debit' back to the association by making 'credit' on future sales of products and services. It is noteworthy that they do not necessarily have to return gifts to the person who originally offered them, but to a third party. This means not only that reciprocity is unnecessary, but also that reciprocal exchange is only an ideal that each participant should refer to, because such a situation is realised only when every account equals zero, but is unattainable in reality. The 'credit money' that is individually and spontaneously created in LETS circulates within the association and gradually vanishes through multilateral cancellation among participants. Owing to such properties, LETS can be 'money' or 'credit', but, at the same time, does not transform itself into capital. It is true that competition among participants, though not always in terms of profit, still exists, but its inherent properties enhance co-operative ethics and mutual trust all the more. In his *Critique of the Gotha Programme*, Marx mentioned:

a higher phase of communist society ... after labour has become not only a means of life but life's prime want; after the productive forces have also increased with the all-around development of the individual, and all the springs of co-operative wealth flow more abundantly.

(Marx 1989: 87)

Conclusion

This 'higher phase' of society is conceivable as an association of both free individuals and spontaneously formed associations without any control by the state, where labour power as a commodity and the state as an authority structure are both abolished. The slogan 'from each according to his ability, to each according to his needs!' can be realised by using LETS, albeit partially. Although many instances of LETS have so far been formed by small groups of people in villages or towns, we should not presume that it can work only in a small community whose inner human relationships are transparent and face-to-face. LETS is able to transform the meaning of sociability and the intermediacy of the 'cash nexus' in capitalist market economies and to create a new view of money and the market. It has the potential to make a capitalist market economy evolve into an associative one.

References

Bray, J.F. (1839) *Labour's Wrongs and Labour's Remedy*. Leeds: David Green.
Gray, J. (1831) *The Social System. A Treatise on the Principle of Exchange*. Edinburgh: William Tait.
Hodgskin, T. (1825) *Labour Defended against the Claims of Capital*. London: Knight & Lacey.
Marx, K. (1976 [1847]) *The Poverty of Philosophy*, in K. Marx and F. Engels, *Collected Works* 6. Moscow: Progress, 105–212.
Marx, K. (1985a [1864]) *Inaugural Address of the Working Men's International Association*, in K. Marx and F. Engels, *Collected Works* 20. Moscow: Progress, 5–13.
Marx, K. (1985b [1866]) *Instructions for the Delegates of the Provisional General Council. The Different Questions*, in K. Marx and F. Engels, *Collected Works* 20. Moscow: Progress, 185–94.
Marx, K. (1986 [1857–58]) *Economic Manuscripts of 1857–1858 (Grundrisse)*, in K. Marx and F. Engels, *Collected Works* 28. Moscow: Progress, 5–590.
Marx, K. (1987 [1859]) *A Contribution to the Critique of Political Economy*, in K. Marx and F. Engels, *Collected Works* 29. Moscow: Progress, 257–417.
Marx, K. (1989 [1875]) *Critique of the Gotha Programme*, in K. Marx and F. Engels, *Collected Works* 24. Moscow: Progress, 75–99.
Marx, K. (1996 [1867]) *Capital*, vol. 1, in K. Marx and F. Engels, *Collected Works* 35. Moscow: Progress, 7–852.
Marx, K. (1998 [1894]) *Capital*, vol. 3, in K. Marx and F. Engels, *Collected Works* 37. Moscow: Progress, 5–982.
Marx, K. and Engels, F. (1976 [1848]) *Manifesto of the Communist Party*, in K. Marx and F. Engels, *Collected Works* 6. Moscow: Progress, 477–519.
Menger, A. (1886) *Das Recht auf den vollen Arbeitsertrag in geschichtlicher Darstellung*. Stuttgart: J.G. Cotta.
Nishibe, M. (2001a) 'Ethics in exchange and reciprocity', in Y. Shionoya and K. Yagi (eds), *Exchange and Reciprocity, in Trust, Cooperation and Competition*. Berlin and Tokyo: Springer-Verlag, 77–95.

Nishibe, M. (2001b) 'LETS ron' (originally in Japanese), in *Hihyo Kukan [Critical Space]* III–1, 27–52. 'On LETS' (translated from the original; unprinted) http://www.econ.hokudai.ac.jp/~nishibe/works01/On_LETS.pdf.

Owen, R. (1813) *A New View of Society, Essays in the Formation of Human Character*. London: Cadell & Davies.

Owen, R. (1821) *Report to the County of Lanark of a Plan for relieving Public Distress*. Glasgow: Wardlaw & Cunninghame.

Proudhon, P.J. (1888 [1846]) *System of Economical Contradictions: or, the Philosophy of Misery*. Boston: Benj. R. Tucker.

Proudhon, P.J. (1898 [1840]) *What is Property? An Inquiry into the Principle of Right and of Government*. London: William Reeves.

Ricardo, D. (1819) *On the Principles of Political Economy, and Taxation*, 2nd edn. London: John Murray.

Thompson, W. (1824) *An Inquiry into the Principles of the Distribution of Wealth most conducive to Human Happiness*. London: Longman.

Thompson, W. (1827) *Labour Rewarded: The Claims of Labour and Capital Conciliated*. London: Longman.

Part III

The reception of Marx into modern Japan

8 The Japanese concept of civil society and Marx's *bürgerliche Gesellschaft*

Hiroshi Mizuta

Introduction

In the English translation of the works of Marx and Engels, the term 'civil society' is sometimes used as a translation of *bürgerliche Gesellschaft*. This is an apparent distinction from 'bourgeois society' as another translation of the same German term. However, 'civil' or 'civilised society' also occurs in the works of the Scottish Enlightenment, including Adam Smith and Adam Ferguson. In the history of Japanese Marxism and communist thought since 1922 (when the Communist Party of Japan was established illegally), and especially after 1932 when the Communist International issued the *Theses on the Situation in Japan and The Task of the Communist Party*, there have been a few Marxists and their followers who have tried implicitly or explicitly to identify *two* civil societies.

This tendency was strengthened by the Adam Smith scholarship of the 1930s, which was a refuge for Marxist scholars under the Fascist regime in Japan. The aim of the present chapter is to explain how this seemingly peculiar identification of the Marxian term 'civil society' with the Smithian one was possible at all, and what it came to mean in the historical context of Japan and what it means for Marx scholarship in general. As I will first discuss, the problem in translating *bürgerliche Gesellschaft* is by no means unknown to Anglophone Marxists.

To avoid possible confusion in terminology, I would like to make it clear, first, that I am not going to discuss the fashionable usage of the term which seems to have originated with Gramsci. Although I am not neglecting the importance of the Gramscian usage and the discussions originating from it, I think Gramsci's concept of *società civile* was bred in the tradition of Roman civil law and is not directly connected with the subject matter of the present chapter. Needless to say, this does not mean that either Smith or Marx was a stranger to the broad tradition of Roman jurisprudence.

What I would also like to make clear is that the term 'civil society' is used in this chapter as a translation of the Japanese term *shiminshakai*, which means literally 'society of citizens', and also as a translation of the German *bürgerliche Gesellschaft*.

Bürgerlich Gesellschaft – meaning and translation

Roy Pascal, the first English translator of *The German Ideology* (*Die Deutsche Ideologie*), translated *bürgerliche Gesellschaft* as 'civil society', and annotated this as follows:

> *Bürgerliche Gesellschaft*. This term is often wrongly translated as 'bourgeois society'. On the one hand it has the meaning of 'civilized society', i.e. society with government, laws, etc., as opposed to 'natural' or primitive society; and also serves to denote the personal and economic relations of men as opposed to political relations and forms. In particular it arose and was used in the seventeenth and eighteenth centuries amongst bourgeois theoreticians as a theoretical attack on political forms which prevented the free accumulation of private property ... The present context indicates the faultiness of rendering 'bourgeois society'.
>
> (Marx and Engels 1947: 203)

This note is especially relevant to the present subject matter because it is based on Pascal's study of the Scottish Enlightenment, which was then called the Scottish Historical School. Pascal was professor of German at the University of Birmingham when he contributed an article 'Property and society – the Scottish Historical School of the eighteenth century' to the first volume of *Modern Quarterly* in 1938. As a communist confronted with the menace of Nazism on the eve of World War II, Pascal tried to criticise the reactionary character of the German Historical School of the time, including Friedrich Meinicke, in contrast with the positive and progressive character of the Scottish Historical School of the 18th century, including Adam Smith, Adam Ferguson and William Robertson. Although adding a reservation concerning 'the present context', Pascal rejected 'bourgeois society' as a correct translation of *bürgerliche Gesellschaft* and put 'civil' or 'civilised' society in its stead. No doubt he had in mind Adam Smith's civilised society, identical with commercial society, in which 'every man ... becomes in some measure a merchant' (Smith 1976b: 37).

Pascal's reservation shows that he admitted some possibility of using 'bourgeois society' with a negative sense. An editor's note in the *Collected Works* of Marx and Engels reads:

> The term *bürgerliche Gesellschaft* was used in two distinct ways by Marx and Engels: 1) to denote the economic system of society irrespective of the historical stage of development, the sum total of material relations which determine the political institutions and ideological forms, and 2) to denote the material relations of bourgeois society (or that society as a whole), of capitalism. The term has therefore been

translated according to its concrete content and the given context either as 'civil society' (in the first case) or as 'bourgeois society' (in the second).

(Marx and Engels 1976: 593)

The note correctly explains the dual meaning of *bürgerliche Gesellschaft* but completely misconstrues the content of the first one. Nobody can understand Marx and Engels by making their concept of society historically neutral, particularly after Engels declared that he did not know any science other than history.

When Pascal wrote in his note that it was wrong to translate *bürgerliche Gesellschaft* as 'bourgeois society', he meant to say that at least in this particular case Marx and Engels used the term affirmatively or positively, as was also the case in the terminology of the Scottish Enlightenment. He was quite right to point out that Marx and Engels sometimes used the term more affirmatively or positively than did other writers. However, while there was no room for a negative meaning in the usage of the Scottish Enlightenment, the terminology of Marx and Engels was not so simple. For them, *bürgerliche Gesellschaft* was a necessary stage in the history of mankind immediately before socialist society. In spite of the exploitation of the working classes and the alienation of all human beings, the development of culture and productive forces under a capitalist regime is a prerequisite to socialism.

When Marx and Engels wrote in *The German Ideology* about civil society in its various stages as the basis of all history, readers may have been led to think that the passage justifies the note by the English translator mentioned above, in which he commented that Marx and Engels used the term irrespective of historical context. However, a few pages later we read 'civil society as such only develops with the bourgeoisie'. According to Ferguson, who wrote *An Essay on the History of Civil Society* (1767), any society with government and private property may properly be called a civil society, but in the natural course of things it is bound to become a civilised or *commercial society*, as in Adam Smith's conception. The English translator wrongly took the concept to be the result of historical necessity or of the natural course of things, irrespective of history.

In the so-called *Economic Manuscripts of 1857–58*, which have hitherto been known as the precursor to *A Contribution to the Critique of Political Economy* (1859), Marx sketched the natural course of things as follows:

The further back we go in history, the more does the individual, and accordingly also the producing individual, appear to be depending and belonging to a larger whole. At first, he is still in a quite natural manner part of the family, and of the family expanding into the tribe; later he is part of a community, of one of the different forms of community which arise from the conflict and the merging of tribes. It is not until the 18th century, in 'bourgeois society', that the various forms of social nexus confront the individual as merely a means towards his private ends, as external necessity. But the epoch which produces this standpoint, that of the isolated individual, is precisely the epoch of the hitherto most highly developed social (according to this standpoint, general) relations.

(Marx and Engels 1986: 18)

Although the translator used 'bourgeois society', it is clear that Marx used the term *bürgerliche Gesellschaft* affirmatively in a full sense. Thus there is no need to make a distinction between 'civil society' and *bourgeois society* in the translation.

In his system of political economy, including the magnum opus *Das Kapital* (1867), Marx tried hard to show, through a critical and objective analysis of capitalist society, that it was the highest stage of the historical development of human society, and that it produced huge productive forces and an organisation of labour beyond its own control, before being replaced by a socialist society. Marx thought that capitalism was an inevitable historical stage which was to develop into socialism, so in his letter to Vera Zasulich (1881), in which he admitted that his theory of capitalist development was valid only for Western Europe, he was hesitant to apply his theory to Russia, where capitalism had not yet ripened. This means that he thought that a socialist society would come only after a capitalist society (Marx and Engels 1992: 71–2).

Marx and Engels had inherited from Hegel the idea of necessary historical stages in the history of mankind. Although Hegel had studied the political economy of Sir James Steuart, and perhaps that of Adam Smith, the idealist character of his philosophy did not allow him to put full stress on the materialist base of human life. In his philosophy of law, the system of need is entirely absorbed into the state, while Marx and Engels thought, thanks to their historical materialism, that the productive forces of capitalist society as a whole, including even well-trained workers, should be taken over by socialist society. Thus they transformed the Hegelian dialectic into their dialectical materialism, according to which they evaluated the achievement of capitalist society much more affirmatively than did Hegel.

Their affirmative evaluation of capitalism has been strengthened in Japan mainly for two reasons: the backward character of Japanese society, and the peculiar development of Adam Smith scholarship in Japan. Paradoxically, the first caused the second.

Westernisation of Japan

As it is well known nowadays, Japan started to open its doors to the West in 1854 and subsequently modernised its state and society under the imperial restoration in 1868. As a latecomer into the world of imperialism, the new government found it an urgent necessity to modernise the nation as a whole, allowing a certain range for individual freedom but at the same time strengthening national unity against possible Western invaders and their ideological weapons of liberalism. The ideas of Western liberalism were needed for modernisation but at the same time they were thought dangerous to the national unity which the government was trying to build on the basis of the Chu Hsi sect of Confucianism.

A Japanese version of Chu Hsi's teaching was adopted by the Tokugawa Shogunate government during the 18th century as the fundamental principles of government and social organisation, and this was inherited by the new Meiji imperial government. The principles which were inherited from the feudal era by the apparently modern government may be characterised as the family analogy of politics and political organisation, in which the emperor is a benevolent but almighty father. Under this semi-feudal regime, the transplantation of modern Western ideas had to take a somewhat truncated form. For example, Hobbes's *Leviathan* was translated and published in 1883 by the Ministry of Education, omitting the first book, in which Hobbes declared that everyone had an inviolable natural right of self-preservation on which 'civil society' should be founded. It is true that there had been a long controversy about Hobbes's political stance, but it is at the same time true that he laid a cornerstone for the history of democratic thought through his idea of the state of nature of mankind. However, the Japanese government tried to use the truncated translation to justify absolute imperial power. (However, it must be noted that the democratic aspect of Hobbes's idea of civil society or state of nature was appropriated later by Adam Smith scholarship.)

As early as 1871 the Ministry of Education was established to start a national system of education, including compulsory primary schools. The system worked so successfully that primary schools accepted 31.53 per cent of school age children in the first year, and 93.23 per cent in 1903, just before the Russo-Japanese war of 1904–5. This development of literacy was unrivalled among developing nations. The Japanese economy had just passed through the industrial revolution before the end of the century. The development of education itself was by no means bad for Japanese people in general but the government operated the system to bring up a clever but obedient nation whose citizens would have no suspicion about the divine and inviolable regime of the emperor. To ensure the effectiveness of the system, or to keep it within a desirable limit, the imperial message on education was issued in 1890, following the imperial constitution of 1889. The message – an adaptation of Chu Hsi's teaching mentioned above – was addressed to the great family of the empire under the divine emperor, and it asked people to be loyal to the emperor and to their family elders. In addition, it was ordered that the message should be read at every school ceremony by formally dressed schoolmasters. Order had been strictly kept until Japan's defeat on 15 August 1945. The message was a bible for Japanese who had grown up from 1890 to 1945. Even the present writer, who finished primary school more than 70 years ago, can repeat at least a part of it word-for-word. To safeguard this system of loyalty education, educational sentinels encircled the nation's life. They consisted of schoolteachers and lesser military officers who were recruited as clever boys of poor families by means of stipends. They were usually found in rural areas where peasants suffered from rack rents or feudal rents levied by absentee landlords, in addition to the climate being not quite suitable for rice production. In the northern districts the economic and natural conditions were much more severe for the lower strata of peasants than for others. In the years of bad harvests, some of the poor people had to sell their daughters to whorehouses. It was natural that these districts provided breeding grounds for military coups to overcome bourgeois corruption by means of an imperial dictatorship.

The government was fully aware of the dangerous situation in the country in which class differentiation and antagonism were superimposed on feudal and semi-feudal relations. Although Marx and Marxism were known to Japanese readers as early as 1881, rigid censorship did not allow the full translation of his works. They were published in a truncated form or suppressed entirely, as was the case with the *Communist Manifesto*. After the establishment of the Communist International in 1919 and of the illegal Communist Party of Japan in 1922, the government became more and more nervous about the infiltration of dangerous thought. Therefore, in 1923 they did not allow a Russian ship to enter Tokyo Bay, despite the fact that it was carrying wheat for the victims of the great earthquake in the Tokyo area. Perhaps it was partly because of the fact that the ship was named after Lenin.

Promulgation of universal manhood suffrage on 2 March 1922 was followed immediately on 7 March by the notorious *Maintenance of the Public Order Act*, directed against any attempt to abolish the imperial regime and to threaten private property. A few years later it was extended to cover any organisation which made a similar attempt, and all the members of any organisations of that kind; moreover, the penalty was enhanced to include death. The red hunt by Special Higher Police and Military Police was expanded to preventive detention similar to that of the Nazis in the Dachau Concentration Camp in Bavaria. In the confusion after the great earthquake mentioned above, a leading anarchist was killed by a captain of the Military Police. Students' reading circles were not safe. In 1939, the present writer had a narrow escape from a group arrest of a reading circle associated with a book on German 'Katheder' or academic socialism written by Kazuo Okochi (1905–84), who was then a young lecturer at Tokyo Imperial University, later becoming president of the same university after World War II. These examples of fierce suppression, fanatical and sometimes rather ridiculous, show on the one hand how desperately the ruling classes felt the crisis of their regime, and on the other hand how deeply and widely so-called dangerous thoughts had penetrated into the working classes and intellectuals. It was said that all the clever students would become Marxists. Some of them came from the families of absentee landlords and had realised through their readings at university that they were parasites. Some of them had returned to the countryside to organise peasants against their fathers. When those students were arrested by the metropolitan police they were treated with esteem by fellow prisoners, although they were tortured by the special police. There was a general red scare among people, on the one hand, but, on the other, some of them imagined communists as heroes in the darkness.

The wide diffusion of Marxism among students, young intellectuals and trade unions cannot simply be attributed to communist propaganda. There was widespread discontent with several features of the establishment, for example, the existence of the god-emperor, theocratic principles in education, corruption in politics and business, the expansionist policy towards China by means of a national system of conscription, impoverishment of the lower classes by monopoly capitalists and semi-feudal landlords, and so on. To maintain the ammunition industry peasants were forced to buy its by-product as a fertiliser which was unsuitable for their crops. It is true that the government promoted a rational way of thinking among people to the extent that this was useful for increasing the power and wealth of the country, but ironically it naturally and necessarily proceeded beyond the desirable limit. A rational way of thinking enabled many intellectuals to realise the backwardness of their country compared with the West.

In 1932, the Communist International issued *Theses on the Situation in Japan and the Task of the Communist Party*, which stated that the Japanese road to a communist society would be through 'a bourgeois-democratic revolution with a tendency to grow rapidly into a socialist revolution' (*International press correspondence* 1932: 466–72; *Internationale Presse Korrespondenz* 1932: 1303–10). The illegal Communist Party of Japan translated the *Theses* from the German version, in which 'to grow rapidly' was rendered as 'forced [*forcierten*] transformation'. This delicate and important difference between the two versions resulted from the differing political stances taken by the English and German translators of the Russian original. According to the Japanese translation based on the German version, the bourgeois-democratic revolution was a necessary stage, but it was to be transformed by force into a socialist revolution. But according to the English version, the transformation should be accelerated, but not by force. That is to say, a socialist society would come into existence only after capitalist society ripens fully.

As a matter of fact, the difference in translation and interpretation was apparently not striking enough to be expressed in contemporary discussion about Japanese society and its future. In the *Lectures on History of Japanese Capitalism* (*Nihon Shihonshugi Hattatsushi Koza*, 7 vols, 1932–33), edited and written by communists and communist-sympathisers, stress was put on the feudal or pre-capitalist character of Japanese society. It was generally known that the publication was planned in order to justify the *Theses* of the Comintern. Although these books in themselves did no great harm to the establishment, publication was under strict censorship, and one of the four editors was arrested and tortured to death. The remaining three were arrested and forced to resign from chairs at Tokyo Imperial University and Tokyo University of Commerce. Later, though not connected with this, a professor of public finance at Imperial University was arrested because he was a leader of the Marxist popular front movement.

The authors of the *Lectures on the History of Japanese Capitalism* did not form a monolithic group but were called Koza-ha (*Lectures* sect). Moritaro Yamada (1905–84), an associate professor of Tokyo Imperial University and the most influential of those authors, published a book based on his contributions to the *Lectures*. The book was entitled *Analysis of Japanese Capitalism* (*Nihon Shihonshugi Bunseki*, 1934) and called, ironically, a bible for his disciples. It was said that some of them transcribed it like Buddhist monks. As late as 1939, in Manchuria, a puppet state of Japan in northeast China, the present writer met a young Japanese businessman who was proud that he had successfully smuggled Yamada's book through strict censorship at the frontier. He was working for a Japanese company which was exploiting the Chinese proletariat. This may be laughed at now as an expression of intellectual fashion or vanity among young, university-educated Japanese. But at the same time this was evidence that even such a flippant young man as this had agreed with Yamada's analysis concerning the semi-feudal and backward character of Japanese society. He probably recognised his own contradictory position.

Yamada wrote in the preface of his book as follows: 'It is clear enough that Japanese capitalism has deviated from the normal course of capitalist development'. The severest criticism of Yamada was that in his picture of Japanese expansionist capitalism, based on serfdom and feudal agriculture, there was no hope even of a bourgeois-democratic revolution, to say nothing of a socialist one.

Marxist economic history in Japan

Towards the end of the 1930s, that is to say on the eve of the Pacific war (1941–45), some young Marxists who had studied Adam Smith and Max Weber tried to rewrite Yamada's version of Japanese capitalism. Their modifications traced out the normal course of capitalist development and its ideological superstructures.

Hisao Otsuka (1907–96), an associate professor of economic history at Tokyo Imperial University, tried to trace the normal course of capitalist development by relying chiefly on the works of George Unwin (1904). In his *Introduction to the Modern Economic History of Europe* (Oshu Keizaishi Josetsu 1944), he stressed the genealogy of English industrial capitalists, arguing they originated from rural woollen manufacturers. Later, he identified them with the Puritan merchants of the 17th century who appeared in Max Weber's famous essay on the Protestant ethic and the spirit of capitalism (1904–5) and also with Daniel Defoe's *Robinson Crusoe*. Weber's basic idea was taken from Marx's *Capital*, where the typical, normal character and development of industrial capitalism were delineated in clear contrast with those of merchant or commercial capital. In short, Otsuka tried to make it plain that Japanese society was not a normal capitalist society consisting of equal, independent and rational individuals. This means that many Japanese intellectuals read in Marx a theoretical image of a normal, modern society to be realized by means of a bourgeois-democratic revolution as stated in the *Theses* (1932) of the Comintern.

Otsuka may be called a Christian Marxist who saw a model of modern human beings in Puritan merchants and in *Robinson Crusoe*. This identification may seem to western readers to be quite self-contradictory. However, the point is that in pre-war Japan even a radical Christian with a social conscience could become a Marxist. Perhaps that is true to a certain extent even now. There were and are Buddhist Marxists, too. For them, *civil society* was and is a society to be built by means of a revolution of some sort or other.

Kazuo Okochi, who was a great friend of Otsuka, started writing on Adam Smith about the same time. As mentioned above, he was then a lecturer in social policy at the same university. His book was entitled *Smith and List* (*Sumisu to Risuto*) and published in 1943 when Japan's final defeat was becoming clearer day by day. A little earlier, Zenya Takashima (1904–90) published his first book, entitled *The Fundamental Problem of Economic Sociology – Smith and List as Economic Sociologists* (*Keizaishakaigaku no Konponmondai – Keizaishakaigakusha toshiteno Sumisu to Risuto*, 1941). In their books, for the first time in the long history of Adam Smith scholarship, Smith's two great published works were united into a system of social philosophy of civil society. It is true that the relationship of these two works was discussed in Germany in the latter half of the 19th century, chiefly by economists of the historical school, but most of them thought that the 'sympathy' of the first work was incompatible with the 'self-love' of the second work. There were a few who tried to connect Smith with Kant, who admired Smith, by identifying Smith's 'impartial spectator' or 'man within' with Kant's 'conscience', but they ignored Smith's economic analysis of civilised or commercial society.

Okochi read *The Wealth of Nations* (*WN* hereafter) into the *Theory of Moral Sentiments* (*TMS* hereafter) and vice versa. According to him, the picture of free competition of in *WN* was drawn in *TMS* as follows:

> In the race of wealth, honours, and preferences, he may run as hard as he can, and strain every nerve and every muscle, in order to outstrip

all his competitors. But if he should jostle, or throw down any of them, the indulgence of the spectators is entirely at an end. It is a violation of fair play, which they cannot admit of. This man to them, in every respect, as good as he: they do not enter into that self-love by which he prefers himself so much to this other, and cannot go along with the motive from which he hurt him.

(Smith 1976a: 83)

Presumably Okochi thought that in Japanese capitalism, as a latecomer into the imperialist world with a poor domestic market, there was no room for the rules of fair play to avoid corruption and bribery. On the contrary, in civil society in normal capitalism, competitors on equal footings would automatically have established the rule of fair play.

In the following case, Okochi read *TMS* into *WN*. When Smith discussed public revenue he referred to systems of morality as follows:

In every civilized society, in every society where the distinction of ranks has once been completely established, there have been always two different schemes or systems of morality current at the same time; of which the one may be called the strict or austere; the other the liberal, or if you will, the loose system. The former is generally admired and revered by the common people: The latter is commonly more esteemed and adopted by what are called people of fashion.

(Smith 1976b: 794)

Okochi connected the above passage with a statement in TMS which was added to the sixth edition:

In the middling and inferior stations of life, the road to virtue and that to fortune, to such fortune, at least, as men in such stations can reasonably expect to acquire, are, happily in the most cases, very nearly the same. In all the middling and inferior professions, real and solid professional abilities, joined to prudent, just, firm, and temperate conduct, can very seldom fail of success.

(Smith 1976a: 63)

Okochi went on to say that Smith might have had in mind the puritans in Weber's work, which were also referred to by Otsuka. Thus, they were tracing the process of development from simple commodity producers to industrial capitalists in the typical modern society in the West.

Takashima tried to reconstruct Smith's system of civil society as a trinity of moral philosophy, jurisprudence and political economy, that is to say, *TMS*, the Glasgow Lectures on jurisprudence, and *WN*. Both Takashima and Okochi criticised the ethical and nationalist political economy of Friedrich List and his followers, especially with respect to contemporary Japan. They emphasised that even for List, Smith's *civil society* was a normal nation into which a backward German society should develop. According to Okochi, who subtitled the first chapter of his book 'economic logic and economic ethics', Smith's concept of *civil society*, which was expressed in his two books, could absorb List's national system. Takashima also rejected the nationalism and moralism of List, but he thought that List's idea of productive forces could be developed theoretically on the basis of *civil society* as a whole, which Smith had delineated in his three works. In spite of differences like these in their understanding of Smith, they agreed with each other in considering Smith's civil or civilised society to be a model for Japan, or at least to be useful as a theoretical tool for analysing the backwardness of Japanese society.

According to Adam Smith, 'Society may subsist among different men, as among different merchants, from a sense of its utility, without any mutual love or affection' (Smith 1976a: 86). Everybody in society 'is, by nature, first and principally recommended to his own care' (Smith 1976a: 82) and, as quoted above, 'In the race of wealth ... he may run as hard as he can'. Without mutual love they are connected with each other by the exchange of commodities of the same value measured by labour, 'the mercenary exchange of good offices according to an agreed valuation' (Smith 1976a: 86), and mutual sympathies between equals. It must be noted that according to Smith, hierarchical sympathy or veneration of the rich and great is a corruption of the moral sense on the one hand and, on the other, sympathy or compassion for the poor is an ornament unnecessary for the maintenance of society. This is a picture of a society consisting of independent producers in free and fair competition envisaged by many thinkers of the Western Enlightenment, including Smith and Rousseau, and also Marx. Some Japanese Marxists read into Marx the idea of *civil society* characteristic of the Western Enlightenment. According to that view, regardless of what was intended by the *Theses* (1932) of the Comintern, Japan's socialist revolution, via a bourgeois-democratic revolution, absolutely should not lead to Stalinist society. They learned from Smith and Marx the idea of a *civil society* based on radical democracy, including even extraparliamentary movements undertaken by citizens.

Conclusions

Western readers may wonder why I stress the basic condition of *civil society* as extracted from Smith in the foregoing paragraph. It may be said that the urgent problems are love and solidarity as opposed to separation and loneliness, rather than individual freedom and independency. It is true that we have the same problems on the one hand, but on the other hand we are still living among many feudal remnants. The defeat in World War II made the god-emperor descend into a human being, but he is treated with special veneration as the head of the family of Japan. Having him at the top, the family principle dominates the whole nation's life. For example, an overwhelming majority of marriages are arranged by parents, and many parliamentary posts are inherited in family lines. The feudal and semi-feudal bonds were stronger before the defeat than now, and this was one of the reasons for the popularity of Marxism among young intellectuals who suffered from this, including conscription and death in the nameless war.

The Japanese concept of *civil society* is Marx's picture of the early stage of normal capitalism without sharp class antagonisms, but this is superimposed on Smith's civilised or commercial society. In a revolutionary process, what is civil in society is not to be expunged, but rather to be fully realised.

References

Comintern (1932). *International Press Correspondence*. London: Comintern, 466–72.

Marx, K. and Engels, F. (1947) *The German Ideology*, Parts I & III, ed. R. Pascal. New York: Inprecor.

Marx, K. and Engels, F. (1976) *Collected Works*, vol. 5. London: Lawrence & Wishart.

Marx, K. and Engels, F. (1986) *Collected Works*, vol. 28. London: Lawrence & Wishart.

Marx, K. and Engels, F. (1992) *Collected Works*, vol. 46. London: Lawrence & Wishart.

Smith, A. (1976a) *The Theory of Moral Sentiments*. The Glasgow edition of the works and correspondence of Adam Smith, vol. 2. Oxford: Oxford University Press.

Smith, A. (1976b) *An Inquiry into the Nature and Causes of the Wealth of Nations*. The Glasgow edition of the works and correspondence of Adam Smith, vol. 1. Oxford: Oxford University Press.

Unwin, G. (1904) *Industrial Organization in the Sixteenth and Seventeenth Centuries*. Oxford: Oxford University Press.

Weber, M. (1904–5) *Die protestantische Ethik und der 'Geist' des Kapitalismus*. In *Archiv für Sozialwissenschaft und Sozialpolitik*, ed. Werner Sombart, Max Weber, Edgar Jaffé, vol. 20: 1–54; vol. 21: 1–110. Tübingen: J.C.B. Mohr (Paul Siebeck).

9 Marx and J.S. Mill on socialism

Shohken Mawatari

Introduction

Duncan (1973) viewed Marx as a champion of socialism, and J.S. Mill as a champion of liberalism. But this interpretation is not particularly persuasive, because Mill's liberalism is compatible with certain types of socialism, for example, Fourierism. In addition, Mill located liberty as an essential part of human happiness, so far as it does not allow some persons to harm others. In Mill, both liberalism and socialism are based on social utility, i.e. utilitarianism, in a compatible and orderly manner.

Other interpreters have argued that Mill was not a socialist for reasons other than his liberalism. Bain (1882), one of Mill's close friends, stressed Mill's distance from a socialist position. Robbins (1961) also pointed out that Mill's bitterly anti-socialist attitude in the first edition of the *Principles of Political Economy* (1848) resonates with the last unfinished draft of *Chapters on Socialism* (1879), so we should not overrate the pro-communist position in the third edition of the *Principles* (1852). Others, such as Asheley (1921), Losman (1971), Schwarz (1972) and Davis (1985), following the same line of argument, emphasise what distinguished Mill's position from the socialist one.

Even with regard to interpreting Mill, however, this is also misleading. Mill (1851) distinguished socialism from communism. He called supporters of workers' associations or co-operatives 'socialists', by contrast with 'communists', who advocated common property and perfect equality.

In the first edition of the *Principles*, it is true that Mill took a somewhat anti-socialist and anti-communist position, because he could not support Saint-Simonianism and Owenism. In the second edition, however, he evaluated Fourierism and supported it, because it combines workers' initiatives and distributive justice with competition, private ownership, market economy and individual liberty (Mill 1849, vol. III: 982–3; Fourier 1829: 118–19). In the third edition, while maintaining his Fourierist position, Mill accepted, or at least did not deny, the communist position. In that edition, Mill went so far as to write:

The impossibility of foreseeing and prescribing the exact mode in which its [communism's] difficulties should be dealt with, does not prove that it [communism] may not be the best and the ultimate form of human society.

(Mill 1852, vol. II: 207)

This passage was deleted from the fourth edition onwards, but the other passages of the third edition, which are tolerant of communism, remained in the text up until the last edition of the *Principles*, published at the same time as the *Chapters on Socialism*. Mill accepted Fourierist socialism, and left communism 'an open question' which the people of the future would have to decide on.

Mill himself clearly referred to his socialist position: 'our ideal of ultimate improvement went far beyond Democracy, and would class us decidedly under the general designation of Socialists' (Mill 1873, vol. I: 239). 'Our' and 'us' includes Harriet Taylor. On this interpretive basis, Marshall and Schumpeter, and more recently Kuhrer, Claeys and Hollander, and, in Japan, Sugihara and Mawatari, have identified Mill as a socialist and as a liberal at the same time (Marshall 1921: vii; Schumpeter 1954: 532; Kuhrer 1992: 230; Claeys 1987: 145; Hollander 1985: 820–1, 823; Sugihara 1973: 181–242; Mawatari 1997a: 417–52).

Thus Marx and Mill were both socialists in the mid-19th century. Marx's socialist ideas are well known, but Mill's are not. It may be very useful to analyse Marx's socialist ideas from J.S. Mill's point of view, because Mill's ideas are quite different from Marx's and, owing to their difference, Mill's ideas are useful for an objective characterisation of Marxian socialism. We will analyse Marx's socialist ideas from Mill's point of view.

Marx's 'scientific socialism'

Marx's analysis of socialism is often labelled 'scientific socialism', following Engels. That label is better suited for expressing Marx's socialist ideas than 'revolutionary communism', which is also quite often used, because, although the two labels are partly compatible, 'scientific socialism' indicates more generally a methodological feature of Marx's socialist thought, while the term 'revolutionary communism' merely alludes to Marx's means of realising a socialist society. In addition, 'scientific socialism' reflects Marx's life-long activities, particularly after the 1850s, when he began to do serious research regarding political economy. He did not necessarily support revolutionary actions in the later decades of his life. In the preface to the second German edition of the *Communist Manifesto* (1872), Marx and Engels said: 'no special stress is laid on the revolutionary measures proposed at the end of Section II' (Marx and Engels 1872: 174–5). The way of reform thus depends upon the situation of the nation.

We must first fix what is 'scientific socialism' as formulated by Marx. It is closely related to the materialist interpretation of history. He established those basic ideas in the 1840s, particularly in his manuscript *The German Ideology* (1845), with Engels, and also in the *Manifesto of the Communist Party* (1848), with Engels. He also recapitulated the view of the world he had established in the 1840s in his *Preface to A Contribution to Critique to the Political Economy* (1859), as follows (Marx 1859: 262–4):

- The laws and other various forms of the states originate from human economic relations. The whole of these economic relations are called civil society ('bourgeois society').
- We must rely on Political Economy for the anatomy of civil society.
- A man (or a woman) enters into the relations of production independent of his (or her) own will. The whole of these relations of production constitutes the economic structure of society.
- This economic structure is the basis, or substructure, of the society, on which the superstructure of the legal and political relations, also corresponding social consciousness, is built.
- Human social consciousness does not determine human social existence, rather social existence determines social consciousness.
- As a consequence of the development of productive forces, the relations of production and the proprietorship which reflects them, turn into fetters on the further development of the productive forces, which marks exactly when the time of social revolution begins.
- The economic and social constitution of mankind has experienced the eras of the Asiatic, ancient, feudal and modern bourgeois modes of production.
- The modern bourgeois mode of production is the last antagonistic form of society, after which the pre-history of mankind draws to a close.

Marx foresees socialist society as a necessary result of the conflict between productive forces and relations of production in capitalist society. That conflict or contradiction will come about with a necessity, 'which can be determined with the precision of natural science'. Men become conscious of this conflict in legal, political, religious, artistic or philosophic, in short, ideological forms, and fight it out (Marx 1859: 263). Marx viewed periodic economic crises and increasing poverty among workers in every economic crisis as a result of the contradiction between productive forces and relations of production.

Human consciousness is a reflection of people's social way of existence, particularly of their relations of production, so that workers will revolt in response to the economic difficulties arising from their relations of production. Marx viewed utopian advocacy of socialism as arbitrary, not scientific. What 'scientific socialism' means is that socialist society can be foreseen scientifically, as a necessity.

These ideas of Marx have serious implications, which some people have accepted uncritically, while others have denied them completely. In short, these ideas have been subject to comparatively little serious examination, presumably because they are so sweeping and provocative.

Mill might have examined them, but he did not, because he was not familiar with Marx's ideas (the *Critique* was published in German in 1859), and he may never even have known the name of Marx. Or, as Sugihara suggested (1973: 182–3), he might have heard the name of Marx from Odger, who was Mill's friend and the chairman of the first International Working Men's Association. Marx was one of the members of the council of the Association (Mill 1870: 220; Evans 1989: 275).

Mill's methodology of social reform

However, Mill had discussed closely related points in a very different way. Mill was also 'a reformer of the world', to use his own description (Mill 1873: 137). In his *System of Logic* (1843), which treats mainly the methodology of science, he makes a clear distinction between 'science' and 'art', saying that 'science' is related to 'is' or 'do', while 'art' is related to 'ought to be' or 'ought to do'. Mill well knew Hume's guillotine: 'morals do not come from reason' (Mawatari 1982/1983).

Mill went further. He not only separated science from art, but also connected them. The ends must come first; teleological art (in his case, utilitarianism) supplies the ends. Second, science seeks suitable means for the ends, because science knows the causes which bring about the intended ends (results). Third, in practical art, objective and subjective conditions must be taken into consideration in order to put the means into practice. In short, practical art is a joint result of teleology and science in concrete situations. In social practice teleology and science must be united in concrete situations (Mill 1843: 949). Mill exerted considerable influence on Weber (1949: 523; Blaug 1980: 134–5, 140–3). It is evident, then, that Marx's theory of the necessity of socialist society is quite different from Mill's.

Marx was mainly concerned with the objective and subjective conditions of socialist society, the third stage of Mill's connection between science and art. The objective conditions of socialist society will mature 'with the precision of natural science'. Furthermore, even subjective conditions will be prepared semi-automatically, because men facing the contradiction of productive forces and production relations become conscious of their objective conditions. In this connection, for Marx, political economy is vital for predicting the coming economic crisis, and for explaining the scientific basis of social reform.

For Mill, in order to reform society, we must first have the ends of the reform, that is, teleology. What is Marx's teleology, and what are his supreme goods? In the 1840s, when he transformed himself from a young Hegelian and took up his own independent position, Marx insisted on workers' liberation from their depressed mental and material position in capitalist society, labour-alienation, exploitation, oppression, and so on. He often referred to 'general human emancipation' or 'the universal liberation' of 'the labouring class' (Marx 1843: 184–6). We could say that this is the end of the reform that he sought, but 'liberation' is a negation of the present state, not a positive setting of ends and teleology.

Compared with Mill's utilitarianism, Marx's teleology, or his discussions of the ethical basis of his alternative society, is lacking, or at least weak, so that we cannot know what his supreme goods are, how he locates justice, impartiality, liberty, and equality in his order of value. There are many ethical questions unanswered by Marx, such as whether human nature will change in the course of time, how the total or collective good is induced from the good of individuals, and whether or not the life of a proletarian is more important than that of a capitalist.

Marx and Mill also hold different views about the role of science. Marx needs science not to find the rational means to certain ends, but to demonstrate the material basis of social reform as the necessary result of the conflict between productive forces and production relations, from which two consequences follow. First, the rationality of the means for the ends in Marx's case becomes less important than in Mill's case in 'Toward rationality in ethics' (Ryan 1970: 187). Marx and Mill had completely different opinions about revolutionary measures (see Marx and Engels 1848: 505–6; Mill 1879: 709, 737, 749). In addition, for Marx the objective demonstration of the material basis of social reform makes the subjective question of change less significant – who will try to reform existing society and on what basis?

Mill's comparative analysis of social systems

For Marx socialism is the problem of necessity, but for Mill it is the problem of choice. In order to choose, people can and must compare existing society with socialist society. Mill proposed a method of 'comparative analysis of systems' in order to decide which system is better – competition (private property) or co-operation (common property). People will have to choose the better system of the two. Mill's theory of socialism is not a demonstration of the necessity of socialism, but a comparison of two systems from a teleological point of view, specifically the utilitarian ethical standard.

From the very beginning of his discussions with an Owenite communist group at the age of nineteen, Mill proposed a method for the comparative analysis of systems. Thompson (1822: 182) attacked the defects of competition: competition is incompatible with the full operation of the principles of benevolence; in competition it is difficult to apportion supply to demand; labourers suffer from competition with machinery; it is the tendency of competition to make every man a rival to every other, and consequently, the enemy of every other man (Mill 1825: 316–18). Mill criticized each of these points by showing another side of the coin: the merits of competition, and the defects of the co-operative system (Mill 1825: 309–11, 319). It is interesting, in this context, that Mill wondered whether or not under the co-operative system there would be trade, or interchange of commodities. 'If not you are reduced almost to primitive barbarism. But if one Community trades, and exchanges its commodities with other communities, there would be still competition' (Mill 1825: 318). Mill, unlike other socialists of his time, appreciated the market economy and considered it compatible with, and rather necessary for, communist society. Mill pursued market socialism (Mill 1849: 982–3; Mill 1851: 446), whereas Marx wanted a system of central planning (Marx and Engels 1848: 505).

Mill's earliest proposal for a method of comparative analysis of socio-economic systems is as follows:

> The question is not whether a state of Competition is exempt from evil, for we know that evil is mixed up in every human lot; but whether Competition or Cooperation on the whole affords the best chance for human happiness: and it is not by a review of the evils of the Competitive system that this great question can be decided, but by a fair comparison of the evils of the Competitive and the evils of the Cooperative system.
>
> (Mill 1825: 319)

Almost all socialists attacked existing society by pointing out its evils and defects, and so proposed an alternative society which was allegedly to overcome these evils or defects. Marx is no exception. But this way of comparison, according to Mill, is seriously defective and unfair, because the comparison is made between the evils of the existing society and the merits of the alternative society. This comparison sets a very low standard of satisfaction for the alternative society to meet, because it needs only slight merit to overcome some of the existing evils, no matter how serious the evils it would introduce. The results of a comparison in this manner will be almost self-evident. A socialist society is required only to jump over a bar that is intentionally and methodologically set very low.

For us to be fair, argues Mill, we must compare the evils of the existing society with the possible evils of the alternative society, and the merits of existing society with the possible merits of the alternative society. His utilitarian principle supplies the ethical standard for the comparison. We must judge which of these social systems 'afford the best chance to happiness'. His method of 'comparative analysis of systems' allows us to decide which system is better on the whole by comparing both the evils and the merits of the two systems from the point of view of the greatest happiness (Mawatari 1997a: 432–4, 440–3; 1997b: 150).

Evidence that Mill made much of this method of comparison is provided by his frequent references to it and his repeated applications of it for drawing conclusions from his own comparison of the existing system with an alternative one. In the first edition of the *Principles of Political Economy*, he said that in considering the institution of property as a question in social philosophy, we must suppose a community unhampered by any previous possession. The inhabitants must be free 'to choose whether they would conduct the work of production on the principle of individual property, or on some system of common ownership and collective agency' (Mill 1848, vol. II: 201). In the third edition of the *Principles of Political Economy* (1852), which marked Mill's most 'advanced' view of socialism, he again referred to his method for the comparative analysis of systems:

> If the choice were to be made between Communism with all its chance, and the present state of society with all its sufferings and injustices ... all the difficulties, great or small, of Communism would be but as dust in the balance. But to make the comparison applicable, we must compare Communism at its best, with the régime of individual property, not as it is, but as it might be made.
>
> (Mill 1852, vol. II: 207)

In the unfinished *Chapters on Socialism*, 1879:

> What is incumbent on us is a calm comparison between two different systems of society, with a view of determining which of them affords the greatest resources for overcoming the inevitable difficulties of life ... The question is, which of these arrangements is most conductive to human happiness.
>
> (Mill 1879, vol. V: 736, 738)

This comparative analysis of systems is what is most important for Mill, but least important for Marx, because for him it is a self-evident question unworthy of being scrutinised. Marx believed firmly that science can show the necessity, and even superiority, of socialism; he was a socialist prior to being a scientist.

From where Marx's concerns ends, however, Mill's begins. Mill's science of political economy only clarifies the statics and dynamics of a modern market economy, from which no answers are derived for the question 'which of these arrangements is most conductive to human happiness'. In order to draw conclusions about this question, Mill was seriously engaged in the comparative analysis of systems at least three times.

As noted above, Mill distinguished socialism from communism, and he supported socialism of the Fourier-type of association, but not communism. The desirability of communism is an 'open question' for people of the future to decide.

Mill on Fourierism

With respect to socialism, Mill had supported Fourierism, since the time of the second edition of the *Principles of Political Economy*: 'The most skillfully combined, and in every respect the least open to objection, of the forms of Socialism, is that commonly known as Fourierism' (Mill 1849, vol. III: 982). Mill examined Fourierism, focusing on the 'Phalange', as follows:

> This system does not contemplate the abolition of private property, nor even of inheritance: on the contrary, it avowedly takes into consideration, as an element in the distribution of the produce, capital as well as labour. It proposes that the operation of industry should be carried on by associations of about two thousand members, combining their labour on a district of about a square league in extent, under the guidance of chiefs selected by themselves. In the distribution, a certain minimum is first assigned for the subsistence of every member of the community, whether capable or not of labour. The remainder of the produce is shared in certain proportions, to be determined beforehand, among the three elements, Labour, Capital, and Talent.
>
> (Mill 1849, vol. III: 982)

The capital of the community may be owned in unequal shares by different members (labourers), who would in that case receive, as in any other joint-stock company, proportional dividends. The claim of each person on the share of the produce apportioned to talent is estimated by the grade or rank which the individual occupies in the several groups of labourers to which he or she belongs. These grades are in all cases conferred by the choice of his or her companions. The buying and selling operation of the association to the outside world, is performed by a single agent (Mill 1849, vol. III: 982–3).

According to Mill's distinctions in 'On the probable futurity of the labouring classes' in book IV of his *Principles*, Fourierism ('Phalange') is his second type of association. This is 'the association of labourers among themselves', contrasted with 'the association of labourers with capitalists'. As a matter of fact, the section of 'the association of labourers among themselves' was introduced in the third edition, after Mill's acceptance of Fourierism in the second edition. The section also contains his detailed examination of French and British examples of that type of association.

So far as associations are concerned, Mill believed in their feasibility, first of an association of labourers with capitalists, finally of an association of labourers among themselves. There can be little doubt for Mill, 'that the relation of masters and workpeople will be gradually superseded by partnership, in one of two forms: in some cases, association of the labourers with the capitalist; in others, and perhaps finally in all, association of the labourers among themselves' (Mill 1852, vol. III: 769).

For Marx, Fourierism is merely a type of 'critical-utopian socialism', which bears an inverse relation to historical development, and consistently endeavours to deaden the class struggle. 'Phalanstere' (a kind of Fourierist community) is nothing but a castle in the air (Marx and Engels 1848: 515–16). Accusing Fourierism of being utopian, Marx himself planned to get power through communist revolution, and to establish a centralised authority – 'the centralization of credit in the hands of State, by means of a national bank with State capital and exclusive monopoly', 'the centralization of the means of communication and transport in the hands of the State', and 'the extension of factories and instruments of production owned by the State' (Marx and Engels 1848: 505). However, this is what Mill was most seriously against when he examined Saint-Simon. For Mill, it is 'a supposition almost too chimerical to be reasoned against' to construe an absolute despotism for the head of the association to adapt each person's work to his capacity, and to proportion each person's remuneration to his merits' (Mill 1848, vol. II: 211). Mill and Marx had quite different opinions about centralised authorities and their efficacy.

Mill on communism

As to communism, distinct from 'non-communistic socialism' (Mill 1848, vol. II: 210), it was a matter of comparison between existing society and communist society from several points of view: liberty, management activity, work-incentives, equitable distribution, efficiency, equal property and population restraints. Mill thought that the communistic scheme was more favourable for restraining population (Mill 1848, vol. II: 206). The *Chapters on Socialism* contain the most detailed analyses.

Managers' motives

Mill points out that there is a big difference in managers' motives to direct production under the systems of common property and private property. In the system of private property, the incentive for managers is self-interest. Managers do their very best for the efficiency and economy of the operations, so as to gain as much profit as possible. Whereas in the system of common property, the incentive for managers is 'public spirit, conscience, the honour and credit' which can be realised when dividends to all members are made as large as possible (Mill 1879: 739).

At the present stage of human nature, 'the closer the connection of every increase of exertion with a corresponding increase of fruits, the more powerful is this motive' (Mill 1879: 740). It will take a considerable time before a majority, or even a substantial minority, can establish the supremacy of public spirit over self-interest through education. Moreover, so far as a manager no longer has the chance of being better off than any other labourer, he would have no strong inducement to make improvements to the process of production. Then:

> Communistic management would thus be, in all probability, less favourable than private management to that striking out of new paths and making immediate sacrifices for distant and uncertain advantages, which, though seldom unattended with risk, is generally indispensable to great improvements in the economic condition of mankind.
>
> (Mill 1879: 742)

Interestingly, J.A. Schumpeter (1950: 10, 61, 131–4) supported the Marxian materialistic interpretation of history, and believed along with Marx in the end of capitalism, but for a different reason, the decay of entrepreneurship in capitalist society.

Workers' incentives

Under communism, workers would have no interest, except their share of the general interest, in doing their work honestly and energetically. However, Mill reasons that matters would not be worse than they are now for the majority of the producing classes. They, being paid by fixed wages, are so far from having any direct interest of their own in the efficiency of their work, that they have not even that share in the general interest (Mill 1879: 742). Mill viewed the status of hired labourers as 'mere servants under the command of the one who supplies the funds, and having no interest of their own in the enterprise except to earn their wages with as little labour as possible' (Mill 1852, vol. III: 769). Piece-work may be to some extent helpful, but it is not a fundamental solution.

As far as the motivation of ordinary workers to exert themselves is concerned, Mill says, 'Communism has no advantage which may not be reached under private property' (Mill 1879: 743). In plain language, communism is at an advantage, or at least not at a disadvantage, so far as work-incentives are concerned.

Apportionment of labour

If communism adopts 'a simple rule to give equal payment to all who share in the work', this is very imperfect justice, unless the work also is apportioned equally. Different kinds of work are unequal in difficulty and unpleasantness (disutility), so that equal payment is rather inequitable. To cope with this difficulty, communists usually propose 'to make quality equivalent to quantity' and 'to work by turns at every kind of labour' (Mill

1879: 744). Mill is critical of this idea for two reasons. First, job rotation squanders the advantages of a division of labour. It greatly lowers the productivity of labour. Second, to demand the same amount of work from everyone is an imperfect standard of justice. People have unequal capacities to work, both mental and physical. Therefore, there should be a dispensing power, an authority competent to grant exemptions from the ordinary amount of work, and to apportion tasks in some measure to capacities. An authority must decide by general voice of members what in the present system can be left to individuals to decide, each in his own case (Mill 1879: 744). Concerning the apportionment of labour, the question is whether it is an inherent source of discord to decide by the general voice the most important matters to each individual (Mill 1879: 745).

The problem of liberty

For Mill, as he wrote in *On Liberty*, the liberty of individuals, so far as it does not harm other persons, is an essential part of human happiness and the most important means to human progress. Mill does not think that existing society excels at realising human liberty. 'The generality of labourers in this and most other countries, have as little choice of occupation or freedom of location, and are practically as dependent on fixed rules and on the will of others'. Labourers are very close to being in 'actual slavery', to say nothing of the entire domestic subjection of women (Mill 1848, vol. II: 209). But the question is, which system secures human liberty more, with respect to individuality of character, public opinion, relation to others, thoughts, feelings and actions. 'No society in which eccentricity is a matter of reproach, can be in a wholesale state' (Mill 1848, vol. II: 209). The answer to this question in the third edition of *The Principles of Political Economy* is that 'it is yet to be ascertained whether the Communistic scheme would be consistent with that multifold development of human nature' (Mill 1852, vol. II: 209). But *The Chapters on Socialism* are somewhat more against communism than is the third edition of *the Principles of Political Economy*:

> Already in all societies the compression of individuality by the majority is a great and growing evil. It would probably be much greater under Communism, except so far as it might be in the power of individuals to set bounds to it by selecting to belong to a community of persons like-minded with themselves.
>
> (Mill 1879: 746)

In Mill's view, the suppression of individuality by the majority is probably much greater under communism. However, Mill, from all these considerations, did not reject communism, but located it as an open question for the people of the future to decide. His final position is revealed in the *Chapters on Socialism*:

From these various considerations I do not seek to draw any inferences against the possibility that Communistic production is capable of being at some future time the form of society best adapted to the wants and circumstances of mankind. I think that this is, and will long be, an open question, upon which fresh light will continually be obtained, both by trial of the Communistic principle under favourable circumstances, and by the improvements which will be gradually effected in the working of the existing society.

(Mill 1879: 746)

Also in the *Autobiography*, he summarises his position:

The social problem of the future we considered to be, how to unite the greatest individual liberty of action, with a common ownership in the raw material of globe, and an equal participation of all in the benefits of combined labour.

(Mill 1873: 239)

What Mill was seriously engaged in was thus a utilitarian assessment of 'Capitalism Versus Communism' (Riley 1996; Smith 1998: 369–86 deals with much narrower range of assessment).

Conclusion

Marx and Mill were both contemporary socialists. But their socialist ideas are so different that some historians of economic thought have failed to recognise that Mill was a socialist. The difference in ideas between Marx and Mill originates from the method with which each thought about future societies, and in particular from the very different roles that science and teleology play for them. For Marx socialism is a matter of necessity, but for Mill it is a matter of choice. As contrasted with Marx's 'scientific', revolutionary, centralised, planned socialism and communism, Mill promoted utilitarian, evolutionary, decentralised market socialism, and also Fourierism. However, because of his comparative analysis of systems he left communism as an open question. For Mill, the most serious problem with communism was whether it is compatible with individual liberty. The twentieth century witnessed the truth of their ideas about socialism.

References

Asheley, W.J. (1921) 'Bibliographical appendix K', in J.S. Mill, *Principles of Political Economy*. London: Longman.

Bain, A. (1882) *John Stuart Mill: A Criticism with Personal Recollections*. London: Longman.

Blaug, M. (1980) *The Methodology of Economics*. Cambridge: Cambridge University Press.

Claeys, G. (1987) 'Justice, independence, and industrial democracy: The development of John Stuart Mill's views on socialism,' *Journal of Politics* 49: 122–47.

Davis, E.G. (1985) 'Mill, socialism and the English Romantics: An interpretation', *Economica* 52(207): 345–58.

Duncan, G. (1973) *Marx and Mill: Two Views of Social Conflict and Social Harmony*. Cambridge: Cambridge University Press.

Evans, M. (1989) 'John Stuart Mill and Karl Marx: Some problems and perspectives', *History of Political Economy* 21: 273–98.

Fourier, C. (1829) *Le Nouveau Monde Industriel et Societaire*. Paris: Bossagne Père.

Hollander, S. (1985) *The Economics of J.S. Mill*. Toronto: University of Toronto Press.

Kuhrer, O. (1992) 'J.S. Mill and utopian socialism', *Economic Records* 68(202): 222–32.

Losman, L. (1971) 'J.S. Mill on alternative economic systems', *American Journal of Economics and Sociology* 30: 85–104.

Marshall, A. (1921) *Industry and Trade*. London: Macmillan.

Marx, K. (1843) 'Contribution to the critique of Hegel's Philosophy of Law: Introduction', in K. Marx and F. Engels (1973) *Collected Works*, vol. 3. Moscow: Progress.

Marx, K. (1859) *A Contribution to the Critique of Political Economy*, in K. Marx and F. Engels (1987) *Collected Works*, vol. 29. Moscow: Progress.

Marx, K. and Engels, F. (1848) *Manifesto of the Communist Party*, in K. Marx and F. Engels (1976) *Collected Works*, vol. 6. Moscow: Progress.

Marx, K. and Engels, F. (1872) Preface to *Manifesto of the Communist Party*, 2nd edn, in K. Marx and F. Engels (1988) *Collected Works*, vol. 23. Moscow: Progress.

Mawatari, S. (1982/1983) 'J.S. Mill's methodology of political economy', *The Keizaigaku* (Tohoku University) 44(2): 1–19; 44(3): 1–21; 45(1): 33–55.

Mawatari, S. (1997a) *The Economics of John Stuart Mill* (in Japanese). Tokyo: Ochanomizu-shobou.

Mawatari, S. (1997b) *History of Economics* (in Japanese). Tokyo: Yuhikaku.

Mill, J.S. (1825) 'Cooperation: Speeches', in *Collected Works*, vol. XXXVI. Toronto: University of Toronto Press.

Mill, J.S. (1843) *A System of Logic*, in *Collected Works*, vols VII–VIII. Toronto: University of Toronto Press.

Mill, J.S. (1848; 1849; 1852) *Principles of Political Economy* in *Collected Works*, vols II–III. Toronto: University of Toronto Press.

Mill, J.S. (1851) Review of Newman's *Political Economy*, *Westminster Review* 56, in *Collected Works*, vol. V. Toronto: University of Toronto Press.

Mill, J.S. (1870) 'Letter to the General Council of the International Workingmen's Association', after 23 July 1870, in *Collected Works*, vol. XXXII. Toronto: University of Toronto Press.

Mill, J.S. (1873) *Autobiography* and *Literary Essays*, in *Collected Works*, vol. I. Toronto: University of Toronto Press.

Mill, J.S. (1879) 'Chapters on socialism', in *Collected Works*, vol. V. Toronto: University of Toronto Press.

Robbins, L. (1961) *The Theory of Economic Policy in English Classical Political Economy*. London: Macmillan.

Ryan, A. (1970) *The Philosophy of John Stuart Mill*. London: Macmillan.

Schumpeter, J.A. (1950) *Capitalism, Socialism and Democracy*. New York: Harper.

Schumpeter, J.A. (1954) *History of Economic Analysis*. New York: Oxford University Press.

Schwarz, P. (1972) *The New Political Economy of J.S. Mill*. London: Weidenfeld & Nicholson.

Sugihara, S. (1973) *Mill and Marx* (in Japanese). Kyoto: Minerva-shobou.

Thompson, W. (1822) *Labour Rewarded*. London: Longman, Hurst, Rees, Orme, Brown & Green.

Weber, M. (1949) *The Methodology of the Social Sciences*, trans. and ed. E.A. Shils and H.A. Finch. Glencoe: Free Press.

10 A bioeconomic Marx–Weber paradigm

Akitoshi Suzuki

Introduction

The Japanese reception of Marx has employed a framework conceptualised as 'Marx and Weber'. This framework is accepted not only as a confrontation between the two but also as a complementarity, balancing Marx's cosmopolitan idealism with Weber's nationalistic *Realpolitik*. There have been two phases in the way that Japanese social scientists used this complementarity. The reception of Karl Marx, begun in the 1930s and continuing until the 1960s, was the first phase, marked by both confrontation and complementarity. This ambivalence between repulsion and absorption characteristically appeared in the 'dispute on Japanese capitalism' of the interwar period. The *Rōnō* school portrayed the Japanese economy as a developed form of capitalism following the Meiji Restoration; accordingly the next major goal for social movements would be a total reformation of society in terms of socialism (Morris-Suzuki 1989: 87). The opposing *Kōza* school maintained that insofar as the Meiji Restoration was not a bourgeois revolution and was instead the substantial completion of an absolutist military regime, the task of social movements would be, in the first instance, the consolidation of modern capitalism, and only in the second instance, a socialist reformation (Morris-Suzuki 1989: 83). The latter school had implicitly adopted certain Weberian perspectives in order to conceptualise a bourgeois revolution as the primary task. Complementary to Marx, Weber emphasised the historical emergence of liberal civil society and economics, which Marx had analysed historically and evaluated negatively in his chapter on 'primitive accumulation' in *Capital*. According to *Kōza* school tactics, the introduction of Weber's perspective into Marx's views was not absurd. This was the first Marx–Weber paradigm. However, the Japanese polity then turned into a pseudo-Bonapartist regime at the time of World War II, instead of establishing a liberal economic society.

Japanese society has lately experienced liberal democracy and economy through post-war political and economic reforms (see Kersten 1996; Morikawa 1992). Civil rights and national wealth have increased in scope in line with rapid economic growth from the 1960s. Accompanied by economic strength, Japan returned to international society as a developed country. Just as revolutionary passions, caused by poverty and diluted by wealth, seemed to fade from the minds of even Marxists, a new mode of thinking called 'third world theory' emerged beginning in the 1970s (Amin 1976; Frank 1978). Third world theorists, who intended to transform Marxist theory, while keeping to a developmental interpretation, asserted that the revolutionary passions in the international working classes have survived in underdeveloped countries, whereas these passions have ceased in developed countries. They supposed that the world working class is now in opposition to the capitalist class. However, it can be said that this theory is really only the international version of former Marxist theory, albeit intensified with a nationalistic perspective. Contrarily, Wallerstein, who is occasionally classified as a third world theorist, introduced Weber's onto-genetic perspective into his own 'world-system theory', which generated the concept 'historical capitalism' (Wallerstein 1974). This is the second Marx–Weber paradigm, which argues that socialism will not emerge spontaneously through the contradictions between global productive powers and modes of production, but rather that it will be realised historically as a single world government.

The dispute concerning Japanese capitalism

Japanese socialist movements began in the Meiji era with anarcho-syndicalism, helped along by Christian humanism (Morris-Suzuki 1989: 74–5). After the success of the Russian revolution in 1917, Bolshevism was introduced. The struggle between anarchism and Bolshevism resulted in a victory for the latter. Another dispute immediately broke out between two oppositional factions within triumphantalist Bolshevism itself: the confrontation between the *Rōnō* and *Kōza* schools. *Rōnō* refers to a monthly magazine *Workers/Peasants* (*Rōnō*). *Kōza* refers to the serial publication of *Lectures on the Developmental History of Japanese Capitalism* (Morris-Suzuki 1989: 82–3). Within this controversy, *Rōnō* argued that the Meiji regime was a completely modern government owing to its policies, which accelerated the liberation of agrarian land, the enlargement of the money economy and the equalisation of tax burdens. They also claimed that the seigniorial regime, which had its origins in *Tokugawa* Japan, had completely collapsed, and further that there was a rising bourgeois class manipulating a revived ancient monarchy (the Emperor-system). Consequently they asserted that the urgent aim of socialist movements had to be a socialist revolution, following the 'single-step strategy', which required a unified front recruited from anti-establishment groups, with a crucial role for proletarians (Uno 1980: xii–iv). By contrast, *Kōza* emphasised that after the Meiji Restoration the regime was a semi-feudal absolutism rather than totally bourgeois. The seigniorial system established in

Tokugawa Japan had been replaced with a semi-modern landlordism, which emerged with the conversion of the former upper-peasant stratum into parasitic landowners (Otsuka 1969b: 272). These landowners and also financial capitalists, who were former merchants, constituted a ruler class, which manipulated a revived emperor (*Tennō*) as an arbitrator protected by a state bureaucracy of ex-samurai. Consequently *Kōza* maintained that socialist movements had to accept the 'double-step strategy': first, the bourgeois revolution, through which they would smash absolutism and consolidate the position of independent farmers and manufacturers; and then, second, a socialist revolution. They concluded that highly distinct vanguard forces, rather than a unified political front, were the way to accomplish this.

A Weberian perspective

The theoretical leaders of the *Kōza* school, who devoted themselves to studying the nature of the Meiji regime, sympathised with Weber's writings insofar as he was crucially concerned with why and how a Western civil society had emerged, and why and how a progressive bourgeois revolution had been completed. Marx's writings, by contrast, simply assumed the existence of such a society and that attendant social reforms had already been instituted. Marx's main theme was why and how a supposedly harmonious civil society could actually be a brutal capitalist society. These differential aspects led to the production of the first 'Marx and Weber' framework in the Japanese context. Refining Weber's *The Protestant Ethic and the Spirit of Capitalism*, Otsuka conceptualised an 'industrial middle stratum' (Otsuka 1982: 13, 24, 167), whose development not only defeated parasitic landlordism and anachronistic financial capitalists but also produced an advanced civil society, endorsed by manufacturing and agricultural middle strata. According to Otsuka, the progressive trade between independent farmers and manufacturers enlarges not foreign markets but domestic ones, eventually promoting a nationalistic bourgeois revolution, which in turn produces an ideal civil society among nations. In the contrary case, the development of trade between landowners and commercial capitalists facilitates foreign trade, which maintains and enforces a typical semi-feudal economy and society in the home country (Otsuka 1982: 27–8). Otsuka reinforces his view by quoting Marx's words:

> The transformation from the feudal mode of production is two-fold. The producer becomes merchant and capitalist, in contrast to the natural agricultural economy and the guild-bounded handicrafts of the medieval urban industries. This is the really revolutionizing path. Or else, the merchant establishes direct sway over production. However much this serves historically as a stepping-stone ... it cannot by itself

contribute to the overthrow of the old mode of production, but tends rather to preserve and retain as its precondition.

(Marx 1975: 332–3)

Against international trade, Otsuka emphasised the significance of the national economy, composed of three main sectors: agricultural, manufacturing and commercial, along with the enlargement of inland trade and markets, all making progress proportionately. Otsuka confirms that the development of capitalism can proceed favourably only by preserving normal industrial configurations. By contrast, when the industrial configuration of a national economy becomes distorted and cannot retain its normal configuration, the development of capitalism not only has to stagnate to this extent but also has to relinquish the common national interest which sustains democracy, so that the national economy itself loses its independence, issuing in total depression (Otsuka 1969a: 121)

Otsuka's views have had an enduring impact on the Japanese reception of Weber. Until the end of World War II, the industrial middle stratum has scarcely existed in Japanese society, the components of which were independent farmers and manufacturers. What prevailed instead were, on the one hand, parasitic landowners and an exploited peasantry, and on the other hand, financial capitalists (*Zaibatsu*) sponsored by state authorities and supported by their subcontractors (see Morikawa 1992: 3–4; Lockwood 1998: 45). Therefore Otsuka's strategy for urgent social reforms had to make a detour, fixing on independent middle farmers and manufacturers at first, and then afterwards dissolving this formation into progressive capitalists and diligent labourers, from which a mature working class eventually completes a socialist revolution.

Pseudo-Bonapartism

Enlightened members of the Japanese ruling class recognised very well how important it was that landowners returned their land to the peasants as soon as possible, in order to end oppressive landlordism. There was a danger that the peasantry would unite with the working class if land-hunger were not assuaged, thus bringing down the regime. They also recognised that the mainstay of the *ancien regime* was the landowner class, without which it would fall to another kind of disaster, a civil society based on freedom. The Japanese ruling class faced a dilemma: giving in to land-hunger on the part of the peasantry, or giving in to the landowning class which wanted additional rents. They steered towards expedient reforms by creating middle size owner-farmers, without expunging parasitic landlordism. They avoided a crisis in landlordism by a plan for dissatisfied peasants and craftsmen to colonise Manchuria, thus breaking up any potential unity between the peasantry and the working class.

Moreover, it could be said that up to the end of World War II Japan had scarcely generated any independent middle manufacturers with their own stock and capital. The Japanese manufacturing sector had only comprised, on the one hand, huge and privileged conglomerates, and, on the other hand, innumerable petty factories bound together with subcontracts. The latter could not fully function as subcontractors who could demand terms, but were forced instead to contribute very high industrial rents to master companies, rather like peasants in the agricultural sector (see Ohkawa and Rosovsky 1998: 68–9). It is unequivocal that this misery was another version of landlordism, but in the industrial sector. If these manufacturers aimed to be owner-entrepreneurs, they could always go abroad and launch their own companies. Growth within the home market, by contrast, was always threatened by the prerogatives of huge corporations.

From *Shōwa*-era depression to the end of World War II, the Japanese regime was a pseudo-Bonapartism. Bonapartism, so called, refers to a regime in which an apparent arbitrator, working as a puppet of the military powers, constitutes his polity by taking advantage of the standing confrontation between bourgeoisie and proletariat. Pseudo-Bonapartism, on the other hand, refers to a regime in which a semi-feudal arbitrator constitutes his polity by taking advantage of the standing confrontation between a semi-feudal bourgeoisie and a semi-feudal proletariat (Kersten 1996: 146, 151–3). The latter is the deformed instance, in which the bourgeoisie compromises in its struggle against feudal powers. The semi-feudal arbitrator seeks to maintain his position by trading the complaints of the semi-feudal proletariat (peasantry and petty craftsmen) off against their independence and freedom to move their businesses abroad (colonisation). Thus domestic contradictions were exported, and state enterprise was destined to dissolve under pressure from major world powers.

Moderno-centralism and world capitalism

After World War II, Japanese society accepted the political restoration, which comprised three major components: agrarian reforms, social reforms, and economic reforms. The first and second agrarian reforms were radical because they confiscated agrarian land from conventional landowners and then distributed it gratis to the former peasantry, with the result that they eventually became independent owner farmers (Chira 1982). Successive social reforms confirmed extensive rights for labourers: the right to organise trade unions, the right to strike and so forth (Morris-Suzuki 1989: 105). The Japanese economy thereby generated free labourers in a service sector. Economic reforms successfully dissolved some of the huge patrimonial conglomerates (Morikawa 1992: 114–19), which had dominated the greater part of the economy during the ancient regime. They were broken up into many individual companies, which could no longer monopolise the Japanese market. This reform also brought free trade and competition into the Japanese economy (Morikawa 1992:

237–9). Accordingly innumerable small and middle-size but independent manufacturers developed. Otsuka projected the 'spirit of capitalism' onto these owner-manufacturers and owner-farmers as the basis for growth in national wealth, which resulted from continuing nationalistic policies that produced a favourable balance of trade. However, the fact that this success resulted from a rapid economic growth and enrichment moderated any enthusiasm for a further socialist revolution, as had been promised in the 'double-step strategy' of the *Kōza* school. This is why Otsuka and his colleagues were said to be moderno-centralists by their opponents (Kersten 1996: 117).

Uno, one of the successors of the *Rōnō* school, asserted that Marx's thought had to be divided into three major components: pure theory, stages-theory and the empirical analysis of actual circumstances, on the basis of the former two kinds of theory (Uno 1980: xxii–xxiii). According to Uno, pure theory refers to the economic theories demonstrated in *Capital*, accessed through the deletion of the historical descriptions in *Capital* and through the recovery of consistency in pure theory. Uno argued that the age of capitalism comprised three different stages with regard to economic policies: mercantile, liberal and imperialist. However, he adverts that this is not a demonstration of the validity of economic theory but rather an historical account of economic policies at each stage. Uno criticised Marx for confusing theoretical analysis and historical description in his thought, and emphasised that each should be treated separately, whereas Marx combined the two aspects arbitrarily (Albritton 1986: 36–8). Uno proposed that the analysis of status quo will emerge from his frame of reference.

Uno is also notable for his international perspective, emphasising that capitalism has held to its original international character. He criticises Otsuka's analysis of capitalism for its nationalistic point of view, whereas it really requires an international aspect. Uno argues that we should treat modern capitalism as world capitalism, in which some national capitalisms are sub-components. It could be said that in the Japanese context Uno's criticism of Marx and Otsuka was a seedbed for the forthcoming theory of underdevelopment and dependence. Uno concludes:

> Specialized branches of political economy ... must all presuppose the stages-theory of capitalist development; for these specialized branches study the various aspects of the capitalist economy ... in the light of the world-historic 'type' ... *Finally*, with all these preparations, political economy can apply itself to its ultimate aim, namely, the empirical analysis of the actual state of capitalism either in the world as a whole or in each different country.
>
> (Uno 1980: xxiii)

World-systems theory

It is notable that Uno's unique interpretation of Marx's writings, especially his world perspective on capitalist economy, revitalised Otsuka's nationalistic interpretation. However, Uno's conception of world capitalism implies international capitalism, rather than world capitalism, and it leads to the view that each capitalist nation state formed in modern times will gradually generate an interrelationship that will eventually complete a single system of world capitalism. This means that although modern capitalism was born as national capitalist systems, it gradually comes to bear the character of global capitalism. By contrast world-system theory, which arose in the 1970s, differs from Uno's theory discussed above. Among the many world-system theorists, let us choose Wallerstein, who emphasised that 'historical capitalism' was formed, not as an aggregate of national economies, but rather as a single global system, strictly a 'world-system'. This was a unique historic occurrence emerging from a unique historical constellation that succeeded the disruption of feudalism in the West (see Wallerstein 1995; 1979: 161–2). The 'European world-economy' was born from the Atlantic trading region. Economic players in Europe, Africa and the Americas regarded it as an inland sea. Historical capitalism thus emerged as a profit-pursuing system, in contrast to the house-holding system that formerly existed in the 'core region'. Wallerstein points this out:

> I believe it is most plausible to operate on the assumption that the 'crisis of feudalism' represented a conjuncture of secular trends, an immediate cyclical crisis, and climatological decline. It was precisely the immense pressures of this conjuncture that made possible the enormity of the social change.
>
> (Wallerstein 1974: 37)

It was absolutely not the case that national capitalisms consolidated into nation states, which grew gradually, and then enclosed the region. Wallerstein proposed instead that this 'developmental perspective' on history should be replaced by his 'world-system perspective' (Wallerstein 1979: 155). He suggested that historical capitalism is an historically 'individual' instance, in Weber's sense of the word 'individual'. Weber explains:

> But it too concerns itself with the question of the *individual* consequence which the working of these laws in a unique *configuration* produces, since it is these individual configurations which are *significant* for us. Every individual constellation which it 'explains' or predicts is causally explicable only as the consequence of another equally individual constellation which has preceded it.
>
> (Weber 1946a: 73)

Wallerstein abandoned a nomological view of history, which Marx himself adapted in his interpretation of human history, and consequently converted to an idiomatic view of history, which we can trace back to Weber's writings. Whereas the global conception of historical processes that we find among other third world theorists maintains a version of the successive conception of historical development, Wallerstein rejects this developmental and nomological view. The other third world theorists were convinced that the world would be more and more divided into world-bourgeoisie and world-proletariat, and that therefore this confrontation would spontaneously produce world-socialism, conceived as a resolution of global contradictions (see Amin 1976: 293–5; Frank 1978: 146, 171). Wallerstein suggests instead that the people of the world will be more and more divided into world-bourgeoisie and world-proletariat, and that this confrontation will produce a new idea (much like Weber's prophecy), which will instantiate a form of socialism founded on a single world government (Wallerstein 1995: 123–4). Weber indicates something similar:

> Not ideas, but material and ideal interests, directly govern men's conduct. Yet very frequently the 'world images' that have been created by 'ideas' have, like switchmen, determined the tracks along which action has been pushed by the dynamic of interest.
>
> (Weber 1946b: 280)

An evolutionary view of economic history

Wallerstein actually produced a fusion between Marx and Weber, which represents another Marx–Weber paradigm, in accordance with both the rejection of the 'developmental' stages-theory and the introduction of 'historical constellations' of 'individual' instances. This simultaneously involves the abandonment of a nomological view of history and arrives instead at an acceptance of a typological view. As an advocate of developmental theories, Marx declares: 'In broad outline, the Asiatic, ancient, feudal and modern bourgeois modes of production may be designated as epochs marking progress in the economic development of society' (Marx 1987: 263). He continues:

> No social formation is ever destroyed before all the productive forces for which it is sufficient have been developed, and new superior relations of production never replace older ones before the material conditions for their existence have matured with in the framework of the old society.
>
> (Marx 1987: 263)

Wallerstein totally denies this perspective and defines a social formation instead as an historical 'individual' instance (Wallerstein 1979: 142–3). His reversal, however, creates another problem: how a fusion between the typological and developmental perspectives might be possible via a trade-off. Wallerstein asks himself:

> But can there be the laws in the unique? There has been one 'modern world' ... It was here that I was inspired by the analogy with astronomy which purports to explain the laws governing the universe, although (as far as we know) only one universe has ever existed.
>
> (Wallerstein 1974: 7)

Weber solved this problem in such a way that each historical 'individual' instance is unpredictably connected with historical configurations known as 'historical switches', and that some major or a great many minor instances may constitute the mainstream or many sub-streams in universal history. Weber's solution to this problem has been visualised through Karl Jaspers's world-schema (Jaspers 1953: 27). If we accept that this schema is the heir to Weber's vision of the historical process, universal history will then be treated as divergent metamorphoses of generic social and economic systems. This leads eventually not only to another version of the linear developmental stages-theory, which is incompatible with any concept of extinction, but it also helpfully removes from the typological perspective the idea that each type of rational system is absolutely 'individual' (see Boulding 1993: 525–6). Yet the typological approach itself requires rational types to be constructed in independence from each other, namely in a way which does not require any connections between them. A further disadvantage of the typological approach is the presupposition that rational types are static structures which circulate without evolution or other changes. It is evident that we lose historical connections and evolutionary aspects with this approach.

The question of the relationship between these two approaches is still equivocal in Wallerstein's world-system theory. In order to solve this problem, we propose the classification of all economic systems into five species: mini-systems; bureaucratic world-empires; feudalistic world-empires (now dissolved); world-economies; and world government (see Figure 1 below). Because the systems exist as individual social species (see Toynbee 1988: 45, 52–3), they have no certain historical order of development. While they are represented below as the ovals whose lengths indicate their life spans, their widths indicate their relative period of dominance. These species not only rise with innovations but also fall with routinisations in a sequence of genesis, growth, decline and extinction. These species evolve or undergo other changes (see Koslowski 1999: 323). However they also generate innovations in Schumpeter's sense:

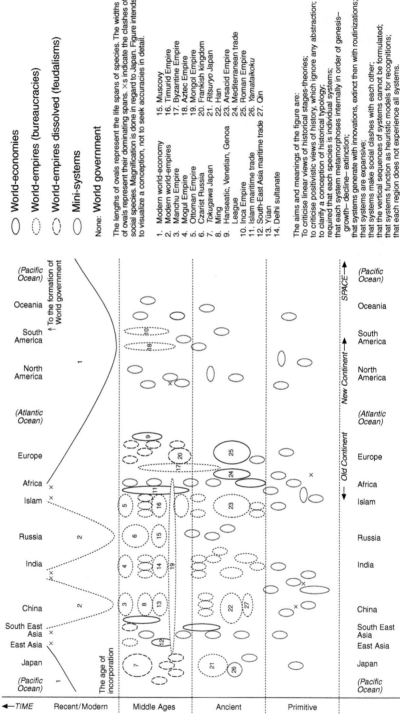

○ World-economies

◌ World-empires (bureaucracies)

◌ World-empires dissolved (feudalisms)

○ Mini-systems

None: World government

The lengths of ovals represent the life spans of species. The widths of ovals represent their dominating spans. ×'s indicate the clashes of social species. Magnification is done in regard to Japan. Figure intends to visualize a conception, not to seek accuracies in detail.

1. Modern world-economy
2. Modern world-empires
3. Manchu Empire
4. Mogul Empire
5. Ottoman Empire
6. Czarist Russia
7. *Tokugawa Japan*
8. Ming
9. Hanseatic, Venetian, Genoa League
10. Inca Empire
11. Islam maritime trade
12. South-East Asia maritime trade
13. Yüan
14. Delhi sultanate
15. Muscovy
16. Timurid Empire
17. Byzantine Empire
18. Aztec Empire
19. Mongol Empire
20. Frankish kingdom
21. *Ritsuryo Japan*
22. Han
23. Arsacid Empire
24. Mediterranean trade
25. Roman Empire
26. *Yamataikoku*
27. Qin

The aims and meanings of the figure are:
To criticise linear views of historical stages-theories;
to criticise positivistic views of history, which ignore any abstraction;
to clarify a conception of historical typology;
required that each species is individual systems;
that each system metamorphoses internally in order of genesis–growth–decline–extinction;
that systems generate with innovations, extinct then with routinizations;
that systems are expansive;
that systems make social clashes with each other;
that the vertical sequences of systems cannot be formulated;
that systems function as heuristic models for recognitions;
that each region does not experience all systems.

By this we should mean that economic development is not a phenomenon to be explained economically, but that the economy ... is dragged along by the changes in the surrounding world, that the cause and hence the explanation of the development must be sought out side the group of facts which are described by economic theory.

(Schumpeter 1951: 63)

Provided that the (x) time-axis represents historical eras from primitive to recent, and that the (y) space-axis represents the geography of major global regions, we can plot these species onto these coordinates. As a result, we can constitute a historical typology which supports the analytical merits of both the evolutionary and typological perspectives (Ghiselin 1999: 21).

Global perspectives

In conclusion, we can make a number of predictions concerning world government. All nation states have been formed from movements, which have abolished regional polities, ranging from tribal to territorial states, including intermediate forms. We believe that today we face certain parallels, which lie between the development of nation states and that of world government. Accepting a global point of view, we regard the status of the present world as a decentralised feudal world, which will complete its role with the emergence of a centralised single polity: world government. It has been beneficial for us to replace some decentralised territorial governments with unified centralised nation states, which have nationalistic perspectives. It will similarly be beneficial for us to replace some decentralised territorial nation states with a unified centralised world-state (O'Hara 2000: 216–17, 300–1). We observe that the processes of political unification along the lines of national agendas repeats itself on a global scale. Finally we will have institutions such as a world parliament, administration, court, police and armed forces in a future world government. Present-day nation states, sooner or later, will be demoted to the level of local governments.

Wallerstein's conception of world government remains unclear. He writes: 'The forms of a socialist world order ... are very unclear, and it seems to me futile to predict' (Wallerstein 1984: 57). While he does not discuss world government in detail, he points out certain defects in the

Figure 10.1 Conceptual figure concerning bioeconomic view of history in regard to socio-economic species. Suzuki improved from Wallerstein 'A world-system perspective on the social sciences', in *The Capitalist World-Economy*. Cambridge: Cambridge University Press, 1979, 152–64.

world economy with respect to its 'universalism', which we interpret as a principle dependent on 'formal rationalities' in Weber's sense (Weber 1978: 85–6). If world government were antagonistic to the world economy, its guiding principle would be 'individualism', which is dependent on Weber's 'substantial rationalities' (Weber 1946b: 331). However, we cannot discuss these details here. Moreover, we wonder whether we will need a new single religion, which will unify all present-day world religions, in advance of the establishment of world government (we do not exclude such possibility). Nevertheless this might require a new political idea transcending all jealous intolerance of national, ethnical, religious and regional differences. It will not be the idea which will reign over all the differences. It will instead be an idea which accepts all the differences in accordance with individualism. The substance of this idea will be loose and defensive in character but will require the conservation of individual diversities as a first priority.

References

Albritton, R. (1986) *A Japanese Reconstruction of Marxist Theory*. Basingstoke: Macmillan.

Amin, S. (1976) *Unequal Development*. Sussex: Harvester.

Boulding, K.E. (1993) 'The basic evolutionary model,' in V. Witt (ed.) *Evolutionary Economics*, 25: 523–47. Aldershot: Edward Elgar.

Chira, S.D. (1982) *Cautious Revolutionaries: Occupation Planners and Japan's Post-war Land Reform*. Agricultural Policy Research Center.

Frank, A.G. (1978) *Dependent Accumulation and Underdevelopment*. London: Macmillan.

Ghiselin, M.T. (1999) 'Darwinian monism: The economy of nature', in P. Koslowski (ed.) *Sociobiology and Bioeconomics*. Berlin: Springer-Verlag, 7–24.

Jaspers, K. (1953) *The Origin and Goal of History*. London: Routledge & Kegan Paul.

Kersten, R. (1996) *Democracy in Postwar Japan*. London: Routledge.

Koslowski, P. (1999) 'The theory of evolution as sociobiology and bioeconomics: a critique of its claim to totality', in P. Koslowski (ed.) *Sociobiology and Bioeconomics*. Berlin: Springer-Verlag, 301–28.

Lockwood, W. (1998 [1954]) 'Foundations of industrialism: the Meiji era', in P. Drysdale and L. Gower (eds) *Routledge Library of Modern Japan*, vol. 1, part 1. London: Routledge, 23–54.

Marx, K. (1975) *Capital*, vol. III, in K. Marx and F. Engels, *Collected Works*, vol. 37. Moscow: International Publishers.

Marx, K. (1987) *A Contribution to the Critique of Political Economy*, in K. Marx and F. Engels, *Collected Works*, vol. 29. Moscow: Progress Publishers.

Morikawa, H. (1992) *Zaibatsu*. Tokyo: University of Tokyo Press.

Morris-Suzuki, T. (1989) *A History of Japanese Economic Thought*. London: Routledge.

O'Hara, P.A. (2000) *Marx, Veblen, and Contemporary Institutional Political Economy*. Cheltenham: Edward Elgar.

Ohkawa, K. and Rosovsky, H. (1998 [1973]) 'A historical introduction', in P. Drysdale and L. Gower (eds) *Routledge Library of Modern Japan*, vol. 1, part 1. London: Routledge, 55–69.

Otsuka, H. (1969a) *Kokumin Keizai (National Economy),* in *Otsuka Hisao Tyosakushū (Collected Papers of Otsuka Hisao)*, vol. 6. Tokyo: Iwanami Shoten, 1–123.

Otsuka, H. (1969b) 'Zettai-ōsei Seiritsu no tameno Kyakkanteki Shojōuken' (Objective Circumstances for the Formation of Absolutism), in *Otsuka Hisao Tyosakushū (Collected Papers of Otsuka Hisao)*, vol. 7. Tokyo: Iwanami Shoten, 270–9.

Otsuka, H. (1982) *The Spirit of Capitalism: The Max Weber Thesis in an Economic Historical Perspective.* Tokyo: Iwanami Shoten.

Schumpeter, J. (1951) *The Theory of Economic Development,* in *Harvard Economic Studies*, vol. 46. Cambridge: Harvard University Press, 1–255.

Toynbee, A.J. (1988) [1972]) *A Study of History.* London: Oxford University Press and Thames & Hudson.

Uno, K. (1980) *Principles of Political Economy.* Sussex: Harvester.

Wallerstein, I. (1974) *The Modern World-System 1.* New York: Academic Press.

Wallerstein, I. (1979) *Capitalist World-Economy.* Cambridge: Cambridge University Press.

Wallerstein, I. (1984) *The Politics of World-Economy.* Cambridge: Cambridge University Press.

Wallerstein, I. (1995 [1983]) *Historical Capitalism with Capitalist Civilization.* London: Verso.

Weber, M. (1930) *The Protestant Ethic and the Spirit of Capitalism.* London: Allen & Unwin.

Weber, M. (1946a) *The Methodology of Social Sciences.* New York: Free Press.

Weber, M. (1946b) *From Max Weber: Essays in Sociology.* Oxford: Oxford University Press.

Weber, M. (1978) *Economy and Society*, vol. 1. Berkeley: University of California Press.

11 Japanese 'cultural eclecticism' and a reinterpretation of Marx and Keynes on the instabilities of capitalism

Makoto Noguchi

Introduction

Cultural eclecticism is often said to have taken root in the Japanese mentality, technology and way of life. After the opening of Japan to the world at the end of the Tokugawa shogunate, the Japanese wavered between adopting Western civilisation and rehabilitating the Japanese pre-modern tradition. At this time they sought some method of integrating modernity and pre-modernity by blending one with the other, or by finding a framework within which to arrange the configuration for the two. In applying Marx's theories of the capitalist economy to analyse pre-war Japanese capitalism, Japanese Marxists faced the similar problem of how to handle the conflict between modernisation and backwardness. Needless to say, Marxists qualified pre-modernity as backwardness in modernisation, whilst cultural eclectics considered pre-modernity to be of no less positive value than modernity. Thus the problem that Marxists and cultural eclectics each tackled was quite different in kind. Nevertheless, the common origin of the problems they addressed lay in the historical conditions in which Japan was placed as a latecomer in capitalist development. Modernity existed side by side with pre-modernity in pre-war Japanese capitalism. This dual character of Japanese capitalism occupied the interest of both Marxists and cultural eclectics.

This chapter attempts to explain how methodological eclecticism grew constructively from the Marxian controversy about the dual character of pre-war Japanese capitalism. As the reception of modernity in Japan led to cultural eclecticism, so the introduction of Marxian theories into Japan also led to methodological eclecticism. I also reinterpret methodological eclecticism as a constructive method of integrating heterogeneous doctrines or theories of capitalist development. Finally I apply this method to evaluating apparently conflicting views of Marx and Keynes on the instabilities of capitalism. In this way, I indicate a new way to incorporate Keynesian insights into the Marxian framework for historical and structural interpretations of capitalist development.

Constructive eclecticism and Uno Kōzō's interpretation of pre-war Japanese capitalism

Marx formulated the economic law of motion of capitalist society, modelling it on England as his best case. In the preface to the first German edition of his masterwork, *Capital*, we find some hints of the methodological procedure through which Marx intended to conceptualise the mode of capitalist production. Marx says that he treats England as the 'classic ground' for the capitalist economy in just the same manner as the physicist 'makes experiments under conditions that assure the occurrence of the phenomenon in its normality'. Although he concedes that such a late-comer as Germany suffers 'not only from the development of capitalist production, but also from the incompleteness of that development', he believes that 'the country that is more developed industrially only shows, to the less developed, the image of its own future' (Marx 1996: 8–9).

Because Japan underwent industrial development much later than Germany, what the history of English capitalism suggests about the future of Japan was a more complicated issue for Japanese Marxists than the future of Germany was for Marx. In rural districts in pre-war Japan there were still many tenant farmers. The growth of the factory system was rapid, but it did not absorb the adult work force sufficiently to alleviate the plight of the surplus rural population. Among Marxist intellectuals a great controversy arose as to how they could explain the historical character of the landlord–tenant relationship in the light of Marx's doctrines in *Capital*. On one side, the Kōza-ha school argued that the landlord–tenant relationship was feudal and constituted the basis of the absolutism of the Emperor system. According to this view, the Japanese working class needs a bourgeois revolution in order to replace feudal relations with democratic relations prior to a socialist revolution. On the other side, the Rōnō-ha school insisted that the tenant system rested on a modern contractual relationship, because the landlord owned and rented commodified land, though they conceded that tenant farming was transitional between feudalism and capitalism. In this view, further capitalist development in Japan, sooner or later, would polarise the peasantry into capitalists and wage workers, and would therefore necessitate a socialist revolution. 'Kōza-ha' means 'lectures school'. The name refers to a series of books, *Nihon shihonshugi hattatsushi Kōza*, or *Lectures on the History of Japanese Capitalist Development*, published in 1932–33. 'Rōnō-ha' refers to 'worker-farmer'. That name ocomes from the title of a socialist journal, *Rōnō*, first issued in 1927. For a bird's-eye view of the controversy, see Nagaoka (1984).

Uno Kōzō did not take part in this controversy, but it was profoundly significant for the grand design of his political economy. It seemed to Uno that Kōza-ha and Rōnō-ha implicitly shared the same method of evaluating the backwardness of Japan in capitalist development, even though both were divided on how to interpret peculiarities of Japanese capitalism.

They both directly contrasted Japan as a less developed country with England as an advanced country, which Marx had regarded as typical of capitalist development. The only frame of reference that they relied on to explain the remnants of pre-capitalist (or non-capitalist) relations, such as tenant farming, was the model of capitalist development explicitly stated in Marx's *Capital*. This was one in which England evolved into a tripartite society composed of capitalists, workers and landlords. In discussing the theory of ground-rent, Marx did as classical economists did, and assumed the universal establishment of capitalist production in all industry, including the agricultural sector (Marx 1998: 608–800). The crucial difference of opinion between Kōza-ha and Rōnō-ha was eventually reduced to this: while the former looked upon the remnants as feudal shackles put on development, the latter treated them as transitional phenomena in the development process.

In a pre-war work Uno cast doubt on the method of applying the development model to Japanese capitalism. His theoretical and methodological interest focused on the prolonged existence of an enormous number of tenant farmers (Uno 1935). Why did rapid industrial development not hasten the differentiation of the peasantry? The doctrines of the two Marxist schools did not offer a satisfactory answer to this question. If feudal fetters had crippled capitalist development, pre-war Japan would not have experienced rapid industrialisation. Inversely, if the remnants of tenant farming had been transitional, they would have been promptly cleared away through rapid industrialisation. Uno investigated the historical and structural conditions, which had eroded the applicability of Marx's development model to Japanese capitalism. It was to two conditions specific to pre-war Japan that Uno attached the highest importance. The first was the rank of latecomer in the capitalist world economy, and the second was the mature formation of finance capital. A backward country which seeks to transform itself into a capitalist society under fierce international competition cannot choose but to transplant to itself a state-of-the-art method of production from an advanced country. Such a pattern of development based on the importation of modern industry not only presupposes a large population of peasants inherited from pre-capitalist society, but also hinders the differentiation of the peasantry, and hence the disappearance of the landlord–tenant relationship. The first reason for this is because the most advanced technology available to a latecomer is much more labour-saving than the one adopted in the classical capitalism of 19th century England, The second reason is because the early introduction of the joint-stock company and the mature formation of finance capital both serve as a powerful lever for catching up; this view bears a close resemblance to Alexander Gerschenkron's model of catching up. This at once brings about a high degree of capital composition through capital centralisation, and it gives rise to a tendency for the state to protect the peasantry politically as a bulwark against growing threat from urban workers. The preservation of the surplus rural population, largely composed of tenant farmers, makes it possible to provide modern industry with an inexhaustible pool of low-wage workers and therefore to bolster international competitiveness in manufacturing industries. Thus the convergence model cannot apply to the process of catching up in latecomer capitalism. This was the outcome of Uno's investigation.

My interest here lies in Uno's methodological innovation rather than in his analysis of pre-war Japanese capitalism. He implicitly distinguished three levels of analysis in attempting to grasp the peculiarities of Japanese capitalism. The first is an application of theories developed in Marx's *Capital*, which are founded on an assumption of development into a tripartite society derived from classical capitalism. The second is an application of the model of capitalist development in latecomer capitalism, the typical pattern for which was Germany, according to Uno. The third is an explanation for the actual situation of Japanese capitalism. This view was methodologically new, but it was not until the works of the post-war period that Uno formulated it more clearly. In the elaborated formulation of Uno's methodology, the first level of analysis is remoulded into principles of pure capitalism as a thoroughly commodified society; the second level into a 'stages theory' that accounts for three historical transformations of capitalism (mercantilism, liberalism and imperialism); and the third level into an analysis of the actual economy, such as the world economy and the national economy, respectively (Uno 1962). However, I think that his pre-war unformulated considerations are heuristically more meaningful than his post-war refined schemata. The core of Uno's methodological contributions is the idea that between the realisation of the essence of the capitalist economy and a causal explanation for its polymorphous existence, there must be an intermediate or middle-range level of analysis. Capitalism has changed its structural character and pattern of motion involving local or national transmutations. The thesis applicable to one specific pattern is therefore not equally true of another. In addition to this, seemingly similar social relationships or economic policies acquire different meanings in diverse capitalist formations. Uno, for instance, took special note of the fact that the peasantry was a heavy drag on primitive accumulation in mercantilist England, but, in laissez-faire England, it was nearly transformed out of existence, and thereafter, in imperialist Germany and pre-war Japan, it was contrarily preserved from decline. Free trade in agriculture assumed quite different roles in laissez-faire England and in laissez-faire Germany, and so did protectionism in agriculture in mercantilist England and in imperialist Germany. In his work Uno (1935) alluded to these facts as well.

Uno's design for a methodology in political economy should be interpreted within the broader context of modernisation in Japan. By introducing a middle-range level of analysis as a sub-frame of reference, Uno opened up the possibilities of explaining polymorphous capitalist development from the viewpoint of an eclectic integration of hetero-geneous elements, such as modern and pre-modern, capitalist and non-capitalist, and market and non-market factors and institutions. He did this while basing his work on some of Marx's insights in *Capital*. The constructive formation of Uno's methodological eclecticism seems to be analogous to that of cultural eclecticism in pre-war Japan (for example, the eclecticism of Fukuzawa Yukichi and Nitobe Inazō), in the sense that either would not have been created if Marxists and cultural eclectics had not embraced the conflict between modernity and pre-modernity. For a discussion of Japanese eclecticism, see Tsurumi (1960). Tsurumi characterised the eclecticism of Fukuzawa and Nitobe as an adaptive attitude of mind towards the situation. Following Tsurumi's terminology, we define Uno's eclecticism as a methodologically adaptive attitude in research. Thus for Japanese eclecticism, the reality of Japan as a latecomer was the common historical environment where the possibility of polymorphous modernity, on the one hand, and polymorphous capitalist development, on the other hand, was grasped by cultural eclectics and Marxian economists respectively. For the possibility of an alternative modernity based on Japanese culture, see Feenberg (1995).

Marxian theory of capitalist accumulation and crisis

By adopting an intermediate or middle-range level of analysis as a sub-frame of reference, we can also comprehend how instability or crisis in capitalism takes on diverse forms in different situations. Capitalism, in its essence, inherently contains the seeds of instability that germinate and develop into serious crises as a consequence. But which seed of instability grows into what sort of crisis depends on historical and structural conditions that transform capitalist development. This problem is at the middle-range level of analysis. What has been regarded often carelessly as a general theory, I will bring down to the middle-range level, and will investigate its conditions of applicability.

In Marx's *Capital*, we find two significant views of the causes of instability that lead to a crisis. In addition to those two, Marx had at least two other views on the instability of the capitalist economy. One concerns the disproportion between various branches of production, and the other concerns the falling rate of profit as a result of the higher composition of capital. However, the first is rectified through a process of apportionment that springs continually from disproportion. The second is only a super long-run tendency that capitalist development might demonstrate under some specific conditions.

One view concerns a possibility that hoarding or a strong demand for money may greatly diminish demand for commodities and bring out a general glut. Marx, intending a criticism of 'law of markets' enunciated by James Mill and J.-B. Say, states that while 'no one can sell unless some one else purchases', 'no one is forthwith bound to purchase, because he has just sold'. As a result, he says, 'if the split between the sale and the purchase become too pronounced, the intimate connection between them, their oneness, asserts itself by producing a crisis' (Marx 1996: 123). The other view is about over-accumulation that causes an acute shortage of inputs, especially labour-power and then a tight profit squeeze. Marx argues that there would be 'absolute over-production of capital' when capital would have grown so rapidly in proportion to the labouring population that 'the increased capital produced just as much, or even less, surplus-value than it did before its increase'. In such a case, he says, 'a portion of the capital would lie completely or partially idle' and 'the other portion would produce values at a lower rate of profit'. This damage to the accumulated capital, 'augmented by the attendant collapse of the credit system', develops into 'violent and acute crises' (Marx 1998: 250–3).

The former view has some connections with Keynesian themes, but, in *Capital* it is suggested without detailed explanation. Marx did not further examine the case where 'no one is forthwith bound to purchase', although he referred to the limits of the 'consumer power of society based on antagonistic conditions of distribution' (Marx 1998: 243). If anything, he largely disregarded the possibilities for disproportion between aggregate demand and aggregate supply. The idea of deficiency in investment demand plays no part in his theorising on capital accumulation and the rate of profit. His theory of over-accumulation, from this point of view, seems to be conceptually incompatible with Keynes's theory of effective demand, which rests upon inquiry into the problem of deficiency in investment. When 'absolute over-production of capital' arises, the rate of profit falls because of an increase in wages due to a shortage of the labour force, and not because of a deficiency in aggregate demand. It remains for us to tackle the question of how to establish the framework within which the two views are made compatible.

Marx had good reason to think that even if there should be any deficiency in aggregate demand, it would be not more than the limits to the consumption power of society. In the 19th century England that Marx treated as a classic model of capitalism, a plan for industrial investment and saving was put into practice, roughly speaking, by the same agent. The major part of fixed investment in manufacturing was financed by an individual proprietorship or a partnership on its own risk. This means that a decision on investment was simultaneous with a decision on saving, and that savings that were not invested were never made. In such an economy, it is natural to think that a decrease in investment simply results from a fall in profit (or surplus-value) that is the main source of savings, and not from a deficiency in investment demand. Even the greatest opponents of the law of markets such as Simonde de Sismondi and Thomas R. Malthus, who ascribed a general glut to insufficient consumption, did not clearly distinguish between investment and saving. In short, the historical condition of classical capitalism is one material reason why Marx could not fully understand the possibility of insufficient investment.

However, the applicability of Marx's theory of over-accumulation is not necessarily confined to classical capitalism. Marx set forth a highly abstract condition as a fundamental premise for the concept of 'absolute over-production of capital'. In his argument, it is supposed that over-accumulation relative to the labour force builds up to such an extent that additional capital produces no surplus value. This presupposition implies that capital expands beyond the limits to the supply of labour. Such a condition, whether or not each decision on investment and saving was made by the same agent, exists in practice whenever a bottleneck in the labour supply occurs. This is one seed of instability that capitalism inherently contains. Nonetheless, how a pattern of instability or crisis develops then hinges on diverse historical-structural conditions of over-accumulation. The pattern of over-accumulation crises in Marx's time is different from that of Keynes's era when a decision on investment was separated from, and independent of, a decision on saving. Laissez-faire capitalism of Marx's time witnessed a periodic panic repeated in a nearly ten-year cycle. Though easily accessible to a disposable industrial reserve army, classical capitalist firms, in the last phase of business prosperity, faced a shortage in the work force in some labour markets, and thereafter fell into a deflationary crisis. By contrast, welfare capitalism in Keynes's era attained long-lasting growth and thus experienced no panics, but, in its last phase, it has instead plunged into an inflationary over-accumulation crisis. The crucial condition that led to the bifurcation in the pattern of over-accumulation crises is the changed relationship between investment and saving. We must specify it more precisely at the middle-range level of capitalist development.

The Keynesian theory of investment and profit in relation to Marxian political economy

Marxian political economy can supplement what Marx grasped with insights gained from Keynesian writings. Some anti-mainstream versions of Keynes's theories of investment, finance and profit are quite helpful in reinterpreting Keynes along Marxian lines. I am concerned here with three pioneers in post-Keynesian or neo-Keynesian economics only: Kalecki, Kaldor and Minsky. They all laid special emphasis on an autonomous role for investment in capitalist development, and they elucidated the patterns of crises that Marx failed to apprehend, owing to the limitations of his model of classical capitalism. Kalecki and Kaldor argue that economic fluctuations are due to investment activity which is not only independent of ex ante profits, but also captures ex post profits. Kalecki shows that under the condition of underutilised capacity, adverse income distribution may trigger a downward cumulative process, while Kaldor explains how at full capacity conflicts over income distribution fuel a wage-price spiral. Minsky calls heterodox economists' attention to the problem of investment financing, and warns against debt deflation, which is offset by forced sale of assets that aims to clear cumulative bad debts. The argument in this section draws largely on Noguchi (1990).

Some transformations of capitalism invalidated the assumption of the simultaneous identity between saving and investment. First, emerging large-scale industry needed a new method of financing that satisfied requirements of massive fixed investment. The new development of heavy and chemical industry as well as the hugely increased capital requirement in the existing light manufacturing outdated the form of the individual proprietorship or the partnership in many enterprises, and undermined the industrial basis of commercial credit such as bill discounting in the banking. Adoption of the form of the joint-stock company and acquisition of extensive industrial credit allows an enterprise access to vast outside funds in addition to its own savings from ex ante profits. Consequently, fixed investment, financed from this widely available outside savings, displays a growing tendency to fluctuate independently of a change in ex ante profits. Second, in large-scale industry, it takes a prolonged gestation period for a huge project to materialise. In other words, an implementation of a plan for installing fixed equipment lags, by a long lapse of gestation, behind a decision on it. The past decision to invest is executed in the present when the investment produces incomes including wages and profits (and therefore savings). Determination of profits or savings is no longer simultaneous with determination of investment. Rather, the past decision to invest determines the present profits or savings, and the ex ante profits or savings does not determine the present investment. Clearly, this is diametrically opposed to the view of Marx or classical economists about capital accumulation.

Kalecki (1971) formulated the above-mentioned anti-classical view of investment in lucid terms. Suppose that both prices and wage rates are stable, savings from wages are zero, and the labour force as well as fixed equipment is underemployed. This supposition reflects the capitalistic reality that business activities in large-scale industry are rarely if ever enhanced to the limit of productive capacity. In Kalecki's simplified model, investment determines profits that equal savings, for workers only consume what they earn. Given the profit share of aggregate income (or the wage share), present profits, as determined by past decisions to invest, in turn determine national income or national output. The Kaleckian formulation of the causal relationships among investment, profits and outputs indicates a possibility that a change in profit share may create another source of instability. If wage-price relations change during the gestation period of investment, previously designed plans for investment are implemented under present but altered circumstances. When wage rates are reduced in relation to prices, the investment realises fewer outputs than it could if they were not reduced, even though profits are constant. Aggregate demand, consisting of investment and consumption, always realises an equal aggregate output. Because investment is unchanged and consumption decreases as a result of wage reductions, aggregate output decreases through wage reductions, while profits remain fixed. Thus, as long as investment is a given, an increasing profit share paradoxically results in decreasing outputs. During a longer period when investment fluctuates, decreasing outputs have an adverse effect on capital accumulation. A decrease in output causes capacity utilisation to deteriorate and discourages a capitalist's motivation to invest. By contrast, in the framework of Marx's theory of over-accumulation, a higher profit share implies a strong incentive to active investment, instead of a collapse. For Marx what is seemingly a driving force in capitalism is for Kalecki a crisis.

While Kalecki aimed chiefly to enquire into the pattern of fluctuation that investment demonstrates in conditions of capitalist stagnation, Kaldor showed a greater interest in the autonomous dynamics of investment when capitalism is expanding. Kalecki's well-known article published in 1943, *Political Aspects of Full Employment*, however, engaged with the problem of a wage-price spiral under a full-employment regime (Kalecki 1971: 138–45). In this article, he poses the question why the capitalist economy cannot sustain full employment. In answering it, he argues, on the one hand, that the strengthened bargaining power of workers arouses a fear of lax factory discipline and political instability in capitalists, and, on the other hand, that a fear of vicious inflation will arise among rentiers. This insight, anticipating the end of the long-lasting post-war boom, represents a starting point for discussing the issue that Kaldor had to raise in examining the conditions for stability when capitalism is expanding. In his pathbreaking paper which framed the neo-Keynesian theory of income distribution, Kaldor boldly adopted the assumption that the capitalist economy operates at full capacity and full employment (Kaldor 1955). Under a full-capacity, full-employment regime an autonomous change in investment demand is subject to supply constraints, and consequently prices will fluctuate. If the ratio of investment to output (i.e. the investment rate) rises, prices will increase in relation to wage rates, and vice versa. In this way, expanded investment, through a reduction in real wage rates, produces an equivalent in increased savings. The flexible relation of prices to wage rates will persist as long as an increase in prices relative to wage rates permits a rise in the investment rate. However, as soon as workers resist a reduction in real wage rates, a price rise will be followed by an increase in wages, and the economy will fall into a vicious spiral of wage-price increases. In such cases, expanded investment will be unable to produce increased savings. This problem is closely associated with the question that Kalecki raised earlier, though somewhat optimistically. Kaldor thought that credit tightening might remove the possibility of a wage-price spiral. Marx might have interpreted this in the context of over-accumulation. However, the instability of a full-employment regime as anticipated by Kalecki and Kaldor tends to accelerate inflation, which is different from the deflationary over-accumulation crisis that Marx described.

Kalecki and Kaldor each elucidate a different mechanism through which investment determines profits in, respectively, stagnating and expanding phases of capitalism. They take much the same view as far as investment financing is concerned. The way we think that demand for investment funds will be satisfied makes a big difference to the analysis of investment financing. Some suppose that the total money supply is exogenously determined by monetary authorities. Others argue that investment funds are endogenously supplied according to demand. Keynes (1973) accepted the former view. By contrast, Kalecki and Kaldor based their theories of effective demand upon the latter view. Minsky (1986), who propounded the 'financial instability hypothesis', advanced the view that the money supply is under institutional constraints and therefore can be endogenously created only to the extent that the institution permits. In this view, the historical evolution of financial institutions alters the elasticity of the money supply (or the supply of funds for investment financing). Whether or not banking provides such funds for investment financing more or less in response to demand depends on the institutional framework. However, as economic expansion proceeds, the evaluation of investor's and lender's risks becomes less cautious, and, sooner or later, banking begins to deviate from the existent norm. Bankers then respond more speculatively to bolder demand by borrowers for funds. In such an expansionary phase, financial innovation imparts an elasticity that the system could not otherwise acquire. This increased financial flexibility transforms a robust financial structure into a fragile one. The enhanced availability of financing permitted by innovation affords borrowers surplus funds that can be invested in various financial assets such as outstanding stocks, existing bonds and real estate, in addition to fixed equipment for production. Consequently soaring asset prices boost the expected rate of return on investments and the value of collateral for loans, and thus fosters short-term financing of portfolio investment, which renders the financial structure highly vulnerable to a rise in interest rates. Loan commitments made in the past are fulfilled only by debt repayments drawn from the present profits. If a steep rise in interest rates or a great decrease in the availability of short-term financing takes place at a time when present profits cannot even meet interest payments, borrowers and bankers will be forced to sell asset holdings or collateral assets in order to fulfil past commitments. This will induce a collapse in asset prices, which in turn may trigger debt deflation, that is, a vicious cycle of accumulating bad debts and aggravating deflation. The financial instability hypothesis indicates not only a process of financial destabilisation which an over-accumulation crisis or an unstable-investment crisis may involve, but also a possibility that a financial crisis may develop independently of any acute difficulty in accumulation or investment of real (not monetary) capital.

Understanding instabilities in modern capitalism: through the eyes of Marx in the spirit of Keynes

The historical and structural conditions that are vitally significant for the development of a Marxian-type over-accumulation crisis are different from those that cause a Kaleckian-type downward vicious circle or a Kaldorian-type wage-price spiral or a Minskyian-type financial instability. A particular type of instability corresponds to the specific structural conditions of modern capitalism that produce such instability. However, any of these crises has some fundamental root in either or both of two major sources of instability inherent in the nature of capitalist accumulation. In integrating Keynesian insights into a Marxian framework, it is essential to distinguish between identifying the universal cause of the instability inherent in capitalism and analysing the diverse appearances of the instability at the middle-range level of capitalist development. Okishio (1986) shows almost no attention to the middle-range level of capitalist development, although in Japan he represents one of the few systematic attempts to interpret Keynes along Marxian lines. Ōuchi (1970) bases his work on Uno's methodology and makes an attempt to incorporate Keynesian policy into a middle-range theory of state monopoly capitalism. However, he explains the role of this policy chiefly in terms of a reduction in real wages through inflation which relieves over-accumulation relative to the labour force. This argument contains an inconsistency, because over-accumulation under a Keynesian policy regime makes a reduction in real wages difficult and so sparks a wage-price spiral. The two are associated with what Marx calls the 'absolute over-production of capital' (a crisis of over-accumulation) and represents the case where 'no one is forthwith bound to purchase' (an unstable-investment crisis). The first, for Marx, means over-accumulation relative to the labour force, but this can be regarded in the broad sense as a supply-side constraint representing a drag on capital accumulation, even if a labour shortage is a major factor. The second generally implies the unstable nature of aggregate demand, but specifically indicates the instability of investment that constitutes the major fluctuations. Taxonomically, the Kaleckian downward spiral in stagnating capitalism belongs to the unstable-investment crisis. The Kaldorian wage-price spiral in expanding capitalism has a dual character, which manifests itself, on the one hand, as an over-accumulation crisis insofar as it is due to over-investment, but, on the other hand, as an unstable-investment crisis insofar as investment overshoots apart from ex ante produced profits. The Minskyian financial crisis can be contingently linked to either of two essential patterns of instability, over-accumulation or unstable investment. The Minskyian financial crisis can be combined with any of the three patterns: Marxian over-accumulation; Kaleckian downward spiral; and Kaldorian upward spiral. Here I will touch on the relation between the Minskyian financial crisis and the Marxian crisis of over-accumulation. It seems that in *Capital* Marx never admits the possibility of an autonomous change in investment except in floating capital. This supposition is approximately consistent with the reality of classical capitalism. When the financing of floating capital is expanded by banking, independently of ex ante profits, an over-accumulation crisis can be 'augmented by the attendant collapse of the credit system', as Marx says.

From the historical-structural viewpoint, the Great Depression that began with the stock market crash in 1929 can be seen as a typical case of a Kaleckian crisis. The boom prior to the crash brought unprecedented prosperity to America, but profit share tended to rise and therefore the power of workers to spend remained feeble. It was this set of historical circumstances that set off the downward spiral of investment and consumption after the stock market crash. Minskyian instability exacerbated that vicious cycle, and as a result the crisis culminated in debt deflation. By contrast, the source of the Kaldorian crisis can be traced back to the institutional peculiarities of the post-war growth regime that warded off the downward spiral. Long-lasting post-war growth was underpinned by a rise in the wage share during the downturn and by a rise in profit share during the upswing. A higher wage share prevented the downward spiral, and a higher profit share ensured accelerated investment and technical progress. The institutional foundation of that mechanism was laid by a workable compromise between capital and labour, despite conflicting interests as to whether to raise productivity or to improve the standard of living. However, over-accumulation when capitalism is expanding undermined its foundations, and so led to the wage-price spiral. In this case Minskyian instability also greatly destabilised the inflationary process. The stagflation of the 1970s is a historical instance that typically illustrates the Kaldorian crisis. Itoh (1980) evinces the first attempt to interpret the inflationary crisis of the 1970s according to Marx by using Uno's theory of over-accumulation. However, more emphasis must be placed on the inflationary spiral resulting from an independent increase in investment demand, combined with supply-side over-accumulation. To sum up, both patterns of crisis, Kaleckian and Kaldorian, represent two potential instabilities, downward and upward, that lurk in modern capitalist systems with highly developed large-scale industrial sectors.

What pattern then can we use to capture new crises that emerge under neo-liberalism after stagflation? Neo-liberal capitalism has experienced an idiosyncratic pattern of crises that may be called a polymorphous appearance of Minskyian instability. Past decisions on debt bind the present production of output flows just as decisions on investment do. This is the fundamental cause of Minskyian instability. This cause of financial instability, combined only loosely with either supply-side or demand-side constraints on real investment, can result in diverse forms of the instability. The historical background of such appearances lies behind rapid financial innovation, as is shown by capital market liberalisation that is taking place globally. Corporate governance that aims at the maximisation of shareholder value is prevailing today, and the scourge of downsizing is nearly wiping out the institutional foundation that previously prevented a downward spiral. Consequently contemporary capitalism seems always threatened with the risk of debt deflation. Nonetheless, Keynesian policy almost never commands much attention because current circumstances are different from the 1930s. The globalisation of capital has spurred on the process of deindustrialisation in advanced countries, and also the process of industrialisation in emerging economies. Over global networks, capital can flexibly use differentiated labour at low cost. Deindustrialisation may relieve advanced countries of some of the inevitable conflicts with organised workers that large-scale industry produced. These circumstances have weakened the social basis for Keynesian policy. For all its relaxation of supply-side constraints on accumulation, neo-liberal capitalism has suffered from repeated financial instabilities, and will also do so in the not too distant future. Investment financed through capital markets exhibits shortsighted behaviour, and therefore responds over-sensitively to short-term changes in profits. Even a mild symptom of some difficulty in real accumulation might arouse a collapse in portfolio investment, and eventually lead to a great contraction in real investment. The Asian financial crisis of 1997–98 exemplifies this possibility. However, it is merely one of the different paths within Minskyian instability leading to a decline in real investment.

Conclusion

Uno's methodological eclecticism, developed from the Marxist controversy concerning the history and development of Japanese capitalism, provides rich potentialities for the reconstruction of Marxian political economy after *Capital*. His innovation in the methodology of political economy consists in introducing a middle-range level of analysis, enabling us to interpret different phases of polymorphous capitalism as diverse transformations in its evolutionary process, instead of reducing capitalism simply to one model. This view is antithetical to a monistic vision of capitalism. The historical evolution of Japanese capitalism from pre-modernity to modernity sparked considerable doubt as to whether every society would converge into a unique model of modernity or capitalism. For the issue of convergence or divergence in the most recent phase of Japanese capitalism, see Noguchi (2001). Uno, in answer to this question, advanced the view that capitalisms transform themselves and diverge in the middle-range world where a latecomer competes with a frontrunner. I have reinterpreted Uno's method of middle-range analysis and applied it to diverse instabilities in capitalism. This method will also be effective in other cases where bifurcations in development or structural differences in capitalism are important.

References

Feenberg, A. (1995) *Alternative Modernity*. Berkeley: University of California Press.

Itoh, M. (1980) *Value and Crisis: Essays on Marxian Economics in Japan*. New York: Monthly Review Press.

Kaldor, N. (1955) 'Alternative theories of distribution', *Review of Economic Studies* 23: 83–100.

Kalecki, M. (1971) *Selected Essays on the Dynamics of the Capitalist Economy*. Cambridge: Cambridge University Press.

Keynes, J.M. (1973) *The General Theory of Employment, Interest and Money*, in *The Collected Writings of J. M. Keynes*, vol. 7. London: Macmillan.

Marx, K. (1996) *Capital*, vol. 1, in K. Marx and F. Engels, *Collected Works*, vol. 35. New York: International Publishers.

Marx, K. (1998) *Capital*, vol. 3, in K. Marx and F. Engels, *Collected Works*, vol. 37. New York: International Publishers.

Minsky, H. (1986) *Stabilizing an Unstable Economy*. New Haven: Yale University Press.

Noguchi, M. (1990) *Modern Capitalism and Theories of Effective Demand* (in Japanese). Tokyo: Shakai Hyōron-sha.

Noguchi, M. (2001) 'The evolution of Japanese capitalism under global competition', in G. Hodgson, M. Itoh and N. Yokokawa (eds) *Capitalism in Evolution*. Cheltenham: Edward Elgar.

Okishio, N. (1986) *Contemporary Capitalism and Economics* (in Japanese). Tokyo: Iwanami Shoten.

Ōuchi, T. (1970) *State Monopoly Capitalism* (in Japanese). Tokyo: Tokyodaigaku Shuppan-kai.

Tsurumi, S. (1960) 'Eclecticism in Japan: an essay on Nitobe Inazō', in *Lectures on the History of Japanese Modern Thought*, vol. 3 (in Japanese). Tokyo: Chikuma Shobō.

Uno, K. (1935) 'The Formation of capitalism and the process of differentiation of the peasantry', *Chūō Kōron*, Nov., reprinted in *Collected Writings of Uno Kōzō*, vol. 8 (in Japanese). Tokyo: Iwanami Shoten.

Uno, K. (1962) *Methodology of Political Economy* (in Japanese). Tokyo: Tokyodaigaku Shuppan-kai.

Part IV

New horizons of Marxology

12 The Brussels Democratic Association and the *Communist Manifesto*

Akihiro Matoba

Introduction

About 150 years have passed since the publication of the *Communist Manifesto* in 1848. Countless research papers dealing with it are available to this day. The *Communist Manifesto* has sold more than ten million copies all over the world. However, it is quite surprising that most writers address it from the standpoint of the history of Marx's and Engels's ideas. The point of view that research papers on the *Communist Manifesto* should be about the development of these ideas is not always wrong, given that it was Marx and Engels who wrote the (anonymously published) *Communist Manifesto*, and that it was Marx and Engels who published its second edition under their own names in 1872. Judging by the enormous impact that their ideas have had on the world in the 20th century, the fact that only two names are mentioned when talking about the *Communist Manifesto* is understandable.

But if we reflect carefully upon the 1848 situation, we will find out that the authors of the *Communist Manifesto* were not Marx and Engels, but the Communist League. The *Communist Manifesto* was the Manifesto of the Communist League written by Marx and Engels at the request of Schapper, their superior. Contemporary readers probably understood it as the manifesto of the international union between democrats and communists, as well as a party programme for the Communist League. The purpose of this chapter is not to emphasise that it was not Marx and Engels alone who wrote the *Manifesto*, but rather that we can better understand the contemporary implications of the *Manifesto* by reading its first edition, which did not include the authors' names. We can also consider the strategic implications of the *Manifesto* for communists and democrats during the 1848 revolutions, as well as Marx's and Engels's opposition to democrats as political opponents.

This chapter intends chiefly to describe relations between the Communist League and the Democratic Association, i.e. the Belgian democrats in Brussels (De Maesshalck 1983; Matoba 1995; 1996). It is necessary to analyse the relations between the Communist League and its main affiliated society (the Fraternal Democrats) and the Democratic Association, in order to understand the contents of the *Manifesto*, which was a programme for the Communist League. Above all, the Communist League had close relations with the Democratic Association in Belgium, of which Marx, who gave final approval to the *Communist Manifesto* before its publication, was vice-president, and with most of the members of the German Workers' Association in Brussels, as well as with members of the communist leagues who had participated in it.

The Fraternal Democrats

The reason why Brussels became one of the centres of the Communist League was not just that its main members, like Marx, Hess, Engels, Bornstedt and Weerth, were already resident there. Indeed, Marx and Bornsted came to live in Brussels after having been deported from Paris in 1845, and they played a major role in establishing the Communist Correspondence Committee, the German Workers' Association and *Deutsche-Brüsseler-Zeitung*.

However, we must bear in mind that the German workers' movement needed Belgian comrades, like V. Tedesco and P. Gigot, who had welcomed Marx and Engels. And we should not forget their personal exchanges with Belgian democrats like L. Jottrand, L. De Potter and C. Spilthorn. Tedesco and Gigot were not only close friends of Marx and Engels, but also had strong ties to the Communist League and were involved in the composition of the *Communist Manifesto*. Through them, the members of the Communist League were able to develop relations with the Belgian democrats.

Marx and Engels also supported friends such as Heinrich Bürgers, Franz Raveaux and Karl D'Ester, who were candidates to local elections in Cologne. The local election in Cologne was held in 1846, and the amount of minimum tax sufficient to obtain suffrage was fixed at over 400 talers a year. There were only 2,304 electors in Cologne out of a population of 80,000 (Seyppel 1991: 39). Their strategy was to back German middle class democrats, since neither suffrage nor eligibility was available to the lower classes. The Communist League was very interested in the Democratic Association because it had the same strategy.

Belgium obtained independence from Holland in 1830, but this revolution was not an easy one, and it created a great many victims. In the battle of September 1830 in Brussels 257 workers were killed by the Dutch Army (Bertrand 1906: 274). On 26 September 1830, after two months, Dutch troops left Brussels as the Dutch Orange regime collapsed there. Both democrats and conservatives had participated in this revolution for independence, the former wanting a republic and the latter wanting the continuation of monarchy. De Potter and C. Rogier joined the provisional government organised just after independence. That government was divided into two parts, one wanting union with France, and the other, independence for Belgium and a republican system of government.

In November 1830 the government drafted a constitution for a monarchy and decided to look for a new king. They had thus nipped democracy in the bud, and then De Potter made the following criticism: 'Did we need to shed blood to get such silly result?' (Bertrand 1906: 39). Leopold I, from Coburg in Saxony, ascended the throne on 4 June 1831. After that, Belgian politics developed around the union between the Liberal Party and the Catholic Party. In the 1830s, some Catholics created a new group of liberals under the influence of Lamenais, and they collaborated with the Liberal Party. In Belgium, socialist ideas had already sprouted in the 1820s through the influence of P. Buonorotti. The Delhasse brothers then became his successors. In 1831 a Saint-Simonian mission group led by H. Carnot and P. Leroux visited Brussels in order to spread their ideas in Belgium. In response to this action, the liberal Rogier, the Delhasse brothers, E. Dupéctiaux and L.A. Quetelet were quite active (Bertrand 1906: 101). Most of those who were significantly influenced were liberals. The Catholic Party was hostile to such action, and the union between the Liberal Party and the Catholic Party was nearly extinguished, especially owing to socialist proposals for community of goods and common property in women.

Though freedom of the press and association were guaranteed by the constitution of 1830 in Belgium, stamp duty and the price of newspapers were both very high, and the meetings of Saint-Simonians were always watched by the police. Therefore the lower classes, which were excluded from local elections, rose up to demand true freedom of association, universal suffrage, compulsory education, progressive taxation and the limitation of rights of inheritance (Bertrand 1906: 139).

In 1833, J. Kats founded the workers' Fraternal Association in Brussels (Bertrand 1906: 146). Its aim was to educate workers for the founding of democracy, and its activities were not far from those of a workers' educational association. We can find in their programmes some activities that are close to those of the democrats, despite the word 'workers' by which they differ. The articles of their programme in *Belgische Volksalmanak voor 1844*, written in the form of a catechism, were as follows:

(1) Principle of equality, (2) universal suffrage, (3) State Annual Expenditure paid by the rich class, (4) compulsory education and the guarantee of life to all children by the State, (5) the guarantee of the right to live to all citizens, (6) the organization of labor, freedom of association and trade, (7) the definition of the responsibilities of bureaucrats, (8) the separation of administrative power from legislative power and submission of the former to the latter, (9) freedom of

the press, festivals, public opinion, association and trade, (10) freedom of association and meeting to discuss the interests of the State, and to educate all citizens to political duties and the law.

(Bertrand 1906: 168)

The democrats differed from the liberals in that they aimed for an improvement in the economic inequality which was caused by liberalism, and the fundamental basis of this goal was much influenced by Saint-Simonism. We can find a sentence explaining the difference between liberals and democrats in *Le Catéchisme Démocratique* (1838), which was written by Alexandre Delhasse:

> Liberalism principally respects the individual reason and richness and it is delighted with the domination of the majority to establish the regime of the submission of the inferior class to the bourgeois. It starts from the antisocial and ambivalent principles to surrender the majority to the domination power of the privileged class. In other words, it starts from individualism which brings selfishness and exploitation of human beings by human beings.

(Bertrand 1906: 177)

The main bulletin of the democratic-socialist organisation was the *Débat Social*, edited by Barthes, Jottrand, the Delhasse brothers and Katz. This bulletin was very influenced by V. Considérant, who visited Belgium from 1838 to 1839 in order to spread Fourierism. Considérant came once more to Brussels in 1845 and then organised the congress in which Rogier, Dupéctiaux, Jottrand, Maynz and the Delhasse brothers participated (Bertrand 1906: 190). An article written by A. Delhasse about the congress was published in *Débat Social*. He said, 'The association will replace selfishness and all combat, and solidarity will unite all people and collect all interests. The meaning of Fraternity is the government of God on the earth' (Bertrand 1906: 192–3).

Until 1847 the democratic movements in Belgium were informed by the alliance of democracy with socialism, Saint-Simonism or Fourierism. In other words, 'democracy' in Belgium in those days was not far from that of socialism. The meaning of the word 'socialist' was naturally very close to that of 'democrat'.

The Democratic Association

The Democratic Association was born at the 'Workers' Banquet' held in Brussels on 27 September 1847 (Jottrand 1838, which includes documents concerning the contract between the Democratic Association and its members; *Deutsche-Brüsseler-Zeitung* 30 September 1847). This banquet was organised by Bornstedt, the editor-in-chief of the *Deutsche-Brüsseler-*

Zeitung, to promote international exchanges between workers. The number of participants at this banquet was 120, and its leaders were General F. Mellinet, Jottrand, J. Imbert and Engels (Bertrand 1906: 209). The Democratic Association thus had close relations with the German Worker's Association in Brussels from the very beginning.

The Democratic Association was founded on 7 November 1847. Its purpose was to associate itself with many fraternal organisations in Europe. Spilthorn, who made an address on 7 November 1847, explained that its aim was 'the fraternity of all people' and that there were no 'limits of nationality, profession and status' to the qualification of participants (Jottrand 1838: 41).

The main members of the administration were Mellinet, Spilthorn and Maynz, and its central committee included Jottrand and Katz, the Belgian democrats' leaders. The presence of interpreters means that this association was mainly multinational. This congress ended on 17 September 1845 with the approval of the contract of the association. The members with their signatures on the contract were Melinet, Imbert, Spilthorn, Maynz, Bornstedt, Heilberg, Kats, Marx, Lelewel, Weerth, Hess, Funck, Gigot, and so forth (Jottrand 1838: 44–5).

Members of the central committee were elected on 15 November 1845. Jottrand was the president, Marx and Imbert were the vice-presidents, A. Packard was secretary, Funk was treasurer, and J. Bejewel, G. Maynz, Spilthorn and G. Weerth were interpreters. The French General Mellinet of the central bureau became honorary president at the proposal of W. Wolff.

The first task of the Democratic Association was to support the nationalist movement in Flanders and the independence movement in Poland. At the third congress held on 28 November 1847, the appeal *From the Democratic Association founded in Brussels with the purpose of collaboration and fraternity of all people of Switzerland* was approved, and at the end we find the signatures of Jottrand, Mellinet, Imbert, Marx and Bornstedt. Furthermore, this appeal was also approved on 30 November 1847 at the German Workers' Association, in which Walla, the president, Moses Hess, vice-president, the treasurer Riedel and secretary Bornstedt signed it (Jottrand 1838: 53–4). The Democratic Association was also planning to strengthen its domestic collaboration by establishing relations with the Ageneses Association and Alliance. This Alliance, founded in the 1840s, was a liberal club and had more than 1,000 members (Bertrand 1906: 215–16). Its policy was to reduce tax, to improve the condition of the working class and to reduce stamp duty. It held a free congress in 1846. The Democratic Association also planned to improve its relations with the other democratic associations in Brussels, as well as with the democratic associations in Tourney, Liége and Ghent. It even made plans for an international congress in 1848 by appealing to the English Fraternal Association and the French Democratic Association (Bertrand 1906: 57). In this respect, the Democratic Association in Brussels was set to become a central organisation for democrats in Europe.

The Congress of the Democratic Association had to resolve language problems as the members of organisation were multinational. They could resolve such problems with the help of talented men like Spilthorn, who had mastered several languages (Bertrand 1906: 60). Concerning the German Workers' Association, Germans and Belgians could make themselves understood, thanks to talented men like the Belgians Gigot and Tedesco, who had mastered the German language.

After the 1848 revolution the political line of the Democratic Association was consistently peaceful. It had applauded the February Revolution of 1848 in France, but it maintained a neutral position afterwards. It was confident that 'The New French Revolution could not be a threatening to us' (Bertrand 1906: 64). Jottrand was also convinced that 'Belgium must be a Republic sooner or later' (Bertrand 1906: 68).

The major crisis of the Democratic Association was the Risquons-Tout Affair. As a result of the subsequent judgment, seventeen of the 32 accused were sentenced to death (Marx and Engels 1977: 404). But all sentences were subsequently reduced to lesser penalties. The police arrested Spilthorn and other important members. F. Becker, who had taken refuge in France, had a plan for invading Belgium to expel the king and to found a republic. Two thousand Belgians living in Paris gathered in arms near the national boundary and were planning to invade Belgium from Lille and Valenciennes. The village they invaded was Risquons-Tout, so they called the invasion after it. The problem for them was whether the members of the Democratic Association, including Spilthorn, had any connection with the affair. The possibility that Germans and other Belgians from the Democratic Association had participated in the revolt was slight. The book *Charles-Louis Spilthorn. The Affairs of 1848 in Belgium* (1872), written by Jottrand, demonstrates Spilthorn's innocence. The most important point for us is that Jottrand emphasised that the Democratic Association did not accept the use of force. The Democratic Association only aspired to the peaceful foundation of a republic, not a violent one.

The Democratic Association and Jottrand

The political programme of the Democratic Association was clearly embodied in the ideas of Jottrand. Felix Delhasse wrote that 'Jottrand considered freedom as the principle and the rule of human life, in other words, the whole of society' (Delhasse 1858: 14). Jottrand was therefore basically a liberal. He thought that Great Britain was the model that Belgium had to imitate. He claimed that Great Britain was a model for peaceful revolution in his *The Association of the People of Great-Britain and Ireland of 6th of August 1838 Proposed as a Model to Belgians*, published in 1838 (Jottrand 1872: 1). He claimed that this was necessary in order to guarantee freedom of the press and association and thus to catch up with Great Britain. He argued that Belgian liberals should take interest in the foundation of the Workers' Association of London, and that they should change from the politics of the privileged to the politics of the people (Jottrand 1872: 6–7).

Jottrand demanded the establishment of democracy and explained the requirements for a workers' government as follows:

> Labor is the only source of richness. Abolish the tax limitation on suffrage. Abolish the conscription system. The expenditure for political cost should be shared by the rich class. Improve or abolish the tax on consumption. The advanced law on inheritance should be introduced in such a way as to abolish the right to inheritance and to collateral inheritance. Property without heirs should revert to the State. Abolish the large land properties. Unite Capital with Labor. Workers should be concerned with the factory, workshop and management. The education of children should be paid for by the State to establish an equality in early life.
>
> (Bertrand 1906: 145–6)

These claims included an improvement in inheritance law, abolition of large landed properties, the foundation of workshops for workers and compulsory custody of orphans by the state. Jottrand fostered international collaboration in a way different from that proposed by workers. He wrote *Return to Belgium via Rheinland Geneva, Switzerland, Savoy, Piemonte, Marseille and the South-west of France starting from Antwerp* (1845), in which he claimed that Belgium, Prussian Rheinland, Baden, Switzerland and Savoy were little states independent from others, and that they had free constitutions and represented the future of European states (Delhasse 1858: 158). According to him, there were two types of political systems, Roman centralisation and Germanic decentralisation (Delhasse 1858: 156). He claimed that the latter was the true European political system. In that respect, the United States of America and Great Britain had in fact adopted the orthodox European political system. There was nothing better for establishing democracy than collaboration between states, such as that between the United States and Great Britain.

The Democratic Association and Marx

From the very beginning, the German Workers' Association in Brussels had close relations with the Democratic Association. The Democratic Association was divided into three sects. The first consisted of the members of the German Workers' Association, with Marx as leader and also including Engels, Weerth, and Wilhelm and Ferdinand Wolff. The second had Bornstedt as its leader, along with as F. Crüger and

L. Heilberg. The third was a neutral sect (Sartorius 1976: 2–3). The German Workers' Association was founded in August 1847 and consisted of 37 Germans, with Wallau as its President (Bertrand 1906: 208).

Marx was absent when the original congress of the Democratic Association was held in September of 1847. Engels wrote a letter to Jottrand to the effect that Marx was the most suitable representative of the German Democratic Association (Sommerhausen 1976: 170). As a result, Marx became vice-president in November 1847 as expected. A few years later, Jottrand wrote about Marx: 'In Belgium, Marx had not spread propaganda on his economy theory which made him famous later. He was not so famous in those days' (Jottrand 1872: 48–9).

Though Marx had already published his book *The Poverty of Philosophy* (1847) in Brussels and had given a lecture on *Wage-Labor and Capital* at the Workers' Association, he was not really known for more than his authorship of the *Speech on Free Trade* (1848), sold at 25 centimes, mostly to members of the Democratic Association. The lecture on free trade made an important contribution to the relationship between the Democratic Association and the Belgian liberals. Marx's view that the development of capitalism, as promoted by free trade, works to destroy feudalism and thus creates a true antagonism between capital and wage-labour, proved that a strategic reconciliation between liberals demanding free trade, the Belgian democrats and the workers' organisation was possible (Jottrand 1872: 59).

The most important role that Marx played in Brussels was as delegate to the general meeting of the Fraternal Democrats of London on 29 November 1847. At the same meeting of the Democratic Association, they expressed their gratitude to F. Flocon, who had supported the Democratic Association at the banquet in Dijon and they were thus positive about developing international collaboration (Jottrand 1872: 56). Marx attended the congress of Fraternal Democrats in November, after arriving in London (*Deutsche-Brüsseler-Zeitung* 9/12 December 1847; Nettlau 1919: 392–401). He spoke as follows:

> The fraternity and the cooperation of all nations is an expression of which all parties, particularly the bourgeoisie of Free Trade, profit today. In fact, there is a sort of fraternity among the bourgeoisies of all nations.
>
> (Sommerhausen 1976: 188)

Marx thus demanded the same fraternal union between all peoples as was the case with the bourgeois class all over the world.

> It is necessary for us to have solidarity of peoples' interests to cooperate. We must break the present condition of property to cooperate in their interests. For it means the exploitation of all people. The imme-

diate interests of all the working class depend on the destruction of the system of property. It is only the working class that should have such means.

(Sommerhausen 1976: 188)

Following Marx, Engels spoke as follows:

It is impossible for one nation to liberate itself while suppressing another nation. The liberation of Germany is not possible without that of Poland from its yoke. Therefore, Germany and Poland have a common interest. German and Polish democrats can cooperate with each other to liberate both nations.

(Sommerhausen 1976: 189)

Marx was referring to mutual international liberation, and he stressed international co-operation. Adolfe Barthes criticised Marx's opinion in the Belgian newspaper *Le Journal de Bruxelles* (Sommerhausen 1976: 190), complaining about the attendance of a German as a delegate for the Belgian Democratic Association. This criticism reflected the essence of co-operation at the Democratic Association. If the Democratic Association in Brussels had been only for Belgians, Barthes's claim would have been right. His claim must have stimulated nationalists in Flanders.

However, Marx replied at once to this claim in the *Deutsche-Brüsseler Zeitung* ('Remarks on the article by Adolphe Bartels'). He explained that the members of the Democratic Association consisted of a mixture of many nationals living in Brussels and that international co-operation was really the essence of the Democratic Association (Marx and Engels 1976: 402). Belgian Democrats had supported this. The climax of the honeymoon between the Democratic Association and foreigners like Marx was the New Year's Eve party of 1847. One hundred and thirty members of the Democratic Association attended this party, held at a restaurant that was the meeting point. This was a grand banquet where Marx's wife Jenny read poems while an orchestra played music so peaceful that it seemed the revolution did not exist.

The Democratic Association and the Communist League in Brussels

The German Workers' Association had meetings twice a week. Its aim was to educate workers and to promote exchanges between their families. Every Sunday, women attended this meeting and read poems aloud. On Wednesday, seminars were held, such as the one for Marx's lecture *Wage-Labor and Capital* (Bertrand 1906: 208).

We can read about the Workers' Association in the documents of Wilhelm Wolff which were confiscated when he was arrested in February of 1848, including a list of names from the German Workers' Association. Looking into this list, we find the names of Marx, Gigot, Wallau, W. Wolff, F. Wolff, Imbert, Bornstedt, Hess, S. Born and C. Vogler, totalling 91 members (Kuypers 1963b: 105).

The German Workers' Association participated in the foundation of an international democratic organisation after a meeting led by Bornstedt on 27 September 1847. Its approach resembled that of the Communist League of Fraternal Democrats and the Chartists in London. This was the strategy of the Communist League, rather than camouflage. Among its aims the Communist League planned to collaborate with the Democratic Association in Belgium to achieve a bourgeois revolution.

At a New Year's Eve party in 1847, Marx toasted the Democratic Association, and commented on the Belgian opposition to absolutism. He mentioned growing support for freedom of association and a constitution which would guarantee freedom of speech (Bertrand 1906: 209). Following Marx, Picard, a member of the Democratic Association, commented on the German contribution to the establishment of democracy and toasted the German Workers' Association. Then Lelewel stood up and expressed his sympathy for democratisation in Germany and his hatred for the political suppression of Poland. Later Bornstedt said that the way to revolution was through international co-operation and that the *Deutsche-Brüsseler-Zeitung* was the only newspaper for the proletariat.

The banquet continued until six o'clock in the morning, with elegant dancing and singing. In his closing address, Hess thanked women for their participation and said that he expected further participation of women in the movement. This banquet showed that the reality of the Workers' Association was far removed from the real situation of workers. Among the participants there were no proletarians, also known (in German) as *die Poebel*. Though I have explained that the German Workers' Association could not promote class struggle so long as proletarians did not take part in that kind of banquet, this group was so aristocratic that proletarians could not be expected to join. As a matter of fact, we cannot deny the aristocratic origin of the members of the Communist League in those days. In addition, we cannot deny that this aristocratic origin actually reflected the state of international democratic co-operation and circumstances of the bourgeois revolutions that arose in 1848.

However, relations between the German Workers' Association and the Democratic Association were about to go downhill. The political situation changed greatly when the Belgian government planned, under pressure from Prussia, to deport many Germans *(Deutsche-Brüsseler-Zeitung,* 20 January 1848). This included a ban on the circulation of socialist ideas into the German states and the deportation of members of the German Workers' Association.

The important problem at this point was the breakdown in relations between Jottrand and Marx. The split started with Marx's criticism of

Jottrand's claim in an article of 6 January 1847 in *Débat Social* in which Jottrand said that it was essential to protect the freedom of the Jesuits and of the supporters of absolutism. Marx replied: 'We cannot serve two masters at the same time' (de Potter 1848: 3). Jottrand's article gave the foreigners in the Democratic Association the impression that it had given Belgians priority over foreigners and that it had broken its pledge of international co-operation. Foreigners like Marx were discontented with the Democratic Association because they suspected that Belgian democrats had changed their policy in order to achieve a domestic consensus.

The changes in the political situation increased the severity of the split. One of these changes was the surveillance by the Belgian government of the democratic movement which was experiencing a surge on the second anniversary of the Crakow uprising in Poland on 16 February 1846. At the anniversary ceremony, on 22 February 1848, Marx explained (in his 'On the Polish question') that communism comprised an aspiration to abolish classes and class discrimination, and that consequently the establishment of democracy meant the abolition of class discrimination (Marx and Engels 1976: 545). The Belgian government took steps to suppress this movement. As a result, it increased the antagonism between the Democratic Association and the Workers' Association. However, both associations had the same purpose, which was to spread 'communism' or 'democracy' in Europe.

De Potter and the 1848 Revolution

The news of the February Revolution of 1848 in France arrived immediately in Brussels. De Potter wrote a pamphlet entitled 'What should we do? We must not hesitate to act' on 1 March 1848. He stated that 'We could legally improve, abolish, reform and change some fundamental laws according to the constitution, thorough legislative power, without a revolution', because there was already some freedom in Belgium (de Potter 1848: 3). 'They had violently upset the monarchy and changed the system of Government in the neighbouring country. Should we do the same?' (de Potter 1848: 3). He argued that Belgians should refuse a revolution, and dare to remain a monarchy, even though it had the possibility of choosing democracy (de Potter 1848: 5). Moreover, he argued that they should accomplish certain reforms within the limits of the constitution:

> Article 25: all powers come from the nation. Article 18: the press is free, Article 19: Belgians have the right to hold the meetings, Article 20: Belgians have the right of association. Article 21: Belgians have the right submit petitions to the authorities with one or more signatures.
>
> (de Potter 1848: 7)

These were the same ideas as those of the Democratic Association. Jottrand defended Spilthorn in court at the trial of the Risquons-Tout Affair. He claimed that the Democratic Association was completely different from a violent revolution. At the congress held on 28 February 1848, he decided to preserve the police force to maintain order in Brussels and to reform certain laws according to the constitution (Jottrand 1872: 63). Spilthorn was dispatched to Paris to explain to the revolutionaries that the Democratic Association was keeping a neutral position with respect to France and England. Apparently Jottrand also formed the assumption that the Belgian monarchy should evolve into a republic. The Workers' Association was opposed to a violent revolution, too. The Brussels police unfairly arrested Germans like Marx on suspicion of carrying arms and then expelled them from Belgium, against the optimistic expectations of the Democratic Association. This was surely pure fiction without evidence. In his article 'The Antwerp Death Sentences' of 3 September 1848, Engels claimed that democrats should never rise in arms, referring to Tedesco and General Melinet who were sentenced to death, but whose sentences were reduced (Marx and Engels 1977: 406).

Tedesco

Tedesco is one of those who have been completely forgotten in the history of the *Communist Manifesto* (Gaspar 1960: 664–9). There are no works referring to the relations that Marx and Engels had with Tedesco except those in Belgium. Tedesco was born in Luxemburg near Trier, and his father was a lawyer like Marx's. Some assert that their fathers were friends and that Marx and Tedesco also became friends. Even if it may not be so, they might have had a relationship. For example, someone asserted that it was Tedesco who brought the manuscripts of the *Communist Manifesto* to London to be printed (Gaspar 1960: 6). The person who brought them to London is still unknown, whereas the person (Friedrich Lessner), who brought them to the printing office, is known for certain. On the basis of Lessner's memoirs, the manuscript of the *Communist Manifesto* arrived at the printing office in London in February 1848, and the news of the February Revolution in France arrived soon after (Lessner 1907: 14). Tedesco translated the *Communist Manifesto* into French, and this was disseminated in Brussels in March 1848. However, he was arrested by the police on the 29 March 1848, so his translation was incomplete (Kuypers 1963a: 415). Because Tedesco's *Catéchisme du Prolétaire* was published in December 1848, and because its contents resembled that of the Manifesto, this small pamphlet was probably written when Tedesco travelled to London with Marx and Engels. That is why it was written as a catechism in a form resembling that of Engels's draft for the *Communist Manifesto*, so it probably constituted one of the draft versions of the *Manifesto*.

The *Catéchisme du Prolétaire* was published by the editorial committee of *Le Peuple* in Liège. It included 34 questions and answers. For example:

1. What are you?
   A[nswer]. I'm a Proletarian. Or if you want, in other words, a worker.
2. What is a proletarian?
   A[nswer]. A proletarian is a man who does not own enough of anything in his life today and who will not own enough of anything tomorrow. – Inheriting nothing in a society where man cannot be rich without labor, he can only have bread as long as he has a master.

(Tedesco 1849: 29)

Tedesco's view on how to overcome the domination of society by capital was no more than a political change achieved through universal suffrage, as advocated by de Potter. However, his opinions were not so different from those expressed in drafts for the *Manifesto* as *Confession of a Communist* (June 1847), the article published in the trial edition of *Kommunistische Zeitschrift* (September 1847) and *About Proletariat and Liberation by True Communism* (October 1847), written by Goertrek. The overall contents are not far from those of Engels's draft *The Principles of Communism* and of the *Communist Manifesto* itself (November 1847). If we distinguish between Tedesco's catechism and the others, we could say that the last two described social change through economic analysis. Therefore, his catechism must have been written before Engels's drafts and the *Manifesto*. If the contents of his catechism resembled those of the Democratic Association, his catechism may have been drafted in close relationship to it.

Tedesco's conclusion is as follows:

And you Proletarian, my brother, the child of many pains. Your incessant propaganda like your work finally reflects your sufferings. This power you spend for your master must be also that of your proletarian brothers. The undivided democratic and social Republic could be established through this holy alliance.

(Gaspar 1960: 43)

Tedesco expected that proletarian liberation might be achieved one day through patient opposition to exploitation. If this means the achievement of communism, his expectation is not far from that of the *Manifesto*.

Conclusion

This chapter has focused on the relations between the Belgian democrats and the communist movement in Brussels. The most important contribution from the Belgian groups to the German communist movements was the promotion of international co-operation across borders and an alliance between democrats and communists. Of course, the movements of the Communist League and the Fraternal Democrats in London were also international and democratic ones. However, the mutual influence developed in Brussels was quite stimulating and strong. Above all, Brussels was the city where Marx lived. His was the final editorial hand on the *Communist Manifesto*. At the same time, the relative position of Brussels in the German communist movement increased due to him. This is why the central bureau of the Communist League was moved to Brussels at the beginning of March 1848.

However, strangely enough, the role of German communist movements in Brussels was completely left out in the history of German communism as well as in accounts of the ideas of Marx and Engels. Lenin and Kautsky noted that the three sources of Marxism lay in German idealist philosophy, French socialism and English political economy, but we cannot find any reference to Belgium anywhere. I dare to say that one of sources of Marxism is Belgian internationalism and the alliance between democrats and communists.

References

Bertrand, L. (1906) *L'Histoire de la démocratie et du socialisme en Belgique depuis 1830.* Brussels: Dechenne.

De Maesshalck, E. (1983) *Karl Marx in Brussel (1845–48).* Brussels: BRT.

de Potter, L. (1848) *Que faut-il faire?, pas plus hésiter que s'agiter, mais agir.* Brussels: D. Raes.

Delhasse, F. (1858) *Ecrivains et hommes politiques de la Belgique.* Brussels: no publisher.

Deutsche-Brüsseler-Zeitung, 30 September 1847.

Deutsche-Brüsseler-Zeitung, 9/12 December 1847.

Deutsche-Brüsseler-Zeitung, 6 January 1848.

Deutsche-Brüsseler-Zeitung, 20 January 1848.

Gaspar, A. (1960) 'Le Manifeste du parti communiste et catéchisme du prolétaires de Victor Tedesco', *Socialisme* 41: 664–9.

Jottrand, L. (1838) *L'Association du peuple de la Grande-Bretagne et de l'Irelande au 6 août 1838, proposé pour modèle au peuple Belge.* Brussels: Leroux.

Jottrand, L. (1872) *Charles-Louis Spilthorn, Evénements de 1848 en Belgique.* Brussels: Ch. Janderauwera.

Kuypers, J. (1963a) 'Les liens d'amitié de Karl Marx en Belgique (1845–1848)', *Socialisme* 58: 410–21.

Kuypers, J. (1963b) 'Wilhelm Wolff und der Deutsche Arbeiterverein (1847/48) in Brüssel' *Archiv für Sozialgeschichte* III: 103–7.

Lessner, F. (1907) *Sixty Years in the Social-Democratic Movement*. London: The Twentieth Century Press.

Marx, K. and Engels, F. (1976) *Collected Works*, vol. 6. London: Lawrence & Wishart.

Marx, K. and Engels, F. (1977) *Collected Works*, vol. 7. London: Lawrence & Wishart.

Matoba, A. (1995) *Marx in Paris*. Tokyo: Ochanomizu Shobo.

Matoba, A. (1996) 'Marx and Brussels', in A. Matoba, T. Shibata and S. Murakami (eds) *Cities and Thinkers*, vol. 1. Tokyo: Hosei University Press, 204–20.

Nettlau, M. (1919) 'Zur Marx' und Engels' Aufenthalt in London, Ende 1847', *Archiv für Geschichte des Sozialismus un der Arbeiterbewegung* 8: 392–401.

Sartorius, F. (1976) 'L'Association démocratique (1847–48)', *Socialisme* 135: 1–19.

Seyppel, M. (1991) *Die Demokratischen Gesellscahft in Köln*. Cologne: Janus Verlags-Gesellschaft.

Sommerhausen, L. (1976) *L'Humanisme agissant de Karl Marx*. Paris, Richard-Masse.

Tedesco, V. (1849) 'Catéchisme du prolétaire', in *Almanach republicain pour l'année 1849*. Liège: A. Charron, 29–43.

13 Louis Blanc, associationism in France, and Marx

Koichi Takakusagi

Introduction

What influence did France's revolutionary socialism have upon Marx's thought? This classical question, first posed in Lenin's 'The three sources and three component parts of Marxism' (1913), is still not satisfactorily answered even today, even though accumulated biographical studies of Marx have grown to enormous proportions. But since supporting evidence concerning such influence is unlikely ever to be found in the literature, we will probably be forced to rephrase the question. In his *The Poverty of Philosophy*, *The Communist Manifesto* and other early works, Marx uses the term 'association', a term borrowed from French, as a crucial concept, for example in this passage from *The Communist Manifesto*:

> When, in the course of development, class distinctions have disappeared, and all production has been concentrated in the hands of a vast association of the whole nation, the public power will lose their character ... In place of the old bourgeois society, with its classes and class antagonisms, we shall have an association, in which the free development of each is the condition for the free development of all.
>
> (Marx and Engels 1959: 482)

Here they take the view that the society of the future will be 'an association'. This concept, which has never been studied in great depth before, is more than sufficient to provoke a re-examination of Marx's thought as a whole.

It is common knowledge that associationism had a tremendous influence in France at the time that Marx was living in Paris (1843–45). Virtually every type of plan for social reform, no matter what their other differences, was built around the concept *association*, and that is why I believe that it is necessary to view Marx as an associationist and to reassess his position within the trends current at that time. Rather than viewing the problem as one of direct influence, what we need to do is to construct tools of historical analysis that may be used to analyse Marx, together with the other thinkers of his time.

My objective here is to provide a general overview of the concept *association* as it existed in the 1840s, as a preliminary step towards analysing Marx's interpretation of it. The main target of this analysis will be the thought of Louis Blanc. I choose to take this path because he was one of the most typical associationists of this time, and because his view of the concept *association* allows us to see both the wide scope of the concept and its inconsistent usage.

Louis Blanc's *Organisation du travail* and the associationist movement

All new concepts, once they come to be widely accepted, begin to vary in their interpretations. Leo Loubère, one of Louis Blanc's biographers, writes that, 'During the July Monarchy the word association acquired the effect of a messianic formula, attracting all groups of the left, whether radical or socialist. Almost cabalistically vague, it lent itself to a variety of meanings' (Loubère 1961: 18). The term *association*, however, was not used exclusively by the left; it was also used as a key concept in works such as Alexis de Tocqueville's *De la démocratie en Amérique* and Eugène Buret's *De la misère des classes laborieuses en Angleterre et en France*. It was against this background that Blanc's *Organisation du travail* (1840), which took the concept *association* as its foundation, became widely popular, and it was the success of this work that eventually lifted Blanc into his position as a member of the provisional government established after the February Revolution in 1848.

It was just before the July Revolution that the Saint-Simonians developed a full-fledged formulation of their own conception of the meaning of *association*. Their dream of abolishing inequalities of birth, of making ability the only criterion upon which people could be judged, and of establishing an association between the formerly divided classes of society was centered around the concept of the worker (*travailleur*) as the linchpin of society. Even at the time when *Doctrine de Saint-Simon* was written, Claude Henri de Saint-Simon's classification of society as consisting of a leisure class and industrialists lived on as a conception of an opposition between the two. It was believed that the end of the exploitation of man by man would be brought about by the creation of a universal association of workers (Bouglé and Halévy 1924: 235–49).

It was after the July Revolution of 1830 that the labour movement began to come into its own. The conception of workers' co-operative associations put forth by P.J.B. Buchez in 1831 came to be viewed within the labour movement as a new type of labour organisation that would replace the *compagnonnage,* and so the movement began actually to create such associations. One might say that it was when the concept 'worker' came to be more strictly understood in conjunction with the increasing industrialisation of society that the ideal of *association* and the movement to create it came into being in the 1840s. This movement consisting of autonomous organisations of workers formed the foundation upon which associationism was built (Magraw 1992: I, 58–90).

After the French Revolution had done away with all privileged intermediate groups in order to create a social structure consisting of only individuals and the state, the historical task facing France was one of creating a new set of non-privileged intermediate groups as a foundation upon which to build a new society. The ideal and movement towards the creation of workers' co-operative associations promoted by *L'Atelier*, a worker's newspaper founded under the influence of Buchez, were natural responses to the needs of the times.

Louis Blanc, together with the Saint-Simonians, viewed associationism as a concept diametrically opposed to individualism. With the exception of a handful of victors, the competition associated with individualism brings only poverty, the source of social evils, to virtually all the people, thus making it a destructive system. Blanc's proposal for a system that would create a society based on associationism instead of individualism was for *ateliers sociaux*, or social workshops. One may say accordingly that Blanc's vision consisted of an extension of the Saint-Simonian conception of association that included autonomous workers' co-operative associations.

Social workshops, however, could only be formed at the behest of the state, and it is here that Blanc's conception differs from that of workers' associations. Blanc stated that, 'The government, considered as the only founder of the social workshops, must determine the statutes regulating them' (Blanc 1840: 109). Under Buchez's plan for workers' associations, the role of the state was limited to lending them money, and Buchez also believed that philanthropic groups could take the place of government in fulfilling this role (Buchez 1831). It is because this view made workers the subjects of the association that it was adopted by *L'Atelier*, and it came to have such a wide influence on the labour movement. Naturally, Blanc did not entirely ignore the view of the independent workers' movement: 'after the first year, these workshops will be able to support themselves, and the role of the government will then be restricted to maintaining relations between all production centers within the same industry and preventing any deviation from the principles of the common regulation' (Blanc 1840: 116–17). The idea of social workshops, however, did not come from the theory underlying the workers' movement. What Blanc was proposing was a system that would replace the one of competition, but which would be capable of governing society as a whole. Unlike the vision proposed in *L'Atelier*, it is only natural to allow the participation of capitalists under this scheme. Social workshops were thus viewed more as something that would make it possible to regenerate the social order that had been destroyed by competition, and Blanc advocated their creation as a means of making special interests and the general interest meet both economically and morally.

The difference between social workshops and workers' co-operative associations is most clearly seen in their provision for the distribution of profits. Under the social workshop system, a portion of the net profits from these workshops would be used to support the old, the sick and the infirm, whereas the Workers' Association Contract (1841) drawn up by *L'Atelier* contained no provisions concerning payments to any of these groups. The reason for this was clearly stated in *L'Atelier*: 'We have intentionally removed such a provision. Indeed, it must not be forgotten that it would be extremely difficult to form associations at this time and that we must fight against competition and most likely other opposition as well' (*L'Atelier* 1841).

The lack of any provision for caring for the needy may be explained not only by its being difficult to do so, but also in terms of the system of thought characteristic of the workers' associations of the July Monarchy. Skilled workers served as the sole force behind the Paris labour movement at the time, and associationism was built upon the foundation provided by the homogeneity of skilled workers (Moss 1976: 9–16). Buchez had clearly stated that factory workers, who were no more than cogs in a machine, were not suited to serving as the foundation upon which workers' associations would be formed. While *L'Atelier* did claim that associations were open to all workers, not only was being 'a good worker' stated as a requirement of membership, but there were also provisions for expelling members as well. One could say accordingly that an unspoken boundary was therefore drawn between different types of workers.

Blanc's criticism of Saint-Simonism was also turned against those who believed in meritocracy. The slogan of the supporters of a meritocratic system was, 'To each according to his ability, to each ability according to its work'. Although Blanc agreed with the first part of this slogan, i.e. that organisations should be based upon ability, he did not believe that workers should be compensated in accordance with the work performed. There is no difference between this and the state of affairs that would exist in a barbarian age in which physical inequality brings about the domination of the weak by the strong. While Blanc did admit that modern society is based on merit, he wanted to construct a system in which differences in ability would not lead to a relation of domination or the subjection of any man. Blanc's ideal was summarised most succinctly in what is effectively the closing sentence of *Organisation du travail*, where he states that, 'it is not in the inequality of remuneration that the inequality of aptitudes should end: it is in the inequality of duties' (Blanc 1840: 131). Louis Blanc does not necessarily insist on equality of pay. His principal insistence consists in severing the bonds between the ability and the right (Gossez 1967: 230–1).

In order to refute those who propounded a meritocratic system, Blanc used the example of the family. The view that a portion of profits should be used to aid the socially disadvantaged may be arrived at by taking a look at the relationship between a father and his children. Blanc posed the question by saying, 'When a father gives out fruit to his children, does he take into consideration any differences in the services they have done? Or does he consider differences in the need they feel?' (Blanc 1841–44: III, 108). Of course, Blanc did not believe in traditional patriarchal rule, an ideology used to justify monarchism. Instead he believed that what should play the role of the father in the state was not a monarch but rather a government that was nothing more than an organisation.

Thus even though *Organisation du travail* contains unifying elements which bring together different ideas from this age of associationism, it remains throughout committed to an opposition to meritocracy. Furthermore, it is because of the unifying nature of this work that it brings out so clearly the opposing elements comprising associationism. In this work one may clearly see the opposition that exists between holism and autonomy and between meritocracy and the principles of family organisation, together with all the other problems faced by associationism.

Workers' associations versus associations of capitalists and workers

In the third edition of *The Principles of Political Economy* (1852), John Stuart Mill, who had watched the February Revolution of 1848 unfold from across the Straits of Dover, greatly changed his views of socialism and communism, compared with the first edition of the same work. In this later edition, he presented his ideal of having workers act on their own to improve their own situation, instead of operating under a paternalistic system in which workers are protected by their employers. Hence he wrote about the historical trend towards the abolition of the employer–employee relationship. In considering associations, Mill described them as a form of partnership, 'in some cases, association of the labourers with the capitalist; in others, and perhaps finally in all, association of labourers among themselves' (Mill 1965: 769). This was a form of partnership that would supersede the relation between a master and his workers. To Mill, these two forms of association are not necessarily mutually exclusive. Instead he viewed 'associations of labourers' as something that might come gradually to replace 'associations of the labourers with capitalists'. Mill's understanding of the concept 'association' might very well be used as a means of gaining an accurate understanding of the term as it was viewed in France under the July Monarchy.

Rather than being a concept restricted merely to workers' associations, the term 'association' came to have completely different meanings as well. For instance, Michel Chevalier, a political economist who was one of the key figures in the Saint-Simonian school, criticised Blanc's *Organisation du travail* severely. His criticisms were based on his own belief that the first thing that had to be done in order to improve workers' living conditions was to raise the general level of production, but he did not criticise the idea of associations as such. In *Lettres sur l'organisation du travail* in 1848, Chevalier discusses his own views of associations.

Chevalier criticised the attempt to purge society of all intermediate groups that had occurred at the time of the French Revolution, and he expressed this most clearly when he said that the law Le Chapelier (1791), banning workers associations, was the gravest of mistakes. He wrote that it had only served to create a social state where nothing could come to be but 'gravel without cement, atoms with no relation to each other' (Chevalier 1848: 267–8). He described association as one of the strongest urges of free men, and viewing association at an abstract and universal level, he saw the spirit of associationism existing in many social systems, such as those of savings banks and pension funds.

In considering actual types of associations, the type that Chevalier believed to be most important were associations in which workers could partake of profits. In other words, the type of associations he was considering were 'associations of labourers with capitalists', with the most common example considered being that of the Paris house-painter Leclaire, which had also been used by Mill in his *The Principles of Political Economy.* Even today there is a Rue Jean Leclaire running from north to south near the Saint-Ouste arch in Paris's 17th arrondisement. Jean Edme Leclaire, originally the son of a poor shoemaker, born in a small village in the Yonne, worked at a variety of trades before he founded a house-painting business in Paris at the age of 25. By 1838 he had become a successful self-made businessman who was employing between 60 and 80 workers. He instituted a variety of different reforms for his workers, and was given many awards in recognition of his work. By instituting a form of profit-sharing as early as 1842, Leclaire made his name one to be remembered in the history books (Fabre 1906: 9–13).

The idea of allowing workers to participate in profits came from a desire to improve their conditions. The viewpoint taken was a philanthropic one: to improve on the existing conditions in which workers were not always assured of having work and in which the wages they earned from their labour were little more than just enough to take care of themselves and their families. At the same time, however, this system was also naturally expected to improve productivity by increasing worker motivation. There was also the problem of slipshod work so often found in the painting business, and one way of solving this problem was to combine the profits of all workers together and to allow workers to participate in those profits, thus creating a sort of bonus system. (Leclaire 1843: 5–7). In the regulations defining the conditions for the administration of the company and the distribution of profits from labour to the core employees and workers of the Leclaire painting company (*Réglement d'administration et de répartition des bénéfices produits par le travail entre les employés et les ouvriers composant le noyau de la maison Leclaire*), it states that 'the number of persons for whom the participation of labourers in profits is to be permitted is unspecified' (Article 3), and that 'the only criterion upon which decisions as to whether to permit participation in profit is that of merit' (Article 8) (Leclaire 1843: 19–22). By thus awarding what were in effect bonuses to dedicated workers, it was possible not only to improve their working conditions but also to improve the management of the company and to make it more successful at the same time. Furthermore, by dividing the workers into core workers and non-core workers, the opposition between capital and labour could be relegated to the background, and the workers could be stimulated to emulate each other.

The reason why Blanc, in the fourth edition of *Organisation du travail* (1845), includes this experiment conducted by Leclaire in an appendix is because Leclaire's experiment had been stimulated in part by a reading of *Organisation du travail*, and the decision to do so may thus be said to have been driven by Blanc's desire to demonstrate the extent of his influence. In a report on the result of his profit-sharing system from 1843, Leclaire writes, 'It would be entirely accurate to say that of all the theories we reviewed, it is the theories of Louis Blanc as described in his book entitled *Organisation du travail* which provided the ideas needed for us to establish a company which would work under actual conditions' (Blanc 1845: 4). The idea of social workshops may also be viewed as a form of association between workers and managers, and even Blanc himself admitted as much. Two different objectives underlie the conception of social workshops: the protection and promotion of the growth of autonomous workers' associations, and the purchasing of businesses and their subsequent structural reformation by the state. Blanc had no clear recognition of the problems that might exist between workers' associations and associations of workers and managers, and it is likely that it was his failure to recognise such problems that led to Blanc's abandonment of the working class in 1848.

When this is considered in conjunction with the fact that Blanc's conception of association was based on familial principles, one sees that this form of 'paternalistic' management might serve as a model for association. However, when Blanc chose to view the organisation of the family as the basis of his notion of association and to draw an analogy between this and the relationship between a father and his children, what he overlooked was the relationship of force and obedience that exists therein. While Leclaire was a caring philanthropist, he was at the same time a stern and shrewd businessman. This can be clearly seen in the massive set of regulations according to which he ran his business. His system was one for controlling his workers through meticulous management: by permitting only specified workers to participate in profits, he succeeded in instilling within them a system by which his workers managed themselves on their own. The example set by Leclaire demonstrates clearly the existence of a deep gulf between associations of workers and manager and workers' associations. (Rancière 1975: 92). The system constructed by Leclaire, in which workers could participate in profits, is a device that forces morals and restrictions from above upon the individuality and autonomy of workers.

The ideal that drove Blanc more than any other was that of national unity. This strong desire to find a place for every group that was prevented from participating socially or politically and to bring social and political unity to all the people is one thing that Blanc carried with him all his life. He believed that political unity is normally achieved through a republican system of government centered around elections, and that associations built upon the premise of republicanism would lead to social unity. Republican government and associations would then together give expression to national unity in both the political and social spheres. A republican government, however, always contains elements that are in opposition to each other. Just as could be seen from struggles for hegemony, once associationism had shifted from the realm of the abstract to the realm of an actual movement, it became impossible to prevent the movement from becoming a place for the clashing of ideals. This unshifting adherence to the ideal of holism, even if it served as a basis from which to criticise the partiality of workers' associations, also serves to conceal the existence of these opposing elements.

Communes and associations

In examining the concept of association as it existed in the July Monarchy, one important aspect that must be considered is the relation between associations and communes. Associations, which are formed according to the intent of free and equal individuals, must be clearly distinguished from communes, born from the land and bloody conflict. It is worth noting, however, that Tocqueville, in addition to recognising the existence of associations formed voluntarily for a variety of different objectives, also analyses communes that consist of 'permanent associations' (Tocqueville 1990: I, 146; trans. 1969: 189). To Tocqueville, the foundation of American democracy was the existence of communes of two to three thousand people. Yet rather than viewing this as a fettering of freedom, he saw it as its very source. Tocqueville, who viewed the American town meeting as a form of commune, put it thusly: 'Local institutions are to liberty what primary schools are to science; they put it within the people's reach' (Tocqueville 1990: I, 50; trans. 1969: 63).

While the relationship between Blanc and Tocqueville has been researched very little, Blanc did in fact write a lengthy critique of *Démocratie en Amérique* in 1835. It is from Tocqueville that he obtained some of his ideas, and he then developed those ideas into his own theory of communes. The most important of these ideas is the distinction drawn by Tocqueville between governmental centralisation and administrative centralisation.

The demand to devolve power to the provinces that came to the fore during the July Monarchy stood in direct opposition to the tradition of Jacobinism, the doctrine that was forged against the background of the struggle between the Girondin movement of 1793 and the Ultra-Royalist bloc. Ferdinand Béchard, author of the *Essai sur la centralisation administrative* (1836–7), was a follower of Joseph de Maistre (Béchard 1836–7: II, 488). To a republican dedicated to the goal of achieving a national unity that included the working classes, demands for power to be devolved to the provinces could never be accepted. However, for men like these, who could never find any theoretical foundation upon which to base their ideas other than that provided in Rousseau's *The Social Contract*, the coming of a new theory of democracy was undoubtedly like a gift from the very heavens (Duquesnel 1839: 96). Tocqueville's greatest innovation was his proposal for a method to overcome the classical opposition thought to exist between centralised and decentralised power. This may be seen in the following passage where Tocqueville describes how rule by the people can coexist with national unity.

> Certain interests, such as the enactment of general law and the nation's relations with foreigners, are common to all parts of the nation. There are other interests of special concern to certain parts of the nation, such, for instance, as local enterprises. To concentrate all the former in the same place or under the same directing power is to establish what I call governmental centralization. To concentrate control of the latter in the same way is to establish what I call administrative centralization.
>
> (Tocqueville 1990: I, 69–70; trans. 1969: 87)

Even though Tocqueville criticised the existence of the repression caused by the forcible imposition of governmental and administrative centralisation in France, Blanc found a way to use those two types of centralisation in order to establish the legitimacy of Jacobinism. According to Blanc, what the Jacobin regime had imposed was governmental centralisation, and the administrative centralisation that came with it was nothing more than an epiphenomenon that fit with the circumstances of the time (Blanc 1835: 160–1).

The effects of administrative decentralisation were also important to Blanc in other ways. The very fact that he held as his goal a national unity based on the ideal of 'a single indivisible republic' meant that he could never deny the need for centralisation. At the same time, in order to prepare for future elections and to make rule by the people a thing of reality, it was absolutely essential to educate the public. In a situation where the republicans lacked large numbers of centres of operation in the provinces, administrative decentralisation could serve as an effective means of creating a body politic centered around the people in such regions. Blanc himself wrote that:

We have a deep conviction of the intimate relationship between municipal freedom and political freedom. People gain feelings of dignity by regular, continuous exercise of power. When they lose frequent use of the ability, people lose consideration of the right, and go from political apathy to subjection. Administrative decentralization is useful, to create the fire of the movement in various places. It liberates the intellect, and gives purpose to all activities.

(Blanc 1835: 158–9)

In 'Commune', a work written in 1841, Blanc expressed his view that France had not yet achieved a sufficient level of political (governmental) centralisation and administrative decentralisation, even though democracy by its nature is a combination of political (governmental) centralisation, which in turn requires political unity, and administrative decentralisation, which in turn brings about social unity (Blanc 1841: 49–51). In this article, he uses the term 'centralisation politique' instead of Tocqueville's 'centralisation gouvernementale'. Political and social unity, however, were what made it possible to escape from the dogma that asserts that special interests stand in opposition to the general interest. Communes thus do not stand in a relation of opposition to the state. Rule by the people is the basis on which democracies are formed, and the role of the government is to provide support for such a foundation. When he wrote that 'The commune represents the idea of unity as well as of the state . . . The state is a building, and the commune is its foundation', he was addressing the question of how it might be possible to achieve social unity based on the commune (Blanc 1841: 65). He further notes that 'Social unity does not have any basis except that of association. To think, demand, and act jointly comprises association in its strictest, widest meaning' (Blanc 1841: 60).

It is clear that in this article he envisions associations merging with local communities where people have 'frequent, customary and almost daily relations', but the reason why such a merging should come about is never stated clearly (Blanc 1841: 60). Here it is instructive to recall his article 'Réforme électorale', written in 1839. In this article, he propounded his odd theory that it is universal suffrage that creates the conditions needed in order for universal suffrage itself to succeed. In opposition to the doctrinaires who argued that political sophistication was a precondition for the assignment of political rights, Blanc argued that the collective sophistication of the people could be developed by allowing them to exercise their voting rights (Blanc 1839: 306). In his essay 'Le suffrage universel' published in 1850, he argued that political life can only exist where voters assemble to discuss their ideas and feelings with each other (Blanc 1850a: 453). Thus it is only when the people are given the chance to participate in popular elections that communes function as associations. In order to exercise their right to vote or to recall elected officials, commune members must be able to 'think, demand, and act jointly'. The participation of the people in public affairs thus transforms the commune as a whole into a political forum.

Here one can see the point at which Blanc and Tocqueville differ. Tocqueville had seen how the communes of the United States were supported by its direct democracy, and because of this he viewed the commune as a bastion of democracy (Tocqueville 1990: I, 51; trans. 1969: 64). There is no sign, however, of any mention of a direct link to a democratic system in Blanc's commune reform plan. It is true that he recognised the danger of a possible tyranny of the majority within direct democratic systems (Blanc 1850a: 442–5). In the 1850s, Blanc took a stand against direct democracy in his arguments against Littinghausen, Victor Considerant, Ledru-Rollin and other proponents of 'direct government of the people by the people' (Blanc 1851a; 1851b). Yet it is also possible to recognise another reason for his opposition. When speaking about the two different types of life represented by the life of communes and the life of the citizenry (Blanc 1847–62: III, 445), Blanc was aware of the problems that could be raised by governmental centralisation and administrative decentralisation, problems that had not been adequately recognised by Tocqueville. In contrast to Tocqueville, who believed that the affairs of a commune were the concern only of the commune itself, Blanc believed that a commune's affairs were also affairs of the state (Blanc 1841: 61). As long as a commune is viewed as a bastion of democracy that possesses its own culture, it must be independent in order to exist. Yet as long as the residents of a commune are also citizens of nation in which their interests extend over wider areas, they cannot be independent. This conflict between the opposing goals of national unity and the assurance of self-rule by the people may have made Blanc's vision of the commune an ambiguous one.

The relation between the Blanc's social workshops and the commune still remains to be addressed. In the ninth edition of *Organisation du travail* (1850), Blanc called for the creation of agricultural social workshops that would stand in conjunction with industrial ones. These agricultural social workshops would consist of a type of agricultural colony where groups of 50 families or so would live and work communally (Blanc 1850b: 112–15). The question remains, however, just what type of relation such agricultural workshops would bear with the commune, and what type of relationship would exist between such workshops and associations other than communes.

Blanc's thought may be characterised by his method of searching for signs of commonality between two things that on the surface appear to stand in opposition and then striving to achieve a harmonious balance between the two. The conservative nature of his thought has made him a constant target for criticism by more radical thinkers, and it is because of this methodology that his thought is regarded today as lacking in personal vision. Yet in fact Louis Blanc's independence could rather be said to lie in the limitless extent of the problems that lie hidden underneath his conservatism. His modern relevance lies in the way that he recognised such problems.

Conclusion

In this chapter I have examined the problems associated with the notion of association, especially in the work of Louis Blanc. The range of this notion extends even into the present day, and many of the different problems that modern society now faces were foreseen by the thinkers of the 19th century. This attempt to reconstruct Marx's thinking by examining the concept of association enables us – as might be expected – not only to explore the possibilities of Marxian thought but also to explore the inconsistencies inherent in modern society at the same time. However, in order to gain a better picture of Marx for the 21st century, we must begin with further study of the historical context of the 19th century and by repositioning Marx within that context. When association and all of its associated problems are considered – holism and autonomy, meritocracy and the principles of familial organisation, labour movements and business reform, rule by the people and national unity – Marx's thought will undoubtedly take on a new life.

References

Anonymous (1841) 'Réforme industrielle: De l'association ouvrière', *L'Atelier*, ère année, no. 5, janvier 1841: 37–8.

Béchard, F. (1836–7) *Essai sur la centralisation administrative*, 2 vols. Marseilles: M. Olive; Paris: Hivert.

Blanc, L. (1835) 'De la démocratie en Amérique', *Revue républicaine, Journal des doctrines et des intérêts démocratiques*, tome V: 129–63.

Blanc, L. (1839) 'Réforme électorale', *Revue du progrès politique, social et littéraire*, tome II, le 15 octobre: 289–308.

Blanc, L. (1841) 'Commune', *Revue du progrès politique, social et littéraire*, tome V, le 1er février: 46–66.

Blanc, L. (1845) *Organisation du travail, quatrième édition, considerarement augmentée, precedée d'une Introduction et suivie d'un compte rendu de la maison Leclaire, Paris*. Paris: Cauville.

Blanc, L. (1850a) 'Le suffrage universel ou la guerre civile: Il faut choisir!', *Le Nouveau monde: Journal historique et politique*, no. 10, le 15 avril: 435–61.

Blanc, L. (1850b) *Organisation du travail, nouvième édition, réfondue et augmentée de Chapitre nouveau*. Paris: Au bureau du Nouveau Monde.

Blanc, L. (1851a) *Plus de Girondins*. Paris: Charles Joubert.

Blanc, L. (1851b) *La République, une et indivisible*. Paris: A. Naud.

Blanc, L. (1847–62) *Histoire de la Révolution française*, 12 vols. Paris: Langlois et Leclercq.

Blanc, L. (1841–4) *Histoire de dix ans, 1830–40*, 5 vols. Paris: Pagnerre.

Blanc, L. (1840) *Organisation du travail*. Paris: Prévot et Pagnerre.

Bouglé, C. and Halévy, E. (eds) (1924) *Doctrine de Saint-Simon, Exposition, première année, 1829*, nouvelle édition publiée avec introduction et notes par C. Bouglé et Elie Halévy. Paris: Marcel Rivière.

Buchez, P.-J.-B. (1831) 'Moyen d'améliorer la condition des salariés des villes', *Journal des sciences morales et politiques*, tome I, no. 3, le 17 décembre: 36–9.

Chevalier, M. (1848) *Lettres sur l'organisation du travail, ou études sur les principes causes de la misère et sur les moyens proposés pour y remédier.* Paris: Capelle.

Duquesnel, A. (1839) *Du travail intellectuel en France, depuis 1815 jusqu'à 1837.* Paris: W. Coquebert.

Fabre, A. (1906) *Un ingénieur social: Jean-Edme Leclaire.* Nîmes: Imprimerie Clavel et Chastanier.

Gossez, R. (1967) *Les ouvriers de Paris: l'organisation, 1848–1851.* Paris: Société d'histoire de la Révolution de 1848.

Leclaire, J.E. (1843) *Des améliorations qu'il serait possible d'apporter dans le sort des ouvriers peintres en bâtiments, suivies des réglements d'administration et de répartition des bénéfices que produit le travail.* Paris: Chez Mme Ve Bouchard-Huzard.

Loubère, L. (1961/1980) *Louis Blanc: His Life and his Contribution to the Rise of French Jacobin Socialism.* Boston: Northwestern University Press; repr. Westport: Greenwood Press.

Magraw, R. (1992) *A History of the French Working Class*, 2 vols. Oxford: Blackwell.

Marx, K. and Engels, F. (1959) *Manifest der Kommunistischen Partei*, in K. Marx and F. Engels, *Marx-Engels Werke*, vol. 4. Berlin: Dietz Verlag, 461–93.

Mill, J.S. (1965) *Principles of Political Economy with Some of their Applications to Social Philosophy*, in J.M. Robson (ed.) *Collected Works of John Stuart Mill*, vol. 3. Toronto: University of Toronto Press.

Moss, B.H. (1976) *The Origins of the French Labor Movement 1830–1914: The Socialism of Skilled Workers.* Berkeley: University of California Press.

Rancière, J. (1975) 'Utopistes, Bourgeois et Prolétaires', *L'Homme et la société: Revue internationale de recherches et de synthèses sociologues*, nos 37–38: 87–98.

Tocqueville, A. de (1990/1969) *De la démocratie en Amérique.* nouvelle édition historico-critique revue et augmentée par Edouard Nolla, 2 vols. Paris: J. Vrin. Trans. George Lawrence, ed. J.P. Mayer. New York: Doubleday.

14 Editorial problems in establishing a new edition of *The German Ideology*

Tadashi Shibuya

Introduction

The German Ideology comprises the manuscripts that Karl Marx and Frederick Engels wrote together in 1845/1846. In these manuscripts historical materialism was first established. Since the first chapter was published by Rjazanov in 1926 several editions have appeared. In the manuscripts, the first draft was largely written in Engels's hand and was then revised by Marx and Engels. Thus the authorial state of the manuscripts is very complicated. The publishing history of *The German Ideology* has been one of attempts to restore the manuscripts completely. However, in spite of repeated improvements, a complete restoration has not yet been realised. Many problems still remain to be solved in editing *The German Ideology*.

I researched the manuscripts of *The German Ideology* in the Internationaal Instituut voor Sociale Geschiedenis (IISG) in Amsterdam from March to December 1995. The editorial defects of previous editions have been cleared up through this research. Then in 1998, I published a new edition of *The German Ideology* in Japanese translation in order to correct the defects of previous editions (Marx and Engels 1998). In this chapter I will first explain the complicated state of the manuscripts, and then discuss the editorial defects of previous editions, i.e.:

1 Rjazanov's edition (Marx and Engels 1926);
2 Adoratskij's edition (Marx and Engels 1932);
3 a new edition published in the *Deutsche Zeitschrift für Philosophie* (Marx and Engels 1966);
4 the *Probeband* of MEGA® (Marx and Engels 1972);
5 Hiromatsu's edition (Marx and Engels 1974).

Finally I explain the way the manuscripts are restored in my edition (Marx and Engels 1998).

The state of the manuscripts

The manuscripts of *The German Ideology* are preserved in IISG, except for the preface (*Vorrede*). This is preserved in the Russian centre for modern history documentation (RC) in Moscow. The manuscripts consist of sheets in folio-size (*Bogen* in German). Therefore each sheet represents four ordinary-size pages. There is a fold in the centre of each sheet, and each is thus divided into right and left columns along the fold. Engels wrote the first draft in the left column. Originally the right column remained blank, presumably for later notes in the margin. Marx and Engels actually revised the first draft at the same time as they continued writing it. Moreover, they revised it later on, too. Their ways of revising and making additions are as follows:

- Revisions were written between the lines, i.e. above the deleted words.
- Several signs (+, + +, F, E) were written in the left column and the corresponding signs were then written in the right column. The insertion for the left column was written after the sign in the right column. These notes in the margin were written later on. The marginal notes directing the place of insertion were included in the text of the left column by all previous editions. However, previous editions did not mention the sign 'F, E'.
- Marginal notes without specific directions as to the place of insertion. These notes are thought to have been written later on.
- On words already written, other words were over-written. Definite and indefinite articles, demonstrative and relative pronouns, etc. were frequently revised in this way.
- Revised words were written just after deleted words. Thus Engels made revisions while he was writing the first draft.
- Some sentences continue from the left column over into the right column.

Editorial problems in previous editions of *The German Ideology*

Rjazanov's edition

In this section I point out the editorial problems in previous editions, beginning with Rjazanov's edition:

- Deleted words are included in text as a matter of principle.
- When a sentence was greatly revised, the first draft is shown in a footnote.
- The words that Marx inserted are referred to in footnotes.

- Necessary information about the state of the manuscripts is placed in footnotes.

Because deleted words are included in the text, it is possible to understand the first draft as well as the process of revision. However, Rjazanov's edition has certain defects. Not all deleted words are noted, so in this sense the edition is incomplete. Moreover, the complicated process of revision is not represented. For example, the beginning of p. 24 (Marx's own pagination) in the manuscripts is described as follows (chevrons, < >, denote a deleted passage):

> This conception of history thus relies on expounding the real process of production – starting from the material production of life itself – and comprehending the form of intercourse connected with and created by this mode of production, i.e., civil society in its various stages <and in its practical-idealistic mirror image, state>, as the basis of all history; describing it in its action as the state.
>
> (Marx and Engels 1926: 259; see Marx and Engels 1976: 53)

According to Rjazanov, after writing 'civil society in its various stages', the words 'and in its practical-idealistic mirror image, state' were written and then deleted. However, from the words 'and comprehending' to 'as the state', the manuscript actually reads as follows:

> and comprehending the form of intercourse connected with and created by this mode of production, i.e., civil society in its various stages, *as the basis of all history* <from it «and in» its practical-idealistic mirror image«, state»>; *describing it in its action as the state.*

The words in chevrons < > have been deleted, and the words in double chevrons « » indicate those that were deleted earlier. Italic type indicates rewritten words between the lines or in the margin.

From the words 'civil society' to 'as the state', the first draft reads as follows: 'civil society in its various stages and in its practical-idealistic mirror image, state'. At the first stage of revision, the first draft was changed to read as follows: 'civil society in its various stages, as the basis of all history from it its practical-idealistic mirror image'. Then at the second stage of revision, the revised sentence was changed again as follows: 'civil society in its various stages, as the basis of all history; describing it in its action as the state'. In this case the first draft was revised in two stages. In Rjazanov's edition, it is impossible to resolve such complicated sentences, so the manuscripts are not accurately represented.

Adoratskij's edition

- The text contains only revised sentences.
- Deleted and inserted words are explained in as textual-variants.
- Marx's handwriting is denoted by a sign (^{m m}) in the textual-variants.

The greatest defect of Adoratski's edition is to change the order of the first chapter 'Feuerbach' in a way that disregards Marx's pagination, so it is impossible to understand the logic of the first chapter. Furthermore, the manuscripts are restored defectively. For example, according to the textual-variants of Adoratskij's edition, the beginning of p. 10 of the first chapter could be restored as follows:

> Certainly Feuerbach has a great advantage over the 'pure' materialist since he realizes that man too is an 'object of the senses'. But apart^m from the fact that he only conceives him as 'object of the senses', not as 'sensuous activity'^m, because he <remains here in the realm of p[ure] theory, he does not come to [ ] «me[n]» the 'actual, individual, corporeal man' not in his given historical connection, not under his existing conditions of life, which [ ] him what> remains here in the realm of theory and conceives of men not in their given social connection, not under their existing conditions of life, which have made them what they are, he never comes to.
> (Marx and Engels 1932: 34, 571; see also Marx and Engels 1976: 41)

The word <me[n]> indicates that it was deleted earlier. The sign '^{m m}' denotes the words added by Marx. Thus, the words from 'apart' to 'activity' were added. Adoratskij's restoration is inaccurate. From the words 'apart from' to 'he never comes to', the manuscript actually reads as follows:

> But apart^m from the fact that he only conceives him as 'object of the senses', not as 'sensuous activity'^m, because he remains here <in the realm of p[ure]> *in the realm of* theory, <he does not come to [ ]> <me[n]> *and conceives of* the 'actual, individual, corporeal> m<a>en' not in <his> *their* given <historical> *social* connection, not under <his> *their* existing conditions of life, which have made <him> *them* what they are, he never comes to.

Chevrons <> enclose deleted words. Italic type represents rewritten words. According to Adoratskij, after all the words in chevrons (from 'remains here' to 'him what') were written, they were then deleted. Subsequently the words from 'remains' to 'he never comes to' were rewritten again. In the original, however, the words 'his' and 'him' were only changed to 'their' and 'them' because the word 'man' (singular) was changed to 'men' (plural). Marx and Engels therefore revised the sentence, making good use of the first draft. Adoratskij's edition misrepresents the process of revision in the manuscripts. That kind of difference ranges over the whole of the manuscripts, so it is impossible in Adoratskij's edition to restore deleted words accurately.

A *new edition for the* Deutsche Zeitschrift für Philosophie

In this edition, four pages were added to its text. These pages had been published by S. Bahne for the first time (1962: 93–104). The manuscripts were arranged according to Marx's pagination. This edition has great significance because it described the textual arrangement of Adoratskij's edition as false. However, this edition gave only a partial indication of deletions, so readers had to rely on Adoratskij's edition in order to get further information about the process of revision.

The Probeband *(1972) of MEGA*②

The editorial policy is as follows:

- In the *Probeband*, the text includes only sentences after revision; the process of revising the first draft is then explained in textual-variants (*Variantenverzeichnis*), similar to Adoratskij's edition.
- In the text, each page is divided into two columns, like the manuscripts.
- In the textual-variants, the process of revision is restored as follows: the first draft is put in the first line and in the following lines the revised sentences are arranged according to the stages of revision. The process of revision is denoted by various signs (|: :|, < >, —, SV).
- Marx's handwriting is denoted by the sign '^mᵐ'.
- The sign 'SV' (*Sofortvariante*) indicates that Engels made revisions while he was writing the first draft. The sign '/' indicates that he stopped writing and began revising (example: was/).

The *Probeband* restored the complex state of the manuscripts using various signs, making restoration more exact than was possible with the Rjazanov and Adoratskij editions. However, the *Probeband* is defective in that the method of restoration is extremely complicated. It is difficult even for specialists to restore the manuscripts by using these various signs. Moreover, the *Probeband* does not give full information about the different ways of revising, e.g. whether the revised words were written between lines or just after the deleted words. It is in fact impossible to restore the manuscripts completely without this information. The Rjazanov edition represents the most comprehensible way of grasping the process of revision, and it is the way to reproduce the manuscripts as they were originally. If that method is followed and also accompanied by other means necessary for an exact restoration of the manuscripts, then it is unnecessary to reproduce the manuscripts in the complicated way that was employed in *Probeband*.

Hiromatsu's edition

In this edition each page is divided into left and right columns, like the manuscripts. The deleted and inserted words are included in text, like the Rjazanov edition, and mostly based on the textual-variants of Adoratskij's edition. Therefore, the Hiromatsu edition makes the same mistakes as the Adoratskij edition. The Hiromatsu edition was not based on the original manuscripts. The supplements and marginal notes in the right column were not reproduced, except for those on certain pages. Independent research is necessary to publish an edition that is true to the original.

The Shibuya edition

My edition aimed at being as true to the original as possible. The editorial policy of my edition is as follows:

Deleted and revised words are included in text, like Rjazanov edition.

- Each page of the manuscripts is divided into left and right columns. In my text, the left-hand page of a two-page spread represents the left column of the manuscript text; the right-hand page then represents the original right column. Text from the original right column of the manuscript is placed in the right column of the new edition, as far as is technically possible. Although marginal notes directing insertions into the left column are included in the text of the left column by all the previous editions, in my edition these notes are put into the right column as they are in the manuscripts. In this case, the signs (+, ++, F, E) directing the place of insertion are placed at the corresponding points in both the left and the right columns. Sentences continuing from the left column into the right column are reproduced as they are in the manuscripts.
- Words rewritten later are indicated in italic type. Marx's handwriting is indicated in Gothic type, so one can grasp the process of revision in the text itself.
- This edition incorporates many deleted words, which I deciphered for the first time, that had not been represented in previous editions.
- Necessary information for understanding the complex state of the manuscripts is contained in more than 2,000 notes to the edition.

Following the above editorial policy, p. 25 of manuscript, for example, is reproduced in my edition as follows:

(left column of p. 25)

[. .] to share <u>the illusion of that epoch</u>. **For instance, if an epoch imagines itself to be actuated <its> by purely 'political' or 'religious' motives F, the historians of that epoch accept this opinion. The 'fancy', the 'conception' of the people in question about their real practice is transformed into the <realistically> sole determining and active force**, which dominates and determines their practice.

(right column of p. 25)

F although 'religion' and 'politics' are only forms of its real motives.

(Shibuya 1998: 80–1; see Marx and Engels 1976: 55)

The words in chevrons < > represent deletions. The words in **bold** type represent Marx's handwriting. The sign 'F' in the right column directs insertion into the corresponding place (after the word 'motives' at the third line) in the left column. The passage quoted above was thus written by Marx and Engels as follows: in the left column, after the words 'that epoch' in the first line as written by Engels, Marx wrote two sentences in order to amplify Engels's point. Subsequent to the words 'active force' at the sixth line, Engels wrote a relative clause (from the words 'which dominates' to the words 'their practice'). A comma before the relative pronoun ('which') also seems to have been written by Engels.

What does this analysis mean? In this passage, Marx's sentences were not written between the lines or in the margin, but in the left column. Therefore, Marx, too, was present while Engels was writing the first draft on that occasion. Marx added sentences which he thought necessary while Engels was writing; while Engels was writing the first draft, Marx stopped him and amplified his point by inserting the sentences beginning with the words 'For instance'. Engels then completed the passage, having stopped Marx. In this particular case, Marx and Engels were co-operating in writing the first draft of *The German Ideology*.

The fact that Marx and Engels were cooperating gives us a key to resolving the problem of authorship in *The German Ideology*. Gustav Mayer, Engels's first biographer, maintained that the authorship of *The German Ideology* could not be attributed by handwriting identification. According to his account, Marx wrote illegibly and Engels legibly, so Engels acted as amanuensis while they agreed a text. However, Mayer enquired into the relative shares each had in the cooperative work for the first time (Mayer 1934: 226–7). Rjazanov hypothesised that Marx had dictated the text to Engels (1926: 217). Hiromatsu (1968) denied both theories and maintained that *The German Ideology* had been written on Engels's initiative.

As mentioned above, Marx and Engels wrote the first draft alternately, at least on p. 25 of *The German Ideology*. The way that my edition restores the manuscripts demonstrates that Marx and Engels cooperated in composing the text itself. In this way the deleted and revised words are included, not in textual variants, but in the text itself. In my opinion, this method facilitates a restoration that is true to the original (Taubert *et al.* 1997: 170–3; Shibuya 1996: 108–16). Only in that way can one see deletions and insertions visibly in text, even if the presentation is complicated. However, if the deleted words (the words within chevrons) are omitted, the final draft appears very clearly. It is important that the restoration of *The German Ideology* is not only accurate but also intelligible to readers.

References

Bahne, S. (1962) '*Die Deutsche Ideologie* von Marx und Engels', *International Review of Social History*, vol. 7: 93–104.

Hiromatsu, W. (1968) *The Process of the Formation of Marxism* (in Japanese). Tokyo: Shiseido.

Marx, K. and Engels, F. (1926) *Die deutsche Ideologie*, ed. D. Rjazanov, in *Marx-Engels-Archiv, Zeitschrift des Marx-Engels-Instituts in Moskau*, I. Band. Moscow: Verlagsgesellschaft M.B.H., 230–306.

Marx, K. and Engels, F. (1932) *Die deutsche Ideologie*, ed. V. Adoratskij, in *Gesamtausgabe*. Erste Abteilung, Band 5. Berlin: Dietz Verlag, 3–67, 565–83.

Marx, K. and Engels, F. (1966) *I. Feuerbach. Gegensatz von materialistischer und idealistischer Anschauung*, in *Deutsche Zeitschrift für Philosophie*, Heft 10: 1199–1254.

Marx, K. and Engels, F. (1972) *Die Deutsche Ideologie 1. Band, 1. Abschnitt*, in *Gesamtausgabe, Probeband*. Berlin: Dietz Verlag, 33–119, 417–507.

Marx, K. and Engels, F. (1974) *Die deutsche Ideologie, 1. Band, 1. Kapitel*, ed. W. Hiromatsu. Tokyo: Kawadeshobo-Shinsha.

Marx, K. and Engels, F. (1976) *The German Ideology*, Part 1, trans. W. Lough, *Collected Works*, vol. 5. Moscow: Progress Publishers, 23–93.

Marx, K. and Engels, F. (1998) *The German Ideology*, ed. and trans. [into Japanese] T. Shibuya. Tokyo: Shinnihon.

Mayer, G. (1934) *Friedrich Engels, Eine Biographie*, 2nd edn, vol. 1. Den Haag: Martinus Nijhoff.

Shibuya, T (1998) 'Probleme der Edition der "Deutschen Ideologie"', *MEGA-Studien* 1996/1: 108–16.

Taubert, I., Pelger, H. and Grandjonc, J. (1997) 'Die Darbietung der Handschriften im Edierten Text und im Variantenverzeichnis: eine Erwiderung auf Kritik am *Probeband* der MEGA^2 von 1972 und an den Editionsrichtlinien der MEGA^2 von 1993', *MEGA-Studien*, 1997/2: 170–3.

Index

Note: Works by Marx and Engels are listed alphabetically by title.

For Product Safety Concerns and Information please contact our EU
representative GPSR@taylorandfrancis.com
Taylor & Francis Verlag GmbH, Kaufingerstraße 24, 80331 München, Germany

www.ingramcontent.com/pod-product-compliance
Ingram Content Group UK Ltd.
Pitfield, Milton Keynes, MK11 3LW, UK
UKHW021829240425
457818UK00006B/127